"In *Power Women* you will discov⟨...⟩ ⟨...⟩s in the wisdom of professor mothers who ⟨...⟩ e in academia and family at the same time, ⟨...⟩ to God's call along the way. The journeys of these mothers will empower both men and women to pursue our dreams, stay resilient amid challenges, and inspire others to do so."

Chloe T. Sun, academic dean and professor of Old Testament at Logos Evangelical Seminary, California

"Refreshingly honest, *Power Women* is an invaluable resource for women of the Christian faith who are scholar-mothers and for those who hope to support them well. While candid, these essays remain hopeful in their proposals for moving forward personally, spiritually, and structurally. They insightfully explore and interrogate the tensions between being an active researcher and educator alongside being an active and present mother. The diversity of cultural perspectives adds to the depth and beauty of the volume as a holistic approach to thriving as a scholar mom. As someone who regularly has conversations with women who want to pursue further scholarship but also want to be moms, this is an especially valuable resource. Family members, colleagues, and administrators will truly benefit from reading this as well."

Christa L. McKirland, lecturer in systematic theology at Carey Baptist College in Auckland, New Zealand, and founder and executive director of Logia International

"Motherhood for women in the academy comes with complexities and opportunities. This collection of essays by accomplished scholars and engaged mothers, shared from deep faith, diverse backgrounds, and varying stages, provides a realistic and hopeful resource for current and future professor mothers."

Deana L. Porterfield, president of Roberts Wesleyan College and Northeastern Seminary

"This book made me feel so seen. With wisdom and humility, these professor mothers offer practical guidance and support for working moms. While a lot of the advice is specific to moms in academia, all caregivers would benefit from reading these biblical reflections on motherhood as a spiritual practice."

Jane Hong, tenured historian and mom

"I appreciate this collection of diverse and compelling essays. They are written by women in different stages of their parenting and careers, yet they all have in common a deep and thoughtful understanding of how their Christian faith informs their work and lives as mothers, professors, ministers, and community members. In its Christian emphasis, it fills an important niche in the existing academic-mother literature. The book also provides many helpful and concrete examples for other 'power women' who feel that God has called them to academia but might wonder how such a calling might look or worry that they won't be able to succeed. The authors advise other women to respond with God. 'Always God.' And that is the best advice a Christian academic could receive."

Joanne Marshall, associate professor at Iowa State University and editor of the Work-Life Balance book series

"Like holy water for a parched soul, *Power Women* refreshes with a clear articulation of what had remained at the level of unspoken thoughts or ephemeral conversations. With this volume, a diverse set of voices speaks to the heart of what all Christian academic mothers hold: a deep sense of vocational calling both inside and outside the home as well as significant challenges to the flourishing of both vocations. Contemplation, conversation, and even institutional change will be the fruits of these faithfully honest words of power."

Amy Peeler, associate professor of New Testament at Wheaton College and Graduate School

"Though powerfully centering the diverse voices of women in the academy, this book is for all of us who strive to pursue an undivided calling as parents and professors in Jesus' name. For me, it is a source of grace and learning."

Robert Chao Romero, associate professor of Chicana/o, Central American, and Asian American studies at UCLA and author of *Brown Church: Five Centuries of Latina/o Social Justice, Theology, and Identity*

"Finally! This is the book I have wanted and needed for more than a decade. Now academic mothers will have easier access to mentors who can help them navigate the challenges and joys of their multiple callings. These essays weave vulnerable personal narratives with sociological research on women's experiences in the academy. The result is a judgment-free zone that makes space for a wide variety of approaches to the intersection of family and academic life. Readers will not only discover that they are not alone, but they will also come away from this book with strategies for thriving in their homes and in their careers."

Carmen Joy Imes, associate professor of Old Testament at Biola University

"Too often, working moms feel the pressure to 'get it all done' and live up to unrealistic expectations. As I read this book, I felt an immediate sense of solidarity with those who hold scholarly work and motherhood in creative tension. *Power Women* does not offer a one-size-fits-all approach to surviving motherhood and the academy as people of faith. Instead, each contributor shares hard-earned, embodied wisdom of how she embraces her complex, God-given vocations. They do this not as martyrs or superheroes but as finite, faithful human beings. This book should be read by those in need of encouragement and those who seek to support the thriving of working mothers in the academy."

Janette H. Ok, associate professor of New Testament at Fuller Theological Seminary

POWER WOMEN

STORIES OF MOTHERHOOD, FAITH & THE ACADEMY

EDITED BY NANCY WANG YUEN
AND DESHONNA COLLIER-GOUBIL

FOREWORD BY
SHIRLEY HOOGSTRA

Academic

An imprint of InterVarsity Press
Downers Grove, Illinois

InterVarsity Press
P.O. Box 1400, Downers Grove, IL 60515-1426
ivpress.com
email@ivpress.com

InterVarsity Press® is the book-publishing division of InterVarsity Christian Fellowship/USA®, a movement of students and faculty active on campus at hundreds of universities, colleges, and schools of nursing in the United States of America, and a member movement of the International Fellowship of Evangelical Students. For information about local and regional activities, visit intervarsity.org.

All Scripture quotations, unless otherwise indicated, are taken from The Holy Bible, New International Version®, NIV®. Copyright © 1973, 1978, 1984, 2011 by Biblica, Inc.™ Used by permission of Zondervan. All rights reserved worldwide. www.zondervan.com. The "NIV" and "New International Version" are trademarks registered in the United States Patent and Trademark Office by Biblica, Inc.™

While any stories in this book are true, some names and identifying information may have been changed to protect the privacy of individuals.

The publisher cannot verify the accuracy or functionality of website URLs used in this book beyond the date of publication.

Cover design and image composite: Faceout Studio
Interior design: Jeanna Wiggins
Image: blue abstract ink strokes: © Hedzun Vasyl / Shutterstock Images

ISBN 978-0-8308-5306-9 (print)
ISBN 978-0-8308-5334-2 (digital)

Printed in the United States of America ♾

InterVarsity Press is committed to ecological stewardship and to the conservation of natural resources in all our operations. This book was printed using sustainably sourced paper.

Library of Congress Cataloging-in-Publication Data
Names: Yuen, Nancy Wang, 1976- editor. | Collier-Goubil, Deshonna, 1977-
   editor.
Title: Power women : stories of motherhood, faith, and the academy / edited
   by Nancy Wang Yuen, PhD, Deshonna Collier-Goubil, PhD.
Description: Downers Grove, IL : InterVarsity Press, [2021] | Includes
   bibliographical references.
Identifiers: LCCN 2021012990 (print) | LCCN 2021012991 (ebook) | ISBN
   9780830853069 (print) | ISBN 9780830853342 (digital)
Subjects: LCSH: Mothers—Religious life. | Women college
   teachers—Religious life. | Motherhood—Religious aspects—Christianity.
   | Professions—Religious aspects—Christianity.
Classification: LCC BV4529.18 .P69 2021 (print) | LCC BV4529.18 (ebook) |
   DDC 248.8/431—dc23
LC record available at https://lccn.loc.gov/2021012990
LC ebook record available at https://lccn.loc.gov/2021012991

P   25   24   23   22   21   20   19   18   17   16   15   14   13   12   11   10   9   8   7   6   5   4   3   2   1

Y   37   36   35   34   33   32   31   30   29   28   27   26   25   24   23   22   21

To powerful professor mothers everywhere

and the children we steward

CONTENTS

FOREWORD

SHIRLEY HOOGSTRA

SOME THINGS YOU HAVE TO JUST LET GO. This was one of the biggest lessons I learned as a mother who also worked outside the home. This was not an easy lesson to learn. It came to me in a small set of circumstances but represented an ingrained mindset of having to do everything the best, a striving to be above criticism as a working mom.

My daughter was three. My son was five. I was working full time as an attorney in a high-pressure law firm. And my husband, a pediatrician, also had a job with complexity. Both of us were hands-on parents from the start. As for childcare, Jeff and I would usually split each day one week, and on the other week the children went to a great family and he or I would pick the children up in the early afternoon. On the week when we split the day, I would go in early in the morning and try to be home by 2:15 p.m. so that he could get to his office by 3:00 p.m. and work until 9:00 p.m., which allowed his practice to have evening office hours—something the parents in his practice loved. I regret how often I was late to what we called the "pass off." I found it hard to pull myself out midday and midstream. It added stress to his day to be racing against the clock to get into his office. On the days when he was home until 2:15 p.m., he would take the children to school. Our youngest, Mary, went to nursery school. It was an excellent little neighborhood Montessori school. Like most parents, we tried to have a stable home life, enjoyable educational and church opportunities, and consistent caregivers who added to our parenting time. But some things—those societal expectations I imposed upon myself—I just had to let go. One small example was how Mary's hair was done for school. In some ways, it was such a silly little thing. But in others, it seemed like a mark of my motherhood. She had long blonde hair, and in my head, I thought it needed to be done in braids or ponytails or headbands or barrettes. I had to learn that her hair wasn't a grade on my choice to work outside the home. I wasn't a bad mother because her hair was just combed with nothing fancy.

As all two-career parents know, family life is largely about what will be prioritized in the hundreds of pivots that happened every week. The drop-offs. The pickups. The sick child. The unexpected work demands. Making supper at the end of the day. Groceries. Getting the wash done. Arranging a playdate. Getting the birthday treat for school. Pivots that are necessary. Pivots that on some days or weeks feel endless. Add to the home pivots the expected and natural responsibilities you carry from having a job with multiple factors, threads, obligations, and expectations.

Amid the complexities, I knew I had a certain calling to be in my legal practice. I was good at it. I was serving others. I had a Christian witness. I was making a difference in the lives of my fellow law partners. I enjoyed mentoring younger men and women. The intellectual stimulation matched my desire to thrive in my legal work. My husband also had a medical calling to be a pediatrician. His patients loved him. He was kind and had a quiet, listening, and patient demeanor. He was a good partner to his fellow doctors and nurses. He was living out a right fit for his intellectual giftedness and his desire to serve his community.

What we committed to when we were married over forty years ago was that we would be for the other and work to ensure the other person could flourish because of our partnership. And that meant learning to do things we had not done before. He had to plan the craft projects for playgroups.

I had to negotiate telling male law partners who loved their families but set a workaholic pace that I needed a more flexible schedule. It meant that we had to practice forgiving ourselves when we didn't do it all very well; when we disappointed each other on the handoffs; when we didn't have enough time for each other because it was taken up by so many other urgencies. Or it meant not blaming if one of us (me) forgot to pick the children up from elementary school at the end of the day and one of the other mothers filled in for me. It was having an attitude that we were in this together and that our choice of living out vocational callings would also be a good role model for our children.

And it has been. Our children have seen a variety of family schedules. Some of their friends had stay-at-home moms, and they benefited from that. Our children had an interesting life with many visitors in our home or conversations that were above their age grade and stretched them. They learned independence and knew that their parents' lives were works in progress. We had to say that we were sorry when things didn't go right and that we loved being together. We valued each moment of the schedule when we were all together. This was the case from the beginning until now. We did not take it for granted. It was the result of grace.

As I look back at forty years of employment, thirty of them with children, I've learned four things. First, it's been worth it. I wouldn't have the opportunities I have today had I not stayed in the workforce in some way—sometimes full time and sometimes part time. Second, expect some regrets. You have regrets whether you chose one path or the other path. Regrets are inevitable. Be intentional about avoiding regrets to the extent you can, but remember that to believe all regrets are avoidable is an illusion. Third, God's vocational call on your life needs to be honored. It's not by accident that you have particular interests, abilities, or opportunities. These circumstantial, or what we might call providential, opportunities need to be read in light of the parable of the talents in Scripture (Matthew 25:14-30). Like the warning in this story, we are not to hide our talents in the ground. We are instructed to multiply them for the good of the kingdom of God. As believers, we can trust God to equip us for our whole lives—not just our work life or just our family life, but our whole God-submitted life. Last, I found that as my children started to discover the calling on their lives, we had much to talk about with them because we also had continued to ask God to reveal to us his calling on our lives. As emerging adults, they joined us on the journey of submitting the complexities of life to God's calling.

This book offers important stories, observations, and insights into one of the most important conversations for men and women faculty of faith in the academy. How do we fulfill God's call to our first promises—to God, our spouses, and our children? How do we fulfill God's call to be good stewards of our gifts and talents? How do we listen intently to when we should step in and should step out of certain rhythms of our lives? What happens when the unexpected happens? In sharing what worked and what didn't, where we failed and where we succeeded, we allow this generation and future generations to have standing stones to guide them. When all is said and done, what we hope God will say is, "Well done, good and faithful servant." And if said to us, frail humans, it will be through a lens of grace by the Author and Creator of grace. We all hope that we gave or are giving our lives up to God as an offering. And the stories in this book reflect those offerings today.

Humbled to be included in this book,
Shirley Hoogstra, president, Council for Christian Colleges and Universities

ACKNOWLEDGMENTS

I THANK ALL OF THE CONTRIBUTORS. They are my professor mother heroes, several of them also precious friends and sister-colleagues. I dedicate this book in honor of my nai-nai, who raised me. Even though she "barely finished high school" (her words, translated from Mandarin), she is one of the sharpest and most capable human beings I've ever known. I appreciate my family for always supporting me, especially my partner who does much more than his share of household chores. He is the antithesis of toxic masculinity. His unconditional love for me is a gift. I am who I am today because of him. I am grateful for my children, who taught me that I could love more than I imagined possible. I give glory to God whose unconditional love, justice, and compassion sustain me through the wilderness. (Nancy)

I am thankful to God for willing this book into existence and allowing me the opportunity of experiencing it firsthand. I am grateful to my children who made me a professor mommy; your curiosity, energy, vitality, and the pure joy that your life gives mine are remarkable and truly what pulled me back from the brink at my lowest point. Thank you to my parents (Bruce and Glenda), my sister and brother in love (Sadania and Michael), and my friends who are like family to me, who have been my amazing support system, enabling me to work on this project to completion. My sorors (Delta Sigma Theta Sorority, Inc., Fairfax County and Pomona Valley Alumnae Chapters), my Link, Inc. sisters (San Bernardino Valley Chapter), colleagues at Azusa Pacific University, and so many others, thank you for surrounding me with love and support on this challenging, beautiful, fun-filled, adventurous ride of being a mom, professor, department chair, and community member. Thank you especially to all of our contributing authors and their families for giving of themselves, their time, and their stories to enhance us all. (Deshonna)

INTRODUCTION

CONSIDERING MOTHERHOOD
AND THE ACADEMY

ACADEMICS LOVE A PERFECT PLAN. Some of us imagine hitting professional and personal milestones in harmonious syncopation: complete grad school in two to eight years, get a tenure-track job immediately afterward, perhaps find a supportive spouse, and have children when everything is settled. But the journey rarely unfolds as we expect. Roadblocks and potholes appear on our best paved roads, forcing us to change routes and veer into unfamiliar, sometimes scary, places. Timing motherhood can be a challenge; as one academic mother shared, "There is no ideal time to have children. In grad school you have more time, but you have no money. Once you become an assistant professor, you have more money, but you have no time."[1]

Nonetheless, professor mothers are on the rise. In 2014, 80 percent of women ages forty to forty-four with a PhD or professional degree had given birth, compared to 65 percent in 1994.[2] Working mothers face many career

---

[1] Quotes are included throughout the text from academic mothers surveyed by the editors.

[2] A. W. Geiger, Gretchen Livingston, and Kristen Bialik, "6 Facts about US Moms," *Fact Tank* (blog), *Pew Research Center*, May 8, 2019, www.pewresearch.org/fact-tank/2019/05/08/facts-about-u-s-mothers/.

hurdles compared to working fathers. To accommodate children, women are more likely to cut back on their work hours just as their careers are taking off, while men with children can often afford to work longer hours and advance in their careers.[3] This unequal division of childcare and household labor can result in a "mom penalty" and a "dad premium." For academic mothers, this translates to fewer work options. They are 132 percent more likely than fathers to end up in low-paid contingent positions.[4] Academic mothers also face a tenure gap: men with children and women without children are three times more likely to get tenure than women with children.[5]

While this book has been in process, the gender gap has widened due to the Covid-19 pandemic with school and daycare centers closures; childcare and homeschooling duties fall disproportionately on mothers. Women's publishing rates have declined relative to men's amid the pandemic across all disciplines.[6] Women are also less likely to start new research projects, which can have long-term consequences for publications down the line.[7] Working moms across industries have been hit hard by the pandemic and the long-term career impacts are still yet to be seen. NPR Journalist Terry Gross expresses the multi-layered repercussions for working moms:

> As a working parent, I can tell you there are only so many months that you can wake up at dawn or work after bedtime in order to get it all done. It's just not sustainable. And so what's happened is that either people have had to figure out their own alternate arrangements or they're just really incredibly burnt out, [with their] mental health really suffering, or else they've had to cut back on work, either quit, cut back their hours, not apply for the

[3]Andrea Hsu, "Even the Most Successful Women Pay a Big Price in Pandemic," *All Things Considered*, NPR, October 20, 2020, www.npr.org/2020/10/20/924566058/even-the-most-successful-women-are-sidelining-careers-for-family-in-pandemic.
[4]Nicholas H. Wolfinger Mason and Marc Goulden. *Do Babies Matter? Gender and Family in the Ivory Tower* (New Brunswick, NJ: Rutgers University Press, 2013), 38.
[5]Mason and Goulden, *Do Babies Matter*, 28.
[6]Giuliana Viglione, "Are Women Publishing Less During the Pandemic? Here's What the Data Say," *Nature*, May 20, 2020, www.nature.com/articles/d41586-020-01294-9.
[7]Viglione. "Are Women Publishing Less."

promotion they wanted. And these things are just going to have really deep, long-term effects on their careers.[8]

This drop in productivity, compounded over time, can disadvantage academic mothers' career advancement and satisfaction. Not only do working mothers prioritize children over careers, they also prioritize them over housework, time with their spouse, and time for themselves.[9] In fact, working mothers are spending as much time with their children today as mothers in the 1960s and 1970s, when more women were stay-at-home moms.[10] As a result, they risk feeling overwhelmed and rushed at all times.

The building blocks for this book began when a group of academic mothers with young children decided to gather together at a Christian university. We experienced both the challenges and joys of raising children as professors and mothers of faith. To avoid emotional and spiritual burnout, we met once a month to support each other through questions of how to balance children, marriage, work, and faith. We called ourselves the "Professor Mommy" group, and our regular lunches became "water cooler" time for talking about career and family. We prayed for one another when there were crises in the workplace as well as trouble at home. Two of our members even crafted what eventually became our university's first official parental leave policy. We formed reading groups and invited special speakers, senior professor mothers who had survived and thrived in the academy, to encourage us in our journeys. Eventually our children grew older and the meetings faded. But we always longed for a book about us: powerful academic mothers of faith. This collection of advice, experiences, and voices of Christian professor mothers from different universities and backgrounds is the culmination of that calling.

Christian academic mothers may have unique experiences. Some face judgment or pushback as working mothers. At her first faculty retreat at a

---

[8]Terry Gross. "Almost a Year Into the Pandemic Working Moms Feel 'Forgotten,' Journalist Says." February 18, 2021. www.npr.org/2021/02/18/968930085/almost-a-year-into-the-pandemic -working-moms-feel-forgotten-journalist-says.

[9]S. M. Bianchi, M. A. Milkie, and J. P. Robinson. *The Changing Rhythms of American Family Life* (New York: Russell Sage Foundation, 2006), 169.

[10]Bianchi, Milkie, and Robinson. *Changing Rhythms*, 169.

Christian university, one of the contributors was repeatedly assumed to be the wife of a professor (rather than a professor herself), likely because she was visibly pregnant with a toddler in tow. Similarly, a pastor's wife was in disbelief that another contributor could be a professor as her young children ran circles around them. At the same time, several contributors to this book who work at Christian universities felt uniquely supported by their department chairs and colleagues who recognized their need for flexible work schedules to accommodate childcare. One of the editors is a more empathetic supervisor of faculty moms in the academy, having firsthand knowledge of the potential pitfalls of being an academic mother.

As editors, we want to arm you with knowledge and wisdom as you journey through motherhood and the academy. You are not alone. Despite all of the challenges and obstacles, we love being mothers, professors, administrators, and daughters of God. We have curated chapters written by professors in different fields including education, science, social science, and the humanities, along with administrators. The contributors have children of various ages and one even has grandchildren. Many teach at private Christian universities while some work at public and private secular ones. While they do not encompass the full diversity of Christian academic mothers, we hope they provide insight into what it means to balance work, family, and faith. We have organized the chapters into four sections: (1) Navigating Academia, (2) Navigating Motherhood, (3) Navigating Multiple Callings, and (4) Navigating Support.

In part one, "Navigating Academia," we share how professor mothers navigate research, teaching, and parental leave. We want to share some good news. Although women with young children experience a dip in publication productivity during those first few years, mothers actually produce more than their peers over time.[11] Over the lifespan of a thirty-year career, women with children outperform childless workers at nearly every stage of the game.[12] Kids, it turns out, are "the ultimate efficiency hack."[13]

---

[11]Jenny Anderson, "The Ultimate Efficiency Hack: Have Kids," *Quartz*, October 10, 2016, https://qz.com/802254/the-ultimate-efficiency-hack-have-kids/.

[12]Anderson, "Ultimate Efficiency Hack."

[13]Anderson, "Ultimate Efficiency Hack."

In chapter one, Dr. Maria Su Wang shares how she manages to carve out time for research as a mother of young children. Besides research, the amount of energy that we devote to our students can feel overwhelming, even more so when caring for young children. In chapter two, Dr. Stephanie Chan demonstrates how mothering and teaching can be symbiotic, allowing one to enhance the other.

Though most universities have parental leave, the decision to take time off is not always simple. There remains confusion about what parental leave entails. Some academic moms have served on promotion committees where men dismiss parental leave as "time off." In chapter three, Dr. Teri Clemons breaks down misconceptions about parental leave to better support new mother academics. For some academic moms like adjunct professors, parental leave will never be an option. In chapter four, Dr. Yiesha L. Thompson describes how, with little institutional support, adjunct mothers may experience external and internal pressures to teach and advise, often at the sacrifice of their families.

In part two, "Navigating Motherhood," we look at how Christian professor mothers often pressure themselves to achieve some sort of idealized motherhood. This section begins by deconstructing the idea of a "good" mother. In chapter five, Dr. Christina Lee Kim, a psychologist and mother of three daughters, encourages readers to reflect on how external expectations combine with their unique experiences to shape their ideals of motherhood. Then we move onto Dr. Ji Y. Son, a cognitive scientist who deconstructs motherhood expectations and urges readers to reconsider their usefulness. In chapter six, she argues that working mothers actually approximate the category of the "traditional dad." Therefore, she proposes that professor mothers—by reconceptualizing themselves—can experience less internal struggle and more joy in parenting. In chapter seven, Dr. Jean Neely ruminates on God's motherly love. She writes: "Beginning to consider God not merely as Father but as Loving Mother has helped to transform my inner life and dislodge deep spiritual anxiety I used to carry around. Giving myself permission to relate to God as Mother, together with the experience of actually being a mom, has been remarkably healing."

In part three, "Navigating Multiple Callings," we feature Christian academic mothers who juggle multiple callings. In chapter eight, Dr. Jenny Pak shares the struggles of occupying multiple roles as a pastor's wife, a mother, and a psychology professor. She reconciles the often-overwhelming demands of ministry, home, and work life by seeing all of it as service to God. Some Christian professors may feel called to ministry as a pastor. In chapter nine, the Rev. Dr. Jennifer McNutt describes how she answered a threefold calling of motherhood, academy, and the pastorate. She reminds us that our desire to "have it all" only works if "what we ultimately mean by that is seeking the imperishable prize already won for us through Jesus Christ."

As educators, some Christian academics may consider homeschooling their children but don't know where to begin. In chapter ten, Dr. Yvana Uranga-Hernandez documents how she homeschools her four children while working as a full-time professor of speech-language pathology. She also emphasizes how asking for help and support from others is essential to balancing multiple roles.

In part four, "Navigating Support," we discuss how support is essential for Christian academic mothers to survive and thrive. More than ever, professor mothers are feeling stretched in their duties to work and family. Whether professor mothers are breadwinners, solo-earners, or part of duo-working families, they need support. In chapter eleven, the editors examine the village that raises a child, focusing on the role fathers play as well as the larger support network in the case of solo mothers. Dr. Deshonna Collier-Goubil details how, as a young widow and solo professor mom, she assembled an extensive support network of family and friends to care for her twins. Given that mothers are now the primary breadwinners in four in ten US families, the breadwinning professor mothers in this book are part of a growing population in higher education and beyond.[14] In chapter twelve, Dr. Joy Qualls relays how she relies on her husband's servant-leadership to thrive as their family's breadwinner.

Professor mothers can also give and receive support through mentorship and self-care. In chapter thirteen, Dr. Doretha O'Quinn, based on her

---

[14]Geiger, Livingston, and Bialik, "6 Facts about US Moms."

vast experience as a higher education administrator, describes how professor mothers can support one another through mentoring. She draws from her expertise as a mentor to mothers within academia and as an instructor of higher education courses on mentorship. Dr. O'Quinn also emphasizes the necessity of self-care to overall wellness.

In the back of the book, we've included questions designed for you to reflect either individually or collectively on how the topics apply to your own lives. We encourage faculty mothers of faith as well as administrators and allies to read this book in reading groups as a way to build community. We pray this book will guide you in your journey—whether you are in the beginning or somewhere along the way, whether for yourself or as an ally. We've gained so much wisdom and strength from our fellow faculty mothers of faith. We hope you will too.

PART ONE

NAVIGATING ACADEMIA

DIVVYING UP LOVE

SCHOLARLY AMBITION AND MOTHERHOOD
AS SPIRITUAL FORMATION

MARIA SU WANG, PhD

IT'S ALMOST THREE O'CLOCK on a Monday afternoon. I'm trying to finish up a bit of writing—frantically skimming and taking notes on a new source that I picked up yesterday—while constantly keeping an eye on the time displayed at the top right-hand corner of my computer screen. Three o'clock, right when my son's school day ends, is when the internal negotiations begin: *Should I keep him at after-school care until four or five, so I can finish taking these notes? Will he be upset that I didn't get him earlier? But I'm in a good writing groove right now, I don't want to lose the momentum. Tomorrow is a long teaching day, so I won't be able to spend as much time with him. Maybe I will just get him sooner and finish up this work later tonight, after he goes to bed.*

This last line of thought, premised on the lure of the academic mother's time flexibility, usually wins out. And just as frequently, at nighttime I don't return to the scholarly work I was doing earlier.

This scenario plays out innumerable times every week. My conflict—choosing between time spent on my scholarship and time spent with my children—resonates with a recent article in *The Atlantic*, where journalist Erika Hayasaki questions the notion, generally assumed in our culture today, that motherhood and the creative life (or fulfilling career/intellectual life) are incompatible. In addition to interviewing several working mothers who shared similar concerns, Hayasaki reveals her own anxieties when she found out she was pregnant with twins:

> How would I manage three kids, even with an all-in partner, while also keeping up my journalistic life? I only had so much energy. I would have to divide it. What portion would each family member receive? What portion would that leave for my work? It was not just about energy. It was about divvying up love.[1]

Hayashi's confession speaks to the heart of the perceived conflict between being a writer and a mother—a conflict of time, attention, and energy between two fiercely important values: the desire to maintain her creative output and the equally strong desire to be an engaged parent. Moreover, her image of "divvying up love" exemplifies a dominant cultural trope that prevails in our current discourse surrounding the difficulties of managing both motherhood and working life—as one of tension, conflict, and self-division.

This essay explores and interrogates the Christian academic mother's attempt to "divvy up love": that is, being keenly aware of the *potential* for more (as a scholar, teacher, and leader) and yet also painfully conscious of one's limited capacity because of this season of life. I probe and reflect on what it means to live in the space of constantly partitioning oneself among many loves, especially as it relates to the yearning to maintain an active scholarly life while remaining an actively involved parent. At the same time, I want to be reflective about the language of "divvying up love" and what it connotes and signifies. The other project of this essay is to interrogate the kind of language we use to describe being torn between many loves

---

[1] Erika Hayasaki, "How Motherhood Affects Creativity," *The Atlantic*, September 13, 2017, www.theatlantic.com/science/archive/2017/09/how-motherhood-affects-creativity/539418/.

and how that language can shape how we think and feel about what we do. My hope is that by being conscious of the terms we use, we can imagine other ways of embodying motherhood and scholarly ambition. I begin by reviewing several recent think pieces written on motherhood and professional life from the past decade, probing their ideas, themes, and language. The second half of the essay will explore how the Bible discusses ambition, identity, and time—using scriptural passages to ponder the weaving of motherhood and scholarly ambition. I will think through how the experience of both motherhood and the research process can be vehicles for sanctification. I conclude with some personal reflection and questions for new academic mothers who desire to continue with an active scholarly life. More than anything, the goal of this essay is to *make visible* and articulate the experience of Christian academic mothers who yearn to be productive in scholarship and feel the pull and responsibility of motherhood. I hope that by simply acknowledging the ambivalence, frustration, and complexity that can accompany the striving for both to coexist, we might actually move forward toward making this coexistence seem less elusive.

WORKING MOTHERHOOD OBSERVED

In the past decade, there have been numerous essays on motherhood and work from academics, journalists, and artists alike.[2] We live in a cultural moment in which women (and some men) are questioning, more intensely than ever, whether being successful in one's career *and* being an active parent are truly possible. One recurring lament that shows up in many of these essays is the fundamental conflict in time and energy between being devoted to our careers and to our children. Time, according to these authors, is a zero-sum game: there is a finite amount, and time spent on one

---

[2]The most notable ones include Anne-Marie Slaughter's cover story, "Why Women Can't Have It All," *The Atlantic*, July/August 2012, https://www.theatlantic.com/magazine/archive/2012/07/why-women-still-cant-have-it-all/309020/, and Mary Ann Mason, "In the Ivory Tower, Men Only," *Slate*, June 17, 2013, https://slate.com/human-interest/2013/06/female-academics-pay-a-heavy-baby-penalty.html. See www.theatlantic.com/business/archive/2012/06/women-having-it-all-the-debate-so-far/258920/ for a summary of articles in response to Slaughter, as well as www.theatlantic.com/debates/women-workplace/ for an archive of related articles, including interviews with Slaughter.

pursuit (writing, work) is time taken from another (family, children). In these essays, work and motherhood are essentially competitive. So how have women managed the conflict of time and energy between work and family life? What have these essays advised about how to resolve the two?

Number of children and my experience. One option toward mitigating the conflict of time and energy is to have only one child. In her essay in *The Atlantic*, Lauren Sandler quotes Alice Walker's famous declaration that women "should have children—assuming this is of interest to them—but only one," since "with one you can move . . . with more than one you're a sitting duck."[3] This prescription makes sense in a certain way. With one child, the number of parents still outnumbers the child. There is a greater possibility of an equitable division of labor, of handing off childcare responsibilities once your partner can relieve you. When I only had my son, I planned an ambitious research agenda that involved me waking up at six every weekday morning so that I could squeeze in an hour of uninterrupted writing time before he woke. Since he was a good sleeper, with regular hours, this was relatively easy to achieve (notwithstanding my own discipline!). For about a year, I set my alarm for 6 a.m., rolled out of bed and made some tea, and then sleepily shuffled to my desk to devote approximately thirty to forty-five minutes to daily writing. I presented at three national and international conferences that year, including the most prestigious one in my discipline. I felt like a professor-mommy rock star. My days were scheduled down to the half-hour block, requiring tremendous care on my part not to "waste" any time. Even when my son got sick, which he inevitably did because of being in daycare, it did not derail my research goals. My husband and I had organized our respective schedules and childcare responsibilities down to a finely tuned science.

By the time my daughter was born, however, such a carefully calibrated life could no longer persist. Not only did she wake up every night to nurse for over a year, she was also a spotty sleeper. While she napped well during the day, I now had another child to consider during those hours, on top of

---

[3]Lauren Sandler, "The Secret to Being Both a Successful Writer and a Mother: Just Have One Kid," *The Atlantic*, June 7, 2013, www.theatlantic.com/sexes/archive/2013/06/the-secret-to-being -both-a-successful-writer-and-a-mother-have-just-one-kid/276642/.

teaching three classes and being involved in a very time-intensive university committee. The thought of waking early to accomplish even a little writing seemed to require monumental effort, which I couldn't muster at the time. Even though I was well-versed in the literature that advocated for a daily writing habit (especially early-morning writing) as the key to long-term research success, I couldn't do it. It felt like it was asking too much of myself, even for a determined, disciplined "morning person" like me. I had to shift my writing goals. I began to attend one conference a year. My drive to write and research declined. I was puzzled, even alarmed, by this reduction at first. How could adding one more child seem to occupy so much of my mental, emotional, and intellectual space? Why did one more child make such a difference, even with a partner who remained as involved as he could?

I am still not completely sure why having an additional child made such a difference. Perhaps it was physical—my kids are four years apart, so I was older when I had my daughter, and thus presumably had less energy than with the first one. It was very likely circumstantial as well: four months after my daughter was born, my husband accepted a new job that would require him to commute an hour to an hour and a half each way every day. That new morning routine alone greatly altered our family rhythms and also meant he was not as present to share in domestic responsibilities. But I suspect that the biggest shift was mental and emotional, and perhaps not even a conscious one. Having two children, for me, meant a general acceptance of, maybe even resignation toward, being enmeshed and embedded in the mundane realities of childcare: of double the scheduling and to-do lists and making sure someone is there at pickup. It meant resigning myself to the increased *mental labor* of caretaking—which is somehow harder to share evenly between two partners once another child is added to the mix. The consequence is that this mental load inevitably falls more on one partner than the other (usually the female one), and thus takes over a greater portion of her mental, emotional, and physical life, all of which distracts from the kind of concentrated focus and deep thinking required to do scholarly work. This happened to me after having my second child, and I acknowledge this reality without regret or resentment. What it meant, however, is that I had to redefine what it looked like for me to pursue a research agenda now that I had less mental space for it.

Given the increased mental labor that comes with having more than one child, another option is to "back down," as Yael Chatav Schonbrun puts it.[4] Schonbrun, a psychologist and assistant professor of psychiatry and human behavior at Brown University, describes the choice of remaining in her academic profession at a reduced capacity as one that "allows [her] to be engaged in multiple roles, as a researcher, therapist and home-based mom." Yet while this choice has enabled her to stay involved in her profession, Schonbrun admits that the greater consequence has been to her sense of self:

> It . . . means that my productivity within each role is limited. . . . More painful . . . is sitting in on a research meeting, listening to my colleagues bounce around new project ideas and talk about complex data analytics or new methods. . . . Where I used to feel like a member of the group, and a leader on some projects, I now feel a half step behind. . . . I will continue to be an unknown in my research community. No one is going to ask me to speak about my scientific contributions, because, in all honesty, I just haven't contributed enough.[5]

Schonbrun honestly admits that the cost of choosing to reduce her research time is a sense of anonymity within her field and the recognition that she cannot participate to the same degree as her colleagues. This diminished sense of professional identity, further complicated by the knowledge of the *potential* to do more, is probably the hardest aspect of choosing to "back down and not bail out" in one's career. On the one hand, Schonbrun illustrates the notion that some kind of scholarly participation, however small it may feel, is better than none at all. On the other hand, that smaller form of participation can further magnify the sense of alienation one feels from one's discipline at large.

---

[4]Yael Chatav Schonbrun, "A Mother's Ambition," July 30, 2014, *New York Times*, https://opinionator .blogs.nytimes.com/2014/07/30/a-mothers-ambitions/.
[5]Schonbrun, "Mother's Ambition."

This paradox—the desire to hold onto my research ambitions and yet being conscious that the very act of holding on means becoming more aware of being a "step behind"—has shaped my own experience of pursuing research as both a mother and a professor at a teaching-intensive institution. It means being constantly satisfied with "enough"—enough time spent on this task, enough sources to fulfill this particular section of literature review, enough revision on the draft as a whole—while recognizing and rejecting the possibility of that alternate self, that fantasy of an idealized writing product "if only" there were more time, institutional resources, or mental space. It is a life of endless circumscription, of compelling myself to restrict, limit, and demarcate. It means resisting the inevitable pull toward expansion. Academia—whether in writing, teaching, or service—is a profession that can always demand more: more time, more energy, and more attention. While this is surely the case for many careers, it is particularly palpable in the exploratory nature of the research and writing process. More time and contemplation spent yields a depth and complexity to one's ideas that cannot be forced in a shorter span. It is what makes the creation of knowledge interesting and meaningful. And yet I continually find myself needing to limit the pursuit of ideas and arguments simply because there is not enough mental space, even though my intellectual being ardently, even fiercely, yearns to do more.

I want to add that I am not saying that setting limits is not a natural part of the research and writing process. It is evident that any kind of research inquiry requires choosing some paths and foreclosing others. But what I am trying to convey, as Schonbrun so poignantly points out, is that feeling of being "half a step behind" and knowing that this is a choice of my own making. That this choice, like the many related to it, is complicated by numerous other considerations that go beyond my desires and individual will. Is feeling half a step behind better than not joining in at all? To put it another way, is it better *not* to attend the top conferences in my field, where I can feel self-conscious and frustrated at my own lack of achievement compared with those around me, or is it better to still attend and aspire? Even though I have chosen the latter, I wonder sometimes whether I would feel less divided, and perhaps (to be honest) less about *myself*, if I were to give up my writing goals altogether and instead devote myself more fully to my teaching and family life, as many of my colleagues have chosen, rather than trying to make room for a little of everything.

Conflicting norms. Trying to make room for everything—research, teaching, service, and motherhood, among others—is a symptom of what Sarah A. Birken and Jessica L. Borelli, drawing on Robert Drago's work, identify as the three norms that make it difficult for "professor mommies" to succeed in the US academy: the motherhood norm, the ideal worker norm, and the individualism norm.[6] To briefly summarize, the motherhood norm refers to the notion that "women should, for little or no pay, care for their families and others in need." In academia, the motherhood norm bears out both in a woman's actual time spent on childcare and in her academic work. For the former, the greater time flexibility afforded in academia often means that women routinely spend more time caring for their children than their spouses. In terms of the latter, it frequently means that women tend to spend more time on teaching and service work compared to male colleagues. The ideal worker norm reflects the idea that the best workers are those who are totally committed to their careers. Given the fluid nature of academic work, in which one can work outside the boundaries of specific locations and certain hours, this norm invariably means that academics could conceivably be working all the time: in the evenings, late at night, and even on weekends. Finally, the individualism norm refers to the idea that institutions should only offer limited help to those in need, effectively leaving many workers fending for themselves when it comes to important supportive services such as childcare.

These three norms, while not specific to academia, are exacerbated by the time flexibility inherent in academic life. Time flexibility is usually considered a good thing, something many commenters have argued actually

---

[6]Sarah A. Birken and Jessica L. Borelli, "Coming Out as Academic Mothers," January 15, 2014, *The Chronicle of Higher Education*, www.chronicle.com/article/coming-out-as-academic-mothers/. See also Mason, "Ivory Tower;" and Robert W. Drago, *Striking a Balance: Work, Family, Life* (Boston: Dollars and Sense, 2007).

supports women's careers.[7] Yet for the academic mother, it actually intensi-
fies the felt impact of the motherhood and the ideal worker norms. The idea
that we can work whenever we want, wherever we want, and thus can adjust
our work hours and rhythms to our children's schedule, combined with the
porous nature of academic work itself, means that theoretically we could be
working all the time, beyond a nine-to-five schedule. The academic mother
thus experiences two opposing, contradictory impulses: we could always be
working (the ideal worker norm), but we could also always be devoting more
time to our children (the motherhood norm). These two conflicting ideals
are further compounded by the fact that the measures of achievement in
academia are relentlessly time bound, encoded in the organizing principle
of that prime document of productivity, the academic curriculum vitae,
which sorts all categories according to yearly progress: time to publication,
annual conference presentations, and so on. Thus, time flexibility for the
academic mother means her time outside of the classroom and committee
meetings can easily go toward her children, yet her scholarly productivity
requires increased time pressure. In other words, her daily life affords a
flexibility tilted toward more intensive parenting that may not support the
scholarly productivity needed for her to earn tenure or advance in her field.

SCRIPTURAL REFLECTIONS

Having considered the plight of an academic mother who desires to maintain an active research agenda through the lens of the motherhood, ideal
worker, and individualism norms, as well as the language of time conflict
that crop up so frequently in discussions of motherhood and professional
life, is it any wonder that many women decide to give up any semblance
of a sustained writing life after they've had children? With few institutional
resources and support, and the pervasive culture of the individualism
norm that conditions us to think that striving for research is simply a
matter of personal determination and effort, many academic moms can
feel defeated before even starting. By pointing out these structural

---

[7]Slaughter actually advocates for this toward the end of her essay, as one way that women can
maintain their careers and still be involved in their families.

obstacles, then, I want to recognize the felt difficulties of women like me, who desire to still participate in the knowledge production of our fields and yet feel constrained by both institutional and personal limits. Given the current discourse, it seems as if the only sensible choice is to have one child or to "back down" and resolve the psychic and emotional ramifications of that choice. These two options, however, are both unsatisfactory. Moreover, a scriptural lens and perspective can soften the presumed hard delineations between work versus family life. So in the remaining half of this essay, I ask, *How might Scripture guide us away from the paradigm of time conflict and competition?* Does Scripture offer a counternarrative to the imagery of tension, conflict, and fracture often invoked in essays on how to manage both motherhood and career?

When I read the Scriptures, several passages stand out regarding how the Bible represents time. Here are some of my general observations. This list is not meant to be exhaustive, but rather a starting point for conversation and reflection.

God's time is not like our time. In 2 Peter 3:8, it says, "But do not forget this one thing, dear friends: With the Lord a day is like a thousand years, and a thousand years are like a day." God is outside of time because he created it. In the Genesis account of the creation of the world, the creation of time—the separation of night and day—occurs on the first day. In those early chapters of Genesis, God creates the physical principles of nature that will govern our world, including time. Yet God is not bound by those same principles. As 2 Peter reminds us, God is not only *not* bound by time, his way of measuring time is vastly different than ours. We, however, since we exist *in* time, are bound by its rules. We must abide by a twenty-four-hour day, by day and night, by seasonal change, and so on.

Our time is finite, both in a daily sense and in terms of our earthly existence. First Peter 1:24-25 reminds us:

> All people are like grass,
> > and all their glory is like the flowers of the field;
> the grass withers and the flowers fall,
> > but the word of the Lord endures forever.

Unlike God, our time on earth is limited, which is why we must steward our time well. As Psalm 90:12 admonishes us, we should "number our days, that we may gain a heart of wisdom." Knowing that our time is finite explains why academic mothers feel so torn over how to apportion their time between work that is personally and professionally significant and our children, who are equally significant and important. While God is outside of time and the creator of it, we must reckon with our physical limits (we need rest, we need breaks) and the truth that our time on earth has an expiration date.

We reap what we sow. Galatians 6:7 tells us, "Do not be deceived: God cannot be mocked. A man reaps what he sows." This verse reminds us about how we spend our time. Just as our research productivity will languish if we do not invest time in it, so our children need our tending and care to help them establish character and values. This verse reminds us that things don't happen without intentionality. Yet our rate of reaping does not always correlate with how much we have invested. That is to say, there isn't a direct line between how much we sow and *when* or *how much* we reap. It is possible to sow for many years without reaping much at all. Or sometimes this may involve sowing in other activities for a time so that you can reap the benefit of additional time toward another endeavor. For example, for a new academic mom, it may be wise to sow additional time and effort into teaching in the earlier years so that you can reap the benefits of having sustained increased margin to pursue research later. At the same time, for the academic mother, this is also an encouragement that even a little sowing into your research, even during times that require more intense parenting, will eventually yield some fruit. But if we do not sow at all, we cannot reap.

Our lives comprise several seasons. The third chapter of Ecclesiastes famously begins with, "There is a time for everything, and a season for every activity under the heavens" (Ecclesiastes 3:1). The chapter goes on to delineate many of these activities, including "a time to plant and a time to uproot" (Ecclesiastes 3:2) and "a time to scatter stones and a time to gather them, a time to embrace and a time to refrain from embracing"

(Ecclesiastes 3:5). This notion of seasons in our lives, where some activities take greater priority than others, also resonates with Jesus' parable of the talents. In this parable, a master gives his three servants varying talents—one talent, two talents, and five talents—and asks them to do something with them while he is gone. The first two servants double the initial amount of talents they received while the last servant, who was only given one talent, buries his. Commentators have often interpreted this parable as one pointing to how we should invest the resources and talents given to us and that each person is given varying capacities. I think we can also see this parable as indicating the varying amounts of resources and capacities appointed at various *seasons* of our lives: sometimes it is one talent, sometimes it is two, and other times it is five. Yet we can't assume how much we are given and *when* those seasons might occur. The key idea in the parable is the notion of faithfulness toward what has been given.

How can these Scriptures redirect the academic mother who is struggling to maintain both her research ambitions and stay present with her family? The first two observations remind me of our position and posture toward God: one of frailty, humility, and dependency on an almighty Father. Hebrews 4:15-16 tells us that we can come before "God's throne of grace with confidence," expecting to receive his mercy and grace in our time of need.[8] As a mother and academic, these verses promise me that even though *I* may be bound by a twenty-four-hour day, limited by my physical weaknesses, I have access to a God who is not similarly limited. Rather, we have access to a God who has infinite wisdom and resources at hand, who created those boundaries in the first place. It means we can ask him how to navigate those boundaries and how to apportion time to each pressing task. It means asking God how to "divvy up our loves," knowing that it is not an exact formula but may look different every single day.

Furthermore, it also means having the confidence to ask God to *multiply* our time and efforts, depending on the available time we have each day.

---

[8]Hebrews 4:15-16 is, in its entirety, "For we do not have a high priest who is unable to empathize with our weaknesses, but we have one who has been tempted in every way, just as we are—yet he did not sin. Let us then approach God's throne of grace with confidence, so that we may receive mercy and find grace to help us in our time of need."

Some days may only permit thirty minutes or less for research and writing because of family needs or teaching demands. Some days are filled with meetings, student emails, and—a frequent concern for those with young children—child illness. I have learned that in those times of lack, when I feel most acutely the time conflict between work and family, that I can come before God and ask him to expand the effectiveness of those meager ten or fifteen minutes at hand. I may be limited by only twenty-four hours in a day, but God is not. I have experienced this grace (and what a grace it is!) many times, especially during my pre-tenure days. Sometimes a mere fifteen minutes of free writing produced the seed of my chapter's entire line of argument. At other times, a brief ten minutes helped me untangle an especially dense and tricky paragraph. At another time, I spent five minutes chasing down a citation that ended up being an especially important source for my work. I learned that time, in God's spiritual economy, similar to material and spiritual resources, is not simply linear and cumulative; rather, if we invite God into how we apportion our time, it can expand beyond those initial moments. Time, in other words, can multiply. I am reminded of Jesus feeding the five thousand in the Gospels. The young boy who approached Jesus only had five loaves and two fish, yet he willingly and humbly offered it to Jesus to do what he could with them. Jesus multiplied that initial small gift tenfold many times over. While we must steward our time carefully and diligently, we don't need to see it only in physical terms. Rather, there is a spiritual dimension as well, reminding us of the One we depend and rely on daily.

The idea of stewarding our time leads me to the second set of scriptural observations above—concerning sowing and reaping and seasons in our lives. These verses point us toward seeing our family and our ambitions as two separate priorities that both require our attention but at varying rates depending on our daily and seasonal contexts. Some days require more time spent on one over the other. This daily fluctuation necessitates flexibility in our thinking and in our daily rhythms. It should actually prompt us to seek more eagerly the presence of God for guiding us in discerning how to apportion our time. I have found that I cannot write in a hurry, just like I cannot love or teach in a hurry. If I am overwhelmed by the weight of all that is to be done, even if I have two hours to write, much of that time is squandered by worry. I have learned that in order to have an unhurried spirit, whether in writing or in being present with my children, I need to sow abundantly in God's presence and his Word in order to reap peace, stillness, and focus for the tasks at hand.

This soul work, I would argue, is just as important, if not more, as the mental work needed for our research. Slowing down and attending to our inner world makes us more aware of the deeper layers within us, the parts of our inner lives that are perhaps often repressed by busyness. I have found that attending to these feelings and bringing them before the Lord actually frees me to pursue my work with less distraction and anxiety. For example, how often have you spent close to thirty minutes of a writing session just trying to settle down in your spirit so you can actually begin writing? While this continues to be a struggle for me, I have also realized that this kind of restlessness is usually a sign that I need to address a deeper spiritual layer within me. Recently I was feeling very anxious and fretful over a conference paper that I needed to finish in a few weeks. Every time I tried to work on it, I found myself dawdling or feeling apprehensive. My initial thought was *I am feeling anxious because I don't have enough time to work on this.* School had just started for my kids, which also meant there had been a spate of minimum days and teacher service days. I started getting irritated with my husband, resenting him for not sharing equally in covering these non–school days. Yet as I probed further into why I was feeling so anxious, I realized that a large part of my resistance to writing this paper was based in feeling insecure about my topic and fearing others' judgment of my ideas. I was worried about their approval, which prevented me from even beginning. Once I realized this fear, I could bring it before the Lord directly. Rather than simply praying, "Lord, help me finish this paper," or, "Lord, free up more time for me to work on this," I could pray more specifically into this area of fear and insecurity: "Lord, release me from the fear of others' approval and judgment in writing this paper. Give me courage to express my ideas without worrying whether they sound silly or in line with what X has written." This second prayer gets at the reasons *why* it was difficult for me to complete the paper rather than just asking it to be done. It forced me into a greater awareness of my heart.

AUTHENTICITY AND WHOLENESS

I conclude with this exhortation toward greater soul care and spiritual awareness because I truly believe that this aspect—the spiritual—is key for the Christian academic mother who desires to pursue scholarly ambition and family life. So much of this work involves managing the fears and anxieties that can hinder our writing *and* our parenting. We can easily succumb to the motherhood, ideal worker, and individualism norms described above and feel stressed, divided, and worn out. Yet I think the beauty of both research and parenting is that both are long-term endeavors requiring patience and endurance. Both are also intensive, "all-in" activities. If we are willing, both the pursuit of scholarly ambition and parenting can compel us to strip the layers covering our hidden selves, revealing the vulnerable parts of our inner world that need God's light, and thus point to greater intimacy with Jesus. Both, therefore, are apt vehicles for *spiritual formation*. Through my felt conflict between the pursuit of research and being more present with my family, God has formed my heart and challenged my selfhood in ways that I did not expect. Scripture's counternarrative to the paradigm of time conflict and competition, I would argue, is the *opposite* of self-division: it is one that, paradoxically, leads to greater self-wholeness through the recognition of our limits, propelling us toward greater dependency on and trust in God. This trust manifests in releasing our research "to-do" lists, plans, and eventual outcomes for the day (and even in the future), as James 4:13-16 so wisely reminds us.[9] Learning to give our desires and plans—for our professional accomplishments, for our

---

[9]James 4:13-16 (NLT):
Look here, you who say, "Today or tomorrow we are going to a certain town and will stay there a year. We will do business there and make a profit." How do you know what your life will be like tomorrow? Your life is like the morning fog—it's here a little while, then it's gone. What you ought to say is, "If the Lord wants us to, we will live and do this or that." Otherwise you are boasting about your own plans, and all such boasting is evil. Remember, it is sin to know what you ought to do and then not do it.

children's growth and well-being—over to the Lord daily asks us to be present with our inner lives in a way that is at once freeing and terrifying. That kind of authenticity ultimately yields more wholeness.

So instead of time conflict and fracture, of "divvying up love," which can still *feel* all too true, I submit instead the idea of being honest about our ambitions, desires, and needs—that we want to participate fully in both our intellectual pursuits *and* our children's lives. We begin by acknowledging who we are—scholars and mothers—and we embrace both fully, believing that both identities can coexist in God's spiritual economy. Moreover, we grant that the struggle to realize this coexistence is a special gift for the Christian academic mother, an invitation to question and work out our received narratives and beliefs about our identities as women. As we invite God into the hidden, vulnerable places of our being through our work and parenting, we discover the encompassing love of the Father. We experience his love in a deeper way because we are more honest with him and ourselves, and thus we are transformed by these encounters. Rather than seeing our ambition and our families as mutually exclusive, we can instead see them as both part of our calling to worship God with our whole lives and whole selves, as Colossians 3:17 so aptly encourages us: "And whatever you do, whether in word or deed, do it all in the name of the Lord Jesus, giving thanks to God the Father through him."

THE SYNERGY
OF LULLABY
AND SYLLABI

STEPHANIE CHAN, PhD

WHEN JOE FASSLER of *The Atlantic* asked Celeste Ng, award-winning author of *Everything I Never Told You* and *Little Fires Everywhere*, about her favorite literary passage, Ng answered with *Goodnight Moon*—yes, the classic children's story by Margaret Wise Brown of a bunny going to bed and wishing "goodnight" to all the objects in the room. Ng explained to Fassler that she liked the mysterious and creepy nature of *Goodnight Moon* and its ability to provoke questions in the reader. She states, "So many of the details have this subtle, almost unnerving strangeness. This is a baby rabbit, so why is there a black office telephone beside his bed? Why is a red balloon floating around? And why is the whispering old lady's relationship to the child left so deliberately ambiguous?"[1] Her two novels begin with disquieting settings and

---

[1]Joe Fassler, "What Writers Can Learn from *Goodnight Moon*," *The Atlantic*, September 27, 2017, www.theatlantic.com/entertainment/archive/2017/09/celeste-ng-on-learning-from -goodnight-moon/541128/.

ask the reader to ponder what may have happened. What Ng's inspiration illustrates to me is a beautiful synergy between work and motherhood.

The dominant narrative we hear as professor mothers is that motherhood and academia are incompatible. And we hear it from two ends. From the academic world, we are told that mothers face a "baby penalty" and that kids are a "career killer."[2] From the larger social world, including the Christian world, we hear that mothers should be staying home with their children and not working.[3] Of Americans polled by Pew Research Center in 2013, 51 percent said that "children are better off with mother home" compared to 34 percent who said that "children are just as well off if mother works."[4] Contrast this with the 8 percent who said that "children are better off with father home" compared to 76 percent who said that "children are just as well off if father works." Yet in reality, most mothers work—specifically, 70 percent of them in 2015.[5] In their content analysis of 347 *New York Times* articles from 1991 to 2009 on the problems or benefits of being a working mother or stay-at-home mother, Motro and Vanneman find that the greatest share of these stories were about the "distressed working mother." These comprised 63 percent of the total articles.[6] Only 25 percent of the articles discussed working motherhood positively. Moreover, the number of "distressed working mother" articles had steadily *increased* from 1991 to 2009.

Less heralded are the ways in which syllabi and lullaby, or academic life and motherhood, are compatible and synergistic. This chapter will combine personal narrative with academic research to explore the ways in which being a mother can be beneficial for one's academic career, the ways in which

---

[2]Mary Ann Mason, "The Baby Penalty," *The Chronicle of Higher Education*, August 5, 2013, www .chronicle.com/article/The-Baby-Penalty/140813.

[3]Sally K. Gallagher and Christian Smith, "Symbolic Traditionalism and Pragmatic Egalitarianism: Contemporary Evangelicals, Families, and Gender," *Gender & Society* 13, no. 2 (April 1999), 211-33; Kim Parker, "Women More Than Men Adjust Their Careers for Family Life," *Fact Tank* (blog), *Pew Research Center*, October 1, 2015, www.pewresearch.org/fact-tank/2015/10/01/women -more-than-men-adjust-their-careers-for-family-life/.

[4]Parker, "Family Life."

[5]US Department of Labor, "Working Mothers Issue Brief," June 13, 2016, https://digital.library .unt.edu/ark:/67531/metadc955340/m2/1/high_res_d/Working_Mothers_Issue_Brief.pdf.

[6]Joanna Motro and Reeve Vanneman, "The 1990s Shift in the Media Portrayal of Working Mothers," *Sociological Forum* 30, no. 4 (December 2015): 1017-37.

being an academic can be beneficial for family life, and the ways in which faith can contribute to this positive interaction between work and home.

The academic term for this phenomenon is *work-life enrichment*. Greenhaus and Powell define work-life enrichment as "the extent to which experiences in one role improve the quality of life in the other role."[7] They explain that enrichment can go both ways: "Work-to-family enrichment occurs when work experiences improve the quality of family life, and family-to-work enrichment occurs when family experiences improve the quality of work life."[8] In their review of nineteen studies that measure work-life enrichment with self-report data, they find that "in almost every case in which a study assessed enrichment and conflict, the average enrichment score was at least as high as the average conflict score, and generally was substantially higher."[9] Thus these studies seem to suggest that many of us experience more work-life enrichment than work-life conflict. Yet this aspect of the work-life interface gets little personal or public attention. So let's talk about it more. Let's talk here about the ways in which academic and family lives can enrich one another. As I write this, I don't want to be dismissive about the real conflicts we as professor mothers do experience between academic and family life. They are very real, but they are only one part of the story.

As a way to think through work-family conflict and work-family enrichment, let's look at how social scientists have measured the two. First, let's think about work-life conflict:

- Do you have to miss family activities due to work responsibilities?
- Does feeling emotionally drained from work prevent you from contributing to your family?
- Do the behaviors that make you a more effective worker make you a worse parent or spouse?
- Do you have to miss work activities due to your family responsibilities?
- Does family stress make it difficult for you to concentrate on work?

---

[7]Jeffrey H. Greenhaus and Gary N. Powell, "When Work and Family Are Allies: A Theory of Work-Family Enrichment," *The Academy of Management Review* 31, no. 1 (January 2006): 73.
[8]Greenhaus and Powell, "Allies," 73.
[9]Greenhaus and Powell, "Allies," 75-76.

- Do the behaviors that make you a more effective parent make you a worse worker?

To the extent that you agree with these statements, you are experiencing work-family conflict.[10]

Now, let's think about work-life enrichment:

- Does your involvement in work help you understand different viewpoints which helps you to be a better family member?

- Does your work make you feel happy and thus help you be a better family member?

- Does your work help you feel personally fulfilled and thus help you be a better family member?

- Does your family help you to acquire skills that make you a better worker?

- Does your family put you in a good mood and thus help you to become a better worker?

- Does your family encourage you to use your work time in a more focused manner, which makes you a better worker?

To the extent that you agree with these statements, you are experiencing work-life enrichment.[11]

In taking inventory of my own life with these questions, I realized that, overall, as a professor mother, I experience much more work-life enrichment than work-life conflict. Yet I *think* about work-life conflict more than work-life enrichment, maybe because of all those newspaper articles, but maybe also because we tend to think about the bad things in our lives more than we think about the good things.[12]

---

[10]Russell A. Matthews, Lisa M. Kath, and Janet L. Barnes-Farrell, "A Short, Valid, Predictive Measure of Work-Family Conflict: Item Selection and Scale Validation," *Journal of Occupational Health Psychology* 15, no. 1 (January 2010): 75-90.

[11]Michele, K. Kacmar, Wayne S. Crawford, Dawn S. Carlson, Merideth Ferguson, and Dwayne Whitten, "A Short and Valid Measure of Work-Family Enrichment," *Journal of Occupational Health Psychology* 19, no. 1 (January 2014): 32-45.

[12]Roy F. Baumeister, Ellen Bratslavsky, Catrin Finkenauer, and Kathleen D. Vohs. "Bad is Stronger Than Good," *Review of General Psychology* 5, no. 4 (December 2001): 323-70.

I write this piece from two perspectives—as the child of a professor mother and as a professor mother. My mother and I are at very different stages in our career. I am eight years into my career as a professor and my mother is five years post-retirement. We are different types of academics. She was a health sciences researcher employed for all of her career in a joint appointment with a county medical center and a research university. She spent a majority of her time doing research and helping physicians design studies and interpret statistical findings. She had very few teaching responsibilities and when she did teach, she taught research fellows. I am a sociologist working at a private Christian university and spend the majority of my time teaching undergraduate students with a 4-4 teaching load. While the research expectations are lower, I am still expected to research and publish for promotion. There is also a high expectation at my university for service and for mentoring students. My mother has four adult children (three sons and one daughter) and ten grandchildren, two of whom are my two sons. Despite our differences, we have seen similarities in our experiences of work-life enrichment.

My mother's path did shape mine. Our parents can serve as role models in work-life balance, whether as positive role models of what to do or as negative role models for what not to do.[13] For me, my mother was a positive role model of success in both family and work life. In providing the child's perspective, I want to offer some reassurance to professor moms out there that your kids will turn out just fine. This evidence isn't just personal and anecdotal. In her interviews with daughters of successful working mothers, Jill Armstrong found that "almost all daughters believed that having a mother who worked long hours out of the home in a career that she found satisfying is consistent with feeling well loved and well mothered."[14]

Greenhaus and Powell's theory of work-life enrichment identifies five types of resources that one role can provide for the other.[15] These resources

---

[13]Ioana Lupu, Crawford Spence, and Laura Empson, "When the Past Comes Back to Haunt You: The Enduring Influence of Upbringing on the Work-Family Decisions of Professional Parents," *Human Relations* 71, no. 2 (February 2018): 155-81.

[14]Jill Armstrong, "Higher Stakes: Generational Differences in Mother and Daughters' Feelings about Combining Motherhood with a Career," *Studies in the Maternal* 9, no. 1 (August 2017): 11.

[15]Greenhaus and Powell, "Allies."

are (1) skills and perspectives, (2) psychological and physical resources, (3) social-capital resources, (4) flexibility, and (5) material resources. In reflecting on my life as a professor mother and as a daughter of a professor mother, I have found that work has enhanced my family life primarily in terms of skills and perspectives, psychological resources, and flexibility. I have also found that my family life enhances work particularly in terms of skills and perspectives and psychological resources. I will talk about each of these areas in turn. Then I will discuss how my Christian faith influences the work-life interface. While faith may seem to add increasing demands to the plate of a Christian professor mother, in reflecting on my own experiences, I find that faith contributes more resources for work-life balance and enrichment.

WORK ENRICHING FAMILY

Skills and perspectives. Work has given me certain skills and perspectives that enrich family life. One thing we academics are good at is gathering sound information and organizing this information. Knowing how to research and how to find reputable sources of information has given me greater tools to advocate for my children in educational and healthcare settings. Sociologist Annette Lareau found that the children of middle- and upper-class parents have an advantage when it comes to advocating for their children in institutional settings.[16] This is definitely the case for the children of professor mothers. When I was researching preschools for my first child, I read up on all the different preschool educational philosophies (Reggio Emilia, Montessori, High/Scope, Waldorf). I visited different preschools and used my qualitative research skills (ethnography and interviews) to analyze each preschool. I compiled these into an Excel spreadsheet and rated them on different criteria in order to compare them and determine the best one. Because I had taught Tobin and his colleagues' *Preschool in Three Cultures Revisited*, I knew what the National Association for the Education of Young Children (NAECY) was and why it was

---

[16]Annette Lareau, *Unequal Childhoods: Class, Race, and Family Life* (Berkeley: University of California Press, 2003).

important to enroll my child in a NAECY-accredited school.[17] I knew not to be worried when all it seemed like the kids were doing in preschool was playing—because from research we know that this is how kids learn the best. Probably not coincidentally, I ended up enrolling my child at the same preschool as another sociologist who lives in my area. I consulted research when deciding whether or not it would be wise to have my son repeat a year of preschool since he has an October birthday and would be one of the youngest in his class. (By the way, it's not entirely clear whether or not this benefits children, but I read more research indicating there could be a slight advantage at least in the earlier years.)

As a child, I benefited from the skills and perspectives that my mother had as a professor in the health sciences. She was my greatest advocate in healthcare settings and also taught me how to be an informed client of health care services. She taught me to bring a list of questions to my doctor's appointments. She would always research the best doctors. When dealing with medical issues, my mother used her social networks to get us appointments with the top specialists. Thus, in addition to the advantage of a knowledge of medical vocabulary and research skills, her social capital resources made it possible for me to receive the best medical care. I am not in the health sciences, but I still have the research capacity to be a knowledgeable client in health care services for my own children. Certainly, the medical benefits of a full-time academic job are important as well. (And we need the same for contingent faculty!)

My brothers and I also had academic advantages as children. We always had the best science fair projects. My mother was able to take our curiosities and show us how to answer those questions with research and evidence. In junior high, I tested how much of an effect it had on the bounce quality of a tennis ball if you opened the can or left it sealed and whether students identify the same key words in a paragraph. We were exposed to the scientific method very early. We thought through what types of questions we could or should ask, how we could measure things, and how we

---

[17]Joseph Tobin, Yeh Hsueh, and Mayumi Karasawa, *Preschool in Three Cultures Revisited* (Chicago: University of Chicago Press, 2009).

could analyze and present the results. I think as professors, we also converse with our children differently. We welcome and encourage questions. We cultivate critical thinking. When my five-year-old son asks me why most of his teachers are women, I ask him to think of possible explanations. He is already theorizing about society. My husband is a high school chemistry teacher, and I see him doing the same thing. He asks my son questions like "Why are there drops of water on the outside of your cup? How did they get there?"

As a sociology professor, I have the opportunity to be more reflective than the average person about how I am raising my kids. I had one student share with me at the end of taking my intro sociology course that he now had a better idea of how to raise his future children. I was surprised to hear that because I by no means give parenting lessons in this class. But we do talk a lot about why some children succeed and some fail, why some people commit suicide or become criminals, how parents socialize their children, how religion does or does not get transmitted from parents to children, how gender norms influence children, and how people's identities inform their actions. As I discuss these topics with my students, I do apply these lessons to how I am raising my children, and it looks like my students are pocketing these lessons for future reference as well.

Psychological resources. There is certainly a psychological boost that comes from doing meaningful work outside of the family sphere. I think for those of us in academia, intellectual stimulation is important to our psychological well-being. When I was on maternity leave (and I totally appreciated maternity leave for the time that it gave me to physically recover from childbirth and emotionally adjust to adding a new member to the family), I felt myself going stir-crazy. As much as I loved the time to bond with the baby, I craved adult conversation and intellectual stimulation. I felt parts of myself dying as I read the same board books over and over again to the baby, as I kept talking to the baby with no conversational response, and as I felt stuck in the endless cycle of feeding, burping, changing diapers, and soothing. So, while I was on maternity leave, I started "SNACs," which stood for "Stephanie Needs Adult

Conversation." SNACs were dinners with friends and offered a break from the monotony of early parenthood. Once I went back to work, I found that I didn't need SNACs anymore. A lot of the need I had for adult conversation and intellectual stimulation was provided by work in conversations with colleagues and students, attending talks, teaching, and writing. I didn't need SNACs anymore because work provided a regular MEAL ("Mother Engaged in Academic Life").

Sociologist Arlie Hochschild writes about how work becomes a refuge for working parents. She was wondering why parents were not taking advantage of the family-friendly policies at their workplaces and what she found was that people liked being at work.[18] Upon interviewing employees at a family-friendly company, she discovered that they liked work because it was easier than dealing with the difficulties of being at home. Work was the place they felt the most valued and most appreciated. Here's how one of her interviewees, Linda, described life at home:

> I walk in the door and the minute I turn the key in the lock my older daughter is there. Granted, she needs somebody to talk to about her day. . . . The baby is still up. She should have been in bed two hours ago and that upsets me. The dishes are piled in the sink. My daughter comes right up to the door and complains about anything her stepfather said or did, and she wants to talk about her job. My husband is in the other room hollering to my daughter, "Tracy, I don't ever get any time to talk to your mother, because you're always monopolizing her time before I even get a chance!" They all come at me at once.[19]

Meanwhile, here's how Linda described her life at work:

> I usually come to work early just to get away from the house. I get there at 2:30 p.m., and people are there waiting. We sit. We talk. We joke. I let them know what's going on, who has to be where, what changes I've made for the shift that day. We sit there and chit-chat for five or ten minutes. There's laughing, joking, fun. My coworkers aren't putting me down for any

---

[18]Arlie Russell Hochschild, "The Time Bind: When Work Becomes Home and Home Becomes Work," in *Mapping the Social Landscape: Readings in Sociology*, ed. Susan Ferguson (Thousand Oaks, CA: Sage, 2018).
[19]Hochschild, "Time Bind," 513-14.

reason. Everything is done with humor and fun from beginning to end, though it can get stressful when a machine malfunctions.[20]

Work became a refuge for Linda from the stresses of home. I'm sure that many of us can relate.

My mother reduced her work hours and then ultimately retired so that she could help me care for my children. When she retired, she did not linger in academia as many emeritus professors do. She fully immersed herself in her new grandma duties. One day I asked her, "What's harder, Mom, taking care of the baby or going to work?" She said, "Definitely, taking care of the baby. Work is easy compared to this." I said, "I agree." One of my colleagues perhaps put the psychological benefits of work best when she told me that the reason why she returned to work was because she felt depressed as a stay-at-home mother. She joked, "I chose to return to work because it's cheaper than therapy."

In this era of intensive mothering, it is probably more important than ever to have a place of respite. Sharon Hays identifies intensive mothering ideology as the socially appropriate form of mothering in contemporary society.[21] She explains, "The model of intensive mothering tells us that children are innocent and priceless, that their rearing should be carried out primarily by individual mothers and that it should be centered on children's needs, with methods that are informed by experts, labor inten- sive, and costly."[22] The opening passage from Allison Pearson's novel, *I Don't Know How She Does It,* perfectly and satirically depicts what the pressures of intensive mothering ideology look like today:

Monday, 1:37 a.m.

It is the morning of the school carol concert and I am hitting mince pies.

[W]ith a firm downward motion—imagine enough pressure to crush a small beetle—you can start a crumbly little landslide, giving the pastry a pleasing homemade appearance. And homemade is what I'm after here.

---

[20]Hochschild, "Time Bind," 514.

[21]Sharon Hays, *The Cultural Contradictions of Motherhood* (New Haven, CT: Yale University Press, 1996).

[22]Hays, *Cultural Contradictions*, 21.

Home is where the heart is. Home is where the good mother is, baking for her children.

All of this trouble because of a letter Emily brought back from school ten days ago, now stuck on the fridge with a Tinky Winky magnet, asking if 'parents could please make a voluntary contribution of appropriate festive refreshments' for the Christmas party they always put on after the carols. . . .

When they write 'parents' what they really mean, what they still mean is *mothers*. . . . As for 'appropriate festive refreshments,' these are definitely not something bought by a lazy cheat in a supermarket. . . .

But what's the alternative [to faking these homemade mince pies]? Go in to school this afternoon and brazen it out, slam a box of Sainsbury's finest down on the table of festive offerings? Then, to the Mummy Who's Never There and the Mummy Who Shouts, Emily can add the Mummy Who Didn't Make the Effort. Twenty years from now, when my daughter is arrested in the grounds of Buckingham Palace for attempting to kidnap the king, a criminal psychologist will appear on the news and say, 'Friends trace the start of Emily Shattock's mental problems to a school carol concert where her mother, a shadowy presence in her life, humiliated her in front of her classmates.'[23]

When I read this passage to my husband, he said, "That's ridiculous. Of course she should just buy something from the supermarket." He could not relate. But I can. That's the difference between the expectations society places on fathers versus mothers. Society is constantly judging mothers by how much they are conforming to this ideal mother. "How long did you breastfeed your child? You know breast is best." "Are you reading to your child daily? You know how important that is for literacy." "What extracurricular activities are you enrolling your child in? Mine are in soccer, baseball, and fencing." "Are you feeding your baby homemade purees made from only organic fruits and vegetables? If not, you should."

In Armstrong's study of working mother-daughter pairs, she found that there was a generational difference in the expectations of parenting.[24]

---

[23]Allison Pearson, *I Don't Know How She Does It: The Life of Kate Reddy, Working Mother* (New York: Knopf, 2002).
[24]Armstrong, "Higher Stakes."

The grandmothers in the study noticed that their daughters face "more pervasive public judgment and more extensive pressure over the many specific ways in which mothers are expected to entertain, monitor, and direct their children."[25] This confirms the finding of Hays that intensive mothering continues to grow increasingly intense.[26] Although the daughters of these professional mothers all reported that they felt well-mothered and were on high status career paths, they also felt that their ideal job situation would be to work part-time so that they could have "the best of both worlds." Armstrong argues that this pressure to work part-time derives from the escalation of intensive mothering culture and that it could have the negative consequence of hurting women's careers.[27] Despite concern that the increase in mothers' entrance into the labor force would decrease time with their children, time-use diaries show that mothers actually spent more time teaching and playing with their children in 1998 than they did in 1965.[28] Due to the increasing demands of mothering, psychological resources which counter them are particularly important at this cultural moment.

Flexibility. Of the ways in which an academic career can enhance family life, flexibility is probably the most discussed. One of my graduate school advisors told me that being an academic is one of the best careers for having children due to the flexible work hours. He and his wife used the strategy of staggering their work hours so that they didn't need outside childcare. He would come to work early while his partner would take care of the morning childcare duties. Then, he would leave work early to take care of the afternoon childcare duties while his wife worked later. My mother often spoke of the benefit of flexibility that comes with an academic career as well and advised me that it was a great career for people with children. She was always present at all of my high school tennis matches, which would not have been possible with someone with a

---

[25] Armstrong, "Higher Stakes." 17.
[26] Hays, *Cultural Contradictions.*
[27] Armstrong, "Higher Stakes."
[28] Liana C. Sayer, Suzanne M. Bianchi, and John P. Robinson, "Are Parents Investing Less in Children? Trends in Mothers' and Fathers' Time with Children," *American Journal of Sociology* 110, no. 1 (July 2004): 1-43.

nine-to-five job. I never remember her missing any important event in my life due to work. I see children on our campus all the time—those who have a day off of school or a short day or those who are under the weather. I see them eating lunch with mom or dad at the cafeteria, reading a book during their parents' meeting, waiting in the lounge for the parent, or accompanying college students who have been hired as babysitters by faculty. On my campus visit, I met with a female professor who had pillows on the floor of her office, and she mentioned that those were there for her kids when they came on campus. This was a huge encouragement to me as I thought about whether or not I could combine work and family at this particular institution.

The time flexibility I have now allows me to take care of my family in ways that I would not otherwise be able to do. It allows me to chaperone my children's field trips, to attend their performances that are scheduled during normal working hours, and to accompany them to their doctor and dentist appointments. Both of my pregnancies were high risk and required weekly ultrasounds during my second trimester of pregnancy. I remember sitting in the waiting room for these ultrasounds in the high-risk clinic wondering how all these other mothers were managing to make it to all these appointments. At supportive institutions, professors can select their teaching schedules to fit their family lives. When I was an administrative assistant for an academic department, I had one faculty member who always requested that I schedule her classes from 10 a.m. to 2 p.m. every day because she wanted to be able to send her daughter to school and pick her up every day. This is an extreme example, but it shows how flexible a professor's schedule can be. In addition to being able to flex our teaching times, a lot of academic work (at least for social scientists in the era of the internet—reading, writing, analyzing data, prepping for classes, grading, responding to emails) is work that can be done from virtually any location and at any time.

And, we have "summers." Summer for an academic does not translate into no work, but it does mean even greater flexibility in work hours, a positive mix-up in the rhythm of work and rest, and more quality time with the family. I have thirty weeks (58 percent) out of the year with a fixed teaching schedule and twenty-two weeks (42 percent) out of the year that I have control over my own schedule. We recently took a trip with my extended family, and I was the only one among my siblings who was able to stay for the entire four-day (Friday through Monday) trip. Both of my doctor brothers had to work, and my realtor brother had to show property on one of the days.

FAMILY ENHANCING WORK

Skills and perspectives. Not only does work provide skills and perspectives that are beneficial for family life, but being a mother provides skills and perspectives that are beneficial for being a professor. I think one of the greatest skills that women gain from mothering that can enhance their work is the ability to humanize people. Before I became a parent, I used to empathize with people by putting myself in their shoes, but now I have this new "mother lens." After I became a mother, I started seeing people differently. I started to look at people and think, *That could be my child.* Parents often care about their children more than they care about themselves. If a kid gets sick, the kid must go to the doctor immediately. If I am sick, oh, that can wait. When you have this new perspective of "that could be my child," you have an extra measure of care and concern for someone. How this translates to my life as a professor is that when I have students who are struggling in my class or who I am counseling in my office, I think, *That could be my child.* I think about how I would want a professor to treat my child. A respondent in a study of how motherhood affects faculty women similarly expressed:

> Being a mother makes me a more sensitive person. . . . A student is sick and can't come to class or a student who is going through some kind of ordeal or problem—I'm a whole lot more understanding. I just don't let things go, but I look at students now and they are somebody's child. I'm thinking this could be my child, how would I want people to treat this person? So, I think I'm a more compassionate . . . faculty member because of being a mother."[29]

---

[29]Elizabeth K. Laney, Lisa Carruthers, M. Elizabeth Hall, and Tamara Anderson, "Expanding the Self: Motherhood and Identity Development in Faculty Women," *Journal of Family Issues* 35, no. 9 (July 2014): 1227-51.

I think being a mother also helps me to be a more relational teacher. David Schoem writes about the value of relational teaching and learning.[30] He says, "The deepest classroom learning takes place when we recognize that teachers and students come to class and community as whole persons and not simply as intellects and brain power. We learn best in community and amid a community of learners."[31] Not only does motherhood help us to see our students as whole persons, but it provides some of the best real-life illustrations of sociological concepts. When you talk about your son's Paw Patrol T-shirt missing the female pup or his lack of self-consciousness while wearing a Power Rangers costume at Target, they remember gender socialization and the stages of socialization. It also helps students to see me as a whole person. I think students need to know that you have good and legitimate reasons for not responding to their emails at midnight. We are modeling work-life balance for them as well.

Motherhood can make you a more efficient and effective worker. My mother is the most efficient and effective person that I know. She finished her PhD in three years, giving birth to her first child in the second year of her doctoral program. By retirement, she had published hundreds of articles while raising four children. Perhaps having four children while working and a baby while in grad school was not an obstacle to overcome but a reason for her efficiency. While working, she always kept to strict working hours: Monday through Friday, 9:00 a.m. to 4:30 p.m. All work had to get done in that time. I never saw her working at home. She said that knowing that she only had that limited amount of time to work made her incredibly focused during the time that she did have.

This is a consistent theme I hear both in personal conversations as well as in academic studies. Increased sense of efficiency post-motherhood was one of the central findings from Ward and Wolf-Wendel's study of

---

[30]David Schoem, "Relational Teaching and Learning: The Classroom as Community and the Community as Classroom" in *Teaching the Whole Student: Engaged Learning with Heart, Mind, and Spirit*, ed. David Schoem, Christine Modey, Edward P. St. John (Sterling, VA: Stylus Publishing, 2017), 79-99.
[31]Schoem, "Relational Teaching," 79.

professor mothers with young children.[32] One of their respondents explained, "Clearly having [my child] was a major change in my lifestyle and how I dealt with things, and made my hours change significantly, for the good and the bad. The good was I had to become much more efficient; the other side of it is that I live within my hours at work."[33] Although most of Ecklund and Lincoln's book, *Failing Families, Failing Science*, discusses the challenges of having a family life while pursuing a career in elite academic science, they do present some evidence for how family enhances work life.[34] One scientist mother said that her children make her a better scientist because they cause her to be "extremely efficient with the use of [her] time."[35] This seems to bear out in some studies of motherhood and work productivity. Krapf, Ursprung, and Zimmerman find that "economists with two or more children are, on average, more productive than their peers with only one child or no children."[36] They find that having young children does lessen the productivity of mother economists but that in the long run, they are more productive than those without children. Joecks, Pull, and Backes-Gellner find the same association in their study of female researchers in business and economics: those with children are more productive than those without.[37]

Moving outside of just research productivity, having children may contribute to work in other ways. Kmec finds that "mothers have significantly higher levels of job engagement than fathers."[38] Mothers may also make

---

[32]Kelly Ward and Lisa Wolf-Wendel, "Academic Motherhood: Managing Complex Roles in Research Universities," *The Review of Higher Education* 27, no. 2 (December 2004): 233-57.

[33]Ward and Wolf-Wendel, "Academic Motherhood," 249.

[34]Elaine Howard Ecklund and Anne E. Lincoln, *Failing Families, Failing Science: Work-Family Conflict in Academic Science* (New York: NYU Press, 2016).

[35]Ecklund and Lincoln, *Failing Families*, 112.

[36]Matthias Krapf, Heinrich W. Ursprung, and Christian Zimmermann, "Parenthood and Productivity of Highly Skilled Labor: Evidence from the Groves of Academe" (working paper no. 2014-001A, Federal Reserve Bank of St. Louis, January 2014, 14, http://research.stlouisfed.org/wp/more/2014-001.

[37]Jasmin Joecks, Kerstin Pull, and Uschi Backes-Gellner, "Childbearing and (Female) Research Productivity: A Personnel Economics Perspective on the Leaky Pipeline," *Journal of Business Economics* 84 (June 2013): 517-30.

[38]Julie A. Kmec, "Are Motherhood Penalties and Fatherhood Bonuses Warranted? Comparing Pro-Work Behaviors and Conditions of Mothers, Fathers, and Non-Parents," *Social Science Research* 40, no. 2 (March 2011): 451.

better leaders, according to a study by Dumas and Stanko.[39] In their study of working professionals and executives pursuing MBAs, they "found a significant indirect effect of being married with children on ratings of the respondents' transformational leadership behaviors through their increased family role identification and family-to-work resource transfer, and this effect was stronger for women than men."[40] Leadership skills acquired from family life include helping and developing others, taking positions of authority, interpersonal skills, individualizing interactions, and creativity.[41]

After becoming a mother, I gained a whole new respect for all mothers. My son asked me the other day if there are any real superheroes. Yes. Mothers. They are able to power through their jobs in a constant state of nausea and fatigue while humans grow inside them. They are able to battle through the searing pains of childbirth. They are never able to call in sick for their parenting job. They sustain people's lives who are completely dependent on them for survival. They know how to deal with irrational and temperamental people (a.k.a. toddlers and teenagers). Their minds can hold and manage millions of details at once, including the status of household supplies, school enrollment, fingernail trimming, medication refills, doctor and dentist appointments, follow-up appointments, outfits for school performances, schedules for all extracurricular activities, packing lists for trips down to the Q-Tips, birthday parties, meal plans, home repairs, teacher gifts, thank-you notes, library book due dates, field trip forms, new clothes, vaccination records, milestone timetables, recreation center activities, summer camps, school supplies, haircuts, photo albums, family gatherings, visits to and from relatives, and playdates (just to name a few). Knowing all that mothers do on a daily basis, it is incredibly puzzling to think of a human who has developed these superpowers being discriminated against in the workplace due to conceptions that she might not be an ideal worker due to her

---

[39]Tracy L. Dumas and Taryn L. Stanko, "Married with Children: How Family Role Identification Shapes Leadership Behaviors at Work," *Personnel Psychology* 70, no. 3 (July 2017): 597-633.
[40]Dumas and Stanko, "Married with Children," 618.
[41]Dumas and Stanko, "Married with Children," 605.

motherhood status.[42] Mothers are incredibly well-equipped to multitask, to supervise people, to prioritize tasks, to work efficiently and effectively, to deal with difficult coworkers, to persevere through challenges, to be team players, to think about the long game, to mentor, to train, to individualize interactions, to be good listeners, to understand human behavior, to manage time, to think about the greater good, and to delay gratification. Ask any mother, and she'll probably tell you that she is a much better version of her pre-child self.[43]

Psychological resources. Academic life is psychologically challenging. It is the mental version of the show *Wipeout* in which we see if the contestant can avoid being wiped out by a series of physical obstacles at every turn. For academics, the obstacles are mostly mental. As a graduate student, you must survive the grilling of field exams, the dissertation proposal defense, and the dissertation defense. When trying to publish, you must endure "peer review," subjecting your years of hard work to the merciless reviews of experts who tear it all apart. When applying for jobs, you must give job talks and then face an onslaught of criticism during the "Q&A" portion. The same thing happens at academic conferences when you present a paper. Moreover, every semester, you must confront student course evaluations that inevitably include some attacks on your teaching and maybe even your character. In academia, you are told in a thousand ways you are not good enough. In a blog post on *The Professor Is In*, post-academic job coach Jessica Langer describes the psychological battle of academia so well. She writes, "One of the most significant things I've noticed in my post-academic work with clients transitioning out of academia is the extent to which they have gotten into the habit of extraordinarily harsh and total self-criticism, to the extent that they are sometimes unable to recognize their own accomplishments *as* accomplishments."[44] She speculates the reason for this is

---

[42]Shelley J. Corell, Stephen Benard, and In Paik, "Getting a Job: Is There a Motherhood Penalty?" *American Journal of Sociology* 112, no. 5 (March 2007): 1297-338.

[43]Laney et al, "Expanding the Self."

[44]Jessica Langer, "Self-Criticism and the Academy," *The Professor Is In* (blog), March 29, 2016, http://theprofessorisin.com/2016/03/29/self-criticism-and-the-academy-postac-post-by-jessica-langer/.

that "academia trains you to be abusive to yourself." Academia, she says, trains you:

> To constantly criticize your own work as well as others', and never to be satisfied or even content with your work. To put yourself in situations in which you are infantilized and made powerless within a strict hierarchical system in which you are a waste product, not an intended outcome. To accept negativity from yourself that you would never allow to be directed towards someone you love.[45]

Academia *is* this messed up. This is where the psychological resources of family life (and also of faith) can be really helpful. You really need a supportive community to get you through both the external and internal criticism experienced in academia. You need reminders that you are more than your work—more than that terrible student evaluation, more than Reviewer 2's comments, more than tenure. The late Supreme Court Justice and former law professor Ruth Bader Ginsburg spoke of how her daughter contributed to her success in law school. She wrote:

> My success in law school, I have no doubt, was in large measure because of baby Jane. I attended classes and studied diligently until 4 in the afternoon; the next hours were Jane's time, spent at the park, playing silly games or singing funny songs, reading picture books and A. A. Milne poems, and bathing and feeding her. After Jane's bedtime, I returned to the law books with renewed will. Each part of my life provided respite from the other and gave me a sense of proportion that classmates trained only on law studies lacked.[46]

This has been my personal experience as well, though as an academic and not as a student since I had children later than Justice Ginsburg. I have not reached the "I hate you" phase of parenting yet, so currently the "I love you"s, the giggles, the handmade cards, the hugs, and the toddler dance parties are incredibly therapeutic.

---

[45]Langer, "Self-Criticism."

[46]Ruth Bader Ginsburg, "Ruth Bader Ginsburg's Advice for Living," *The New York Times,* October 1, 2016, www.nytimes.com/2016/10/02/opinion/sunday/ruth-bader-ginsburgs-advice-for-living.html.

I have this timeline I made of my ten-year journey to publishing a recent article. I originally made it to show my students the long and rigorous process of peer review that research goes through before they read it. I then revised it when I gave a talk at my university about how to use your sabbatical wisely, adding in the birth of my children into the timeline. I wanted to show what the timeline realistically looks like from start to finish when you have a 4-4 teaching load, young children, and not a lot of research funding. But as I look at that timeline again, maybe it isn't a story of how having two young children impeded my research but of how they encouraged me to persevere through many years of research and many episodes of rejection.

Moreover, the manual labor of keeping two other human beings alive takes me out of my head—out of overthinking and working to the point of diminishing returns. It allows me to hit the "pause" button and remember the real world that is out there beyond the academic world. When I was in grad school, I liked weeding. I didn't have my own garden, so I weeded at the community park. I weeded at my sister-in-law's house. I loved just doing something with my hands and giving the academic part of my brain a rest. While parenting is not restful, it does provide relief from the mental taxation of academia. It's like weeding, but better. When asked which activities gave them the greatest happiness, people rated "play with children" the highest among forty-five different activities.[47] It impressively outranked listening to music, parties, visiting friends, sports and exercise, and travel!

HOW DOES FAITH INFLUENCE WORK-FAMILY CONFLICT AND ENRICHMENT?

Now where does faith come into all this? How does faith influence work-family conflict or work-family enrichment? Dust and Greenhaus propose that we can think of religion influencing these two areas by affecting demands and resources.[48] Does being a Christian professor mother create

---

[47]Meik Wiking, *The Little Book of Hygge: Danish Secrets to Happy Living* (New York: William Morrow, 2017), 152-53.

[48]Scott B. Dust and Jeffrey H. Greenhaus, "Spirituality and the Work-Home Interface: A Demands-Resources Perspective," *Journal of Management, Spirituality & Religion* 10, no. 3 (September 2013): 282-305.

additional demands or provide additional resources? We may feel that faith adds additional demands to the equation. Conservative Protestant women who are working mothers may experience more work-life conflict due to traditional gender ideologies that stress a woman's work in the home. Those who see their work as sacred, as a calling, may sense greater demands from their work. If this is God's work and not just a job, I need to put my whole soul into it. Church involvement—serving at church, midweek Bible studies and small groups, Sunday worship, prayer meetings, volunteer opportunities, and church events—may also add an additional time demand on top of the time demands of work and family. When I first envisioned writing this chapter, I thought that I would be discussing the triple demands of the spheres of work, family, and faith. Having this opportunity to reflect deeply on the interactions between work, family, and faith in my life, however, I have started to see faith more as a resource than as an additional sphere of demands.

Moreover, I found research bears this out as well. May and Reynolds found that conservative Protestant women experience less work-life conflict than other women.[49] Ammons and Edgell also find that conservative Protestant women do not make more work tradeoffs in favor of family than other women.[50] Along with other researchers, they find that religion influences people in more complex ways than simply a belief that translates into practice.[51] So why do women of faith experience less work-family conflict and potentially greater work-family enrichment than other women?

Greenhaus and Dust provide a helpful framework for thinking about how spirituality can foster work-home enrichment.[52] They identify three personal characteristics and three relational characteristics that faith

---

[49]Matthew May and Jeremy Reynolds, "Religious Affiliation and Work-Family Conflict Among Women and Men," *Journal of Family Issues* 39, no. 7 (May 2018): 1797-826.

[50]Samantha K. Ammons and Penny Edgell, "Religious Influences on Work-Family Trade-Offs," *Journal of Family Issues* 28, no. 6 (June 2007): 794-826.

[51]Gallagher and Smith, "Symbolic Traditionalism;" Melinda Lundquist Denton, "Gender and Marital Decision Making: Negotiating Religious Ideology and Practice," *Social Forces* 82, no. 3 (March 2004): 1151-80; Jennifer Roebuck Bulanda, "Doing Family, Doing Gender, Doing Religion: Structured Ambivalence and the Religion-Family Connection," *Journal of Family Theory & Review* 3, no. 3 (September 2011): 179-97.

[52]Dust and Greenhaus, "Spirituality and the Work-Home Interface."

may provide to support work-home enrichment. The personal characteristics are optimism, hope, and sanctification. The relational characteristics are forgiveness, gratitude, and interconnectedness. The ones that resonate most with my experience are optimism, hope, sanctification, and interconnectedness.

First, faith has provided optimism and hope in dealing with the challenges of both work and home. I derive both strength and inspiration from the Lord in my teaching and research. He helps me to persevere through negative teaching evaluations, manuscript rejections, and difficult workplace dynamics. The calling of Christians to seek justice and love mercy is what motivates the topics I research and my teaching of sociology. Knowing that my children are also children of God helps me to know that I am not alone in my parenting struggles. I know that there is a God who loves me and my children. I pray when my children are not eating well, when they fall ill, when they are behaving destructively, and when I cannot control my anger toward them. I do not have to beat myself up when I make mistakes as a parent because I experience the grace of God. As Christians, we are bolstered by a faith that allows us to view our weaknesses as a source of strength since God enters into and meets us in those weaknesses with his strength (2 Corinthians 12:9-10).

Second, the dual sense of calling that faith provides, or what Dust and Greenhaus call "sanctification," may help to ameliorate work-family conflict. Research shows that those who prioritize both work and family equally experience less work-life conflict than those who either prioritize work or family.[53] Our faith allows us to see *both* the value of work and home, and, thus, experience *less* work-life conflict.[54] In my work, I am called to work as unto the Lord—"Whatever you do, work at it with all your heart, as working for the Lord, not for human masters. . . . It is the Lord Christ you are serving" (Colossians 3:23). I am also called to use the gifts God has given me—"We have different gifts, according to the grace

---

[53]Steward D. Friedman and Jeffrey H. Greenhaus, *Work and Family—Allies or Enemies? What Happens When Business Professionals Confront Life Choices* (Oxford: Oxford University Press, 2000).

[54]May and Reynolds, "Religious Affiliation."

given to each of us. . . . If it is teaching, then teach" (Romans 12:6-7). In my family, I (along with my husband) am instructed to teach my children (Proverbs 1:8-9; 6:20; 22:6) and to manage and provide for my household (Proverbs 31:10-31; Titus 2:5). In their study of Christian working mothers in academia, researchers have found that their perspective of viewing their work at home and in the family as sacred callings helped to reduce the feeling of interrole conflict.[55] Oates, Hall, and Anderson write,

> Stemming from their spiritual beliefs, the women in this study sanctified many of their roles, experiencing them as callings, and their responsibilities in these roles were seen as spiritual endeavors that were part of a greater plan. . . . The women looked at their careers as callings, and this approach provided a framework from which they could deal with their interrole tension.[56]

At the same time, my faith also causes me to give neither work nor family supreme importance or too much importance in my life. Our faith might help us to gain the perspective that while both of these things are important, neither is of ultimate importance, thereby lessening the overbearing demands that come from the "ideal worker" and "ideal mother" ideologies. In regards to work, Jesus tells us, "Do not store up for yourselves treasures on earth, where moths and vermin destroy, and where thieves break in and steal. But store up for yourselves treasures in heaven, where moths and vermin do not destroy, and where thieves do not break in and steal" (Matthew 6:19-20). The Bible also tells us that we "cannot serve both God and money" (Matthew 6:24). It is a gift of God to find satisfaction in our work (Ecclesiastes 3:13), but too much toil in our work can also be meaningless (Ecclesiastes 2:21-23). Work should not be our idol, but neither should family. When I had kids, I realized that it is very tempting to make family an idol. This one is harder to see because in Christian circles,

---

[55]Kerris L. M. Oates, M. Elizabeth Lewis Hall, and Tamara L. Anderson, "Interrole Conflict and the Sanctification of Work in Christian Mothers in Academia," *Journal of Psychology and Theology* 33, no. 3 (September 2005): 210-23; M. Elizabeth Lewis Hall, Kerris L. M. Oates, Tamara L. Anderson, and Michele M. Willingham, "Calling and Conflict: The Sanctification of Work in Working Mothers," *Psychology of Religion and Spirituality* 4, No. 1 (February 2012): 71-83.
[56]Oates, Hall, and Anderson, "Interrole Conflict," 218.

this is often an acceptable god. I was very convicted by an interview with Francis Chan who discussed how Christians tend to get married and have kids and then start to focus on "the Christian version of the American Dream" rather than on loving God and neighbors.[57] We are called to take care of our families (1 Timothy 5:8) but not to worship them and place them above God (Matthew 10:37-38; Luke 14:26). This ability to find purpose and identity in something beyond both the realms of work and family also helps to ameliorate work-life conflict.

Third, faith has provided interconnectedness in the form of a strong community and social support system. Dust and Greenhaus explain, "The spiritual characteristic of interconnectedness leads to enhanced social support and coping, while at work or outside of work, which increases social capital resources and decreases stressful demands."[58] I remember, when I was interviewing for my position at Biola, both the shock and delight I experienced when each person I met on the interview trail prayed for me. I felt incredibly supported even as a candidate. When my first pregnancy ended in miscarriage, I saw both the departments I was part of rally around me in prayer and support. I saw this as well when I was pregnant and gave birth to my two children; they were unequivocally viewed as a blessing in my workplace and not a barrier to my work contributions. I have the deepest and strongest relationships at Biola I have ever had in academia, and I believe that is largely due to these relationships being cemented in a deeper faith. My church has been one of the biggest cheerleaders for my work. I have been asked to teach in my areas of expertise and was even given an award recognizing the work that I do as a professor in teaching about justice. Yet my church family has also been the biggest support in my role as a mother, whether through meal trains when I gave birth or through small group fellowship with other families with young children. In this small group, our conversation often inevitably revolves around parenting and parenting support. But most of the women in the group are

---

[57]Megan Briggs, "Francis Chan: Stop Idolizing Your Family," ChurchLeaders.com, December 4, 2018, http://churchleaders.com/pastors/videos-for-pastors/275963-francis-chan-a-challenge-to-the-church.html.

[58]Dust and Greenhaus, "Spirituality and the Work-Home Interface," 292.

also full-time professionals, and we spend a lot of time offering support and prayer for work stresses as well.

CONCLUSION

One of the consistent pieces of advice I have received from my professor mother is to "think positive." This is her life motto, and I think it is part of the reason why she has been so successful in the area of work-life balance. I hope this piece helps us as Christian professor mothers to think positively about our experiences as mothers, workers, and followers of Christ. This is not meant to be a handy Band-Aid to work-life conflict but to serve as a helpful counternarrative to the predominantly negative messaging we receive from ourselves, society, and even our faith communities. In this chapter, we have explored the synergies of work-family enrichment and seen the ways that family life and academic life can enhance one another through transferable skills, broadened perspectives, psychological resources, and greater flexibility. Moreover, we saw how faith can even further contribute to this synergy by supporting work-family enrichment through optimism, hope, sanctification, and interconnectedness.

Changing our thinking is not enough, though. As a sociologist, I also know that for work-life enrichment to happen we need the right support system in place. What has this positive support system looked like for me? First of all, my professor mother: she has been an enormous source of support both mentally and physically (helping to care for my children). Contrary to the "'distressed working mother' and her suffering children" image that is out there, I am here to testify that my mother was an amazing mother, not in spite of her work but because of her experiences with work. Second, work-life enrichment would not be possible without a supportive husband who values and respects my work and who equally parents our children. In our house, taking care of the kids is not just my job or mostly my job. It is both of our jobs. Third, as mentioned above, I go to a church where being a working mother is supported and is the norm. Fourth, I'm thankful to live in an era of services that help working mothers. I am indebted to my kids' teachers, preschool teachers, and afterschool care providers who are part of my childcare team. I must acknowledge Gobble, a meal delivery service that touts fifteen-minute meal prep (it actually takes about twenty to twenty-five minutes), Stitch Fix (personalized clothes sent to your home for those like me who don't like shopping), and Amazon Prime (no explanation needed). It really takes a village (and these days, it can be virtual).

At an institutional level, I think working at a Christian university is helpful for those who want to be professor mothers. Despite some pressure to conform to traditional gender norms from certain corners of the university, there is overall strong support at my university for balancing work and family. For me, the greatest resource that my university has provided is the lack of a tenure clock. There is no deadline for applying for tenure which means that the family constraints female professors often feel due to the synchronized ticking of the biological and tenure clock is not present for the female professors at my university. This is huge. When catching up with one of my grad school professors at a conference, he asked me about progress toward tenure. I shared with him that our university doesn't have a tenure clock. He gave the best response: "What a humane policy!" For those of us who want to pursue an academic career and have a strong family life as well, this has been the greatest gift. This is not typical of most Christian universities. Ninety percent of schools in the Council for Christian Colleges and Universities (CCCU) do have a tenure clock.[59] There are also discussions at my university for changing this policy, which I would highly discourage if it wants to maintain a family-friendly environment and support female faculty.

There are tangible ways in which my institution communicates the importance of family. Families are invited to certain faculty events. There is always a lot of positive attention given to faculty children who are brought onto campus. You will see pictures of faculty members with their families in their offices. Family needs are viewed as valid reasons for teaching schedule requests. There is now a good maternity leave policy in

---

[59]Scott Harris and D. Barry Lumsden, "Tenure Policies and Practices of American Evangelical Colleges and Universities. Part 2: Institutions Granting Tenure," *Christian Higher Education* 5, no. 4 (December 2006): 346.

place, whereby a new mother gets a semester leave to take care of the new baby. This is made possible by California's Paid Family Leave program, which covered part of my pay during this period. Faculty who so desire can work at 75-percent time (teaching three rather than four classes a semester) to have more time with their families. My building is mostly empty by 5 p.m. Children under five eat free at the school cafeteria. There is also a support group for professor mothers (which is where the idea for this volume came from). What must accompany all of these policies is also supportive colleagues—the administrative assistant and chair who will accommodate your course scheduling preferences, the supervisors and peers who will not disparage your desire to take maternity leave or your desire to still work and put your baby in childcare, and the dean who will hold your baby so that you can take notes during the promotion workshop (yes, true story). With the right support, there can be a beautiful synergy of lullaby and syllabi. Goodnight moon. . . . Good morning students. Good morning computer. Good morning reading. And good morning leading. Good morning office. Good morning chair. Good morning meetings everywhere.

(MIS)PERCEPTIONS OF MATERNITY LEAVE IN THE ACADEMY

TERI CLEMONS, MS, SLPD

A FEW YEARS AGO, I was at a party and struck up a conversation with an older woman. Over the course of our conversation, I found out that she was a retired professor. She saw that I was there with my daughter, and our conversation turned to motherhood in academia. Her stories about hiding her pregnancy at work, returning to work shortly after having her baby, and never talking about her children at work reminded me that we have come a long way with regard to how mothers are treated in the academic world. Despite these changes, women in higher education still feel the need to minimize the impact of having children on their careers and workplace. Female faculty feel pressure to delay having children until after they have obtained tenure.[1] They often attempt to schedule their

---

[1]Victoria Gordon, *Maternity Leave: Policy and Practice* (Boca Raton, FL: CRC Press, 2013); Vera Troeger, "How Maternity Pay Can Fix the Gender Pay Gap and Boost Productivity," *The Conversation*, February 15, 2018, https://theconversation.com/how-better-maternity-pay-can -fix-the -gender-pay-gap-and-boost-productivity-90974.

children to be born during breaks in the school year, the so-called May baby.[2] I did this with my first child, who was born over the summer break, which extended into my maternity leave in the fall semester. I didn't feel external pressure to do this; it was more of a self-inflicted pressure to minimize the impact on my colleagues and also maximize my time at home with my new baby.

This chapter will include an examination of research related to maternity leave and the impact it has on the academic careers of mothers. It will give clarity to the skewed image of maternity leave that can lead others to believe new mothers (and sometimes fathers) receive an unfair advantage in policies related to maternity leave and will promote a new framework for how we view work and parental leave. Finally, this chapter will offer some practical advice to female faculty as they prepare for maternity leave.

MATERNITY LEAVE: AN OVERVIEW

Approaches to maternity leave vary significantly in different countries.[3] Most developed countries, with the exception of the United States, provide some parental leave paid for by the government. The percentage of wages supplemented by the government ranges from 29 to 100 percent, and the length of parental leave varies.[4] For example, Canadian mothers are given seventeen weeks of pregnancy leave and parents can share up to thirty-five weeks of additional leave with 55 percent of their pay. Parents can stay home with their child for up to a year with their job protected.[5] In Norway, parents are given forty-four weeks of leave with full pay that can be shared between the parents. Parents in Norway also have the option of taking another full year of unpaid leave. In the United Kingdom, mothers can take

---

[2]Gordon, *Maternity Leave.*

[3]Johanna Weststar, "Negotiating in Silence: Experiences with Parental Leave in Academia," *Relations Industrielles/Industrial Relations* 67, no. 3 (September 2012): 352-74, https://doi.org /10.7202/1012535ar.

[4]Raquel Plotka, and Nancy A. Busch-Rossnagel, "The Role of Length of Maternity Leave in Supporting Mother-Child Interactions and Attachment Security Among American Mothers and Their Infants," *International Journal of Child Care and Education Policy* 12, no. 2 (January 2018): 1-18, https://doi.org/10.1186/s40723-018-0041-6.

[5]Weststar, "Negotiating," 352-74.

six weeks of maternity leave with 90 percent pay and an additional thirteen weeks of unpaid leave.[6]

In the United States, the Family Medical Leave Act (FMLA) mandates twelve weeks of unpaid leave for mothers, but this provision is not universal as it depends on company size and length of employment. Additional maternity leave provisions in the United States vary greatly from state to state and among employers, with some allowing for time off without pay and others supplementing a portion of an employee's pay. Employers who do not offer paid leave often allow parents taking family leave to use vacation pay benefits to cover their leave. In higher education, this approach to pay is challenging because most faculty operate on a nine-month contract and typically are not given paid vacation.[7] Faculty members' experiences with maternity leave are highly inconsistent across departments, even for individual faculty members who have had more than one child.[8] Research shows that maternity leave policies impact retention of female faculty. One study showed that universities with more generous paid maternity leave on average have double the number of female faculty.[9]

MY EXPERIENCE OF ACADEMIA, PARENTING, AND MATERNITY LEAVE

Perceptions about maternity leave can be particularly skewed in Christian higher education, where some hold the perspective that women with children should not be working at all. I remember chatting with two male faculty members after my return to work from my maternity leave with my first daughter. One of the men inquired about how I was feeling about my transition with returning to work. I responded that although there were elements of leaving my daughter to come to work that were difficult, I felt a calling to both motherhood and my role as a faculty member. The second faculty member assured me that the calling that I felt would likely change

---

[6]Weststar, "Negotiating," 352-74.
[7]Gordon, *Maternity Leave.*
[8]Gordon, *Maternity Leave*; Weststar, "Negotiating," 352-74.
[9]Troeger, "Maternity Pay."

over time, implying that eventually I would figure out that I should be at home full time with my daughter.

I am incredibly grateful for the maternity leave that allowed me to spend time at home with my children without any negative financial impact during that period. I live in a state with one of the most generous maternity leave policies in the country, which allows mothers to take six weeks of pregnancy-related disability and an additional six weeks of paid family leave with 60 to 70 percent of salary covered by the state.[10] In addition, the university that I work for has an excellent maternity leave policy where faculty mothers are permitted an entire semester of leave with the university supplementing the remaining percentage of their salary not covered by state funding. The university also supplements the remaining weeks of the semester that the faculty member is on leave that is not covered by state funding. I have not met anyone who has had maternity leave as good as I was able to have following the births of my two daughters. I am thankful for the administrators and committee members at our university who created this policy, and for the women who came before me who did not have it as good as we do now and helped to draw attention to the need for a policy change.

I am also very thankful for my job as a professor. I am a speech-language pathologist, and prior to coming to teach at the university, I worked as a clinician in a hospital setting with a typical eight-to-five workday including covering weekends and holidays. Working in academia, I have enjoyed having a job with greater flexibility and more autonomy with time management. I work in a supportive department that allows me to schedule my classes and office hours in a way that best accommodates the needs of my family. I am very aware that this is not the reality of most working mothers and not even the reality for many women working in higher education. I also have a spouse who is actively engaged with our children and our home life. I could not raise our children and enjoy the career that I have without his partnership.

---

[10]State of California Employment Development Department. "Paid Family Leave Benefits." Accessed December 17, 2020, www.edd.ca.gov/Disability/paid_family_leave.htm.

For the past four years, I have served on the faculty personnel committee that reviews applications for promotion and tenure. Over the years, I have seen the same topic of conversation come up when reviewing an application from a female faculty member who has been on maternity leave during her current application cycle (which typically runs for two to four years, depending on the rank they are applying for). There is always at least one member of the committee who questions the accuracy, and the fairness, of the female faculty member in question being able to apply for promotion during that promotion cycle because they have been out on maternity leave for a portion of that cycle. Attempts to point to the clearly defined policy at our university that maternity leave does not interrupt the promotion cycle are often met with incredulity and skepticism by the questioning members of the committee. The policy somehow is considered unfair by some, even if the female faculty member in question has met all of the other requirements for promotion.

Where does this misperception that maternity leave is unfair to other faculty come from? I believe it is in part due to a lack of understanding about how female faculty *actually* spend their time on maternity leave, and also because there are differing perspectives about how female faculty *should* spend their time on maternity leave.[11] Maternity leave *is not* a vacation. It is also *not* a sabbatical. When I considered why some of my fellow committee members found it unfair that a female faculty member could be eligible for promotion despite being out on maternity leave for a portion of the time, I realized that the people who had concerns about this were men who had never been on maternity leave. Some of them had no children of their own. Others had children but they had not experienced the daily grind of balancing a stay-at-home-parent role with a job that never fully stops, even when on leave. They didn't understand what it is like because they had no concept of how a mother's time is actually spent while on leave. In interviews collected by Lundquist, Misra, and O'Meara, female faculty retailed stories of colleagues who told them they wished they had

---

[11]Jennifer H. Lundquist, Joya Misra, and KerryAnn O'Meara, "Parental Leave Usage by Fathers and Mothers at an American University," *Fathering* 10, no. 3 (2012): 337-63, https://doi.org/10.3149/fth.1003.337.

maternity leave too so they could "get all sorts of stuff done."[12] Another shared about a department chair who expressed "parental leaves were synonymous with research sabbaticals."[13] There is an assumption (sometimes even by naive new parents) that the baby sleeps all day, so there will be plenty of time to get work done.[14]

In an attempt to bridge this gap in understanding, allow me to share a snapshot of what a day in the life of a woman on maternity leave (more specifically a woman working in academia on maternity leave) is like. Just a caveat, I wrote this synopsis when I was on maternity leave when my youngest daughter was four months old and my older daughter was three. I thought this time frame would best capture the period of my maternity leave beyond the California state-mandated twelve-week time frame in which mothers are technically receiving disability benefits and therefore are not legally supposed to be "working." If I had written this earlier, during the first three months of my daughter's life, it would have included nursing a baby eight times a day, holding my daughter during all of her naps for the first three months of her life because she wouldn't sleep during the day any other way, and dealing with the physical recovery of childbirth and the lack of sleep from having a newborn. At the stage depicted here, I began to focus a few meager hours of my day on work. This timeline will look very familiar to other mothers. My hope is that it can provide some insight for those who have not experienced maternity leave firsthand, including department chairs and administrators who influence decisions about maternity leave for faculty.

5:45 a.m.: The day usually begins somewhere between 5:30 and 6:00 a.m. Sometimes the baby wakes up first, sometimes it's my three-year-old daughter. My husband usually gets up with them first to let me sleep a little longer, but I don't get to sleep too much longer because the baby needs to nurse.

---

[12]Lundquist, Misra, and O'Meara, "Parental Leave," 349.
[13]Lundquist, Misra, and O'Meara, "Parental Leave," 349.
[14]Christy Moran Craft and Jo Maseberg-Tomlinson, "Challenges Experienced by One Academic Mother Transitioning from Maternity Leave Back to Academia." *NASPA Journal About Women in Higher Education* 8, no. 1 (March 2015): 66-81. https://doi.org/10.1080/19407882.2014.987086.

7:00 a.m.: Breakfast time. I fix it while my husband feeds the baby some baby cereal; she goes down shortly after for her morning nap.

8:30 a.m.: My husband is out the door for work. My older daughter and I have some one-on-one time until the baby wakes up. Lately she has been into the show *Cupcake Wars* so playtime consists of some intense competition in her play kitchen.

9:00 a.m.: The baby is awake, so we start to get ready for a morning outing. Getting myself and two kids ready to get out the door always puts us into a time warp in which the minutes rapidly disappear, and we are unable to get anywhere before ten o'clock. While I get myself ready, my older daughter dismantles our bed my husband made and empties several drawers in our room. I nurse the baby again before we head out of the house.

10:30 a.m.: We finally make it out the door and head for some kind of excursion, sometimes doing practical things like running errands (always a joy with two kids in tow) but usually somewhere the kids will enjoy like the zoo, a park, a children's museum, or the beach. I am thankful that I have the time to make these kinds of memories with them.

12:30 p.m.: We head home from our outing for lunch and naptime. I hold the hungry fussy baby in one arm while making lunch for my older daughter with the other, then sit down to spoon-feed the baby while reminding my older daughter that she does, in fact, need to eat.

1:30 p.m.: It's naptime, I nurse the baby and put her down for her nap and get my older daughter settled for what we call her "rest time." She's at the age where she's fighting taking a nap so some days she falls asleep and some days she doesn't, but I am not ready to let go of it yet because these are the only moments of serenity I get during the day.

2:00 p.m.: I haven't had lunch yet, so I throw some food in my mouth while the girls are down and attempt to fly through other household tasks such as laundry, cleaning up after lunch, making phone calls for doctor's appointments, etc. I also try to do some prep for dinner because the baby's fussiest time of the day is around dinner time and I can't accomplish much later in the day when she is only happy being held.

3:30 p.m.: The girls are up, which means diaper changes, nursing the baby again, and snack time. We play more, read books, sometimes do another short outing or errand.

5:30 p.m.: I feed the girls dinner while cooking dinner for my husband and me and try to survive the last—and inevitably the hardest—hour of the day before my husband comes home.

6:30 p.m.: Dad is finally home; we take turns eating while the other bounces a fussy baby and entertains our older daughter.

7:00 p.m.: Bedtime routine commences with baths. I nurse the baby again and put her down for the night. My husband gets our older daughter ready for bed and I pop in for prayer, songs, and snuggles before she goes to sleep.

8:00 p.m.: My husband and I crash on the couch. All I want to do at this point is relax and spend time with my husband, but this is the only time of the day that I can get any work done, so I pull out my computer and spend a few hours answering emails and trying to accomplish other work-related tasks.

10:00 p.m.: Time to head to bed to get some sleep (most likely to be interrupted at some point by at least one of our two children) so we can get up and do it all over again tomorrow.

Yes, this synopsis was written by a mother on maternity leave with a second child. However, I assure you it doesn't look much better with just a first baby in the house. Having your first baby is extremely disorienting. Newborn babies have to eat every three hours. That is every three hours from the time they start eating to the time the next feeding begins. So in reality you are feeding a baby every two to two and a half hours, depending on how long they take to eat. Babies do sleep a lot, but not all day. They typically go through a cycle of eating, being awake, and then returning to sleep in those three hours. I remember my husband and I scheduling what we were going to try to accomplish within each three-hour window because if we didn't, the day would slip by and we would look back and wonder what happened.

In addition to the daily grind of caring for a baby, the reality of working in academia means that there is always more work that can be done outside of the typical responsibilities of teaching, grading, committee work, and advising and mentoring students. This work is not as easy to pause while on maternity leave.[15] For most academics, this relates to research and writing for publication. Much of the research and writing type of work in academia fall into a gray area where there may or may not be a direct relationship to the institution that the faculty member works for, but achievement in these forms of work are necessary to gain promotion and advancement at that institution. For me at this stage in my career, the ever-present work was completing my coursework and dissertation for my terminal degree.

In the field of speech language pathology, a master's degree is required to obtain licensure and certification for clinical practice. It is not unusual for faculty in my discipline to be hired with a master's degree and clinical experience to teach at the university level. I was first hired as an adjunct professor and then joined the full-time faculty with the stipulation that I would obtain my terminal degree in order to advance in the ranks as a faculty member. I started my doctoral program two weeks after my oldest daughter was born. I chose an online program because it felt like the only feasible option that afforded me the necessary flexibility to sustain my family life and remain in the area to keep my current position as a faculty member. Looking back, I was indeed naive to how much having a child would change my life and impact my ability to be productive. I knew obtaining my terminal degree was a necessity, and I was also at the stage where my husband and I were ready to start our family. I knew the two things would have to overlap at some point, and I figured that I would prefer to get it done while my daughter was young and it would hopefully have less of an impact on her. My three-year degree program turned into five-and-a-half long years as I worked to finish my dissertation. Although there were several factors at play, the delay in completing my dissertation was in part due to my choice to have baby number two. I was aware that

---

[15]Lundquist, Misra, and O'Meara, "Parental Leave," 337-63.

having another baby would slow down the completion of my terminal degree, but this was the choice my husband and I decided was right for our family.

My productivity with work at home is also impacted by the conscious choices I make to give my daughters my full attention while they are awake and not spend time on my computer or make work-related phone calls. I do this because I think it is to the benefit of their growth and development to have my full attention. On the rare occasion that I do attempt to get some work done when they are awake, it is futile anyway as I am constantly interrupted by someone's needs. Craft and Maseberg-Tomlinson echo this struggle, describing one academic mother's experience of attempting to work at home while transitioning back to work after maternity leave being thwarted as the immediate "demands of childcare superseded her ability to focus for any significant length of time on her academic work."[16] I had our regular babysitter continue to watch my girls one day a week for most of my maternity leave so that I could work on my dissertation and other work-related tasks. This meant that aside from the few hours in the evening that I tried to work, I typically had about four to six hours a week to accomplish anything that I needed to get done, including working on my dissertation.

The reality is that even after maternity leave, adjusting your life and returning to work after having your first child or adding another child to your family is just *hard*, and it continues to be hard, no matter how generous and long your maternity leave.[17] With my first daughter, my maternity leave coupled with the remainder of the summer break and winter break meant that I returned to work when my daughter was six months old and still primarily dependent on nursing. This meant that all of my time in between classes and meetings was spent in my office, trying to multitask getting work done while pumping. It was exhausting and lonely. I expended time and mental energy every evening thinking ahead to what supplies I needed to bring with me the next day or whether there was

---

[16]Craft and Maseberg-Tomlinson, "Challenges Experienced."
[17]Gordon, *Maternity Leave*.

enough milk stockpiled to meet her needs while I was at work. I would wake at 5:00 a.m. to get myself and my daughter ready and out the door to take her to my parent's house so they could care for her while I was at work. I experienced significant stress trying to find other caregivers to watch her consistently on the other days during the week that my parents were not available. The number of hours I spent in my office declined as I tried to minimize the need for outside childcare. All of this impacted my productivity at work.

DESTIGMATIZING AND REIMAGINING PARENTAL LEAVE IN ACADEMIA

The question of fairness and equity regarding maternity leave is a recurrent theme throughout much of the research on the topic of parental leave. Studies have compared the equity of maternity leave policies in academia in different countries and across institutions.[18] Researchers have examined whether parental leave is equally beneficial for male and female faculty.[19] Studies have examined how a faculty member's fears about how they will be perceived for taking (or not taking) maternity leave impact their decision-making, and analyzed how it might impact decisions toward promotion and tenure.[20] Both female and male faculty express fear of how they will be perceived by colleagues for taking parental leave, leading some to consider not having children and others to not take parental leave that was available to them at their institution.[21] Female faculty who have taken maternity leave are less likely to be promoted in part because the time they

---

[18]Troeger, "Maternity Pay;" Weststar, "Negotiating," 352-74.

[19]Lundquist, Misra, and O'Meara, "Parental Leave," 337-63; Steven E. Rhoads and Christopher H. Rhoads, "Gender Roles and Infant/Toddler Care: Male and Female Professors on the Tenure Track," *Journal of Social, Evolutionary, and Cultural Psychology* 6, no. 1 (January 2012): 13, http://dx.doi.org/10.1037/h0099227. Justin Wolfers, "A Family-Friendly Policy That's Friendliest to Male Professors," *The New York Times*, June 24, 2016, Business, www.nytimes.com/2016/06/26/business/tenure-extension-policies-that-put-women-at-a-disadvantage.html.

[20]Lundquist, Misra, and O'Meara, "Parental Leave," 337-63; Thekla Morgenroth and Madeline E. Heilman, "Should I Stay or Should I Go? Implications of Maternity Leave Choice for Perceptions of Working Mothers," *Journal of Experimental Social Psychology* 72 (April 2017): 53-56, http://dx.doi.org/10.1016/j.jesp.2017.04.008.

[21]Gordon, *Maternity Leave*; Weststar, "Negotiating," 352-74; Lundquist, Misra, and O'Meara, "Parental Leave," 337-63.

spent out on leave delayed them from completing the work needed to achieve promotion.[22]

For male faculty, the stigma of taking parental leave may in part be due to conflicting research about how parental leave and attempts at gender-neutral policies such as delaying the tenure track for new parents may unintentionally result in giving an advantage to male faculty. Rhodes and Rhodes argue that institutions should consider restricting parental leave in the academy only to female faculty because there were reports that male faculty take advantage of the leave from teaching and other responsibilities to advance their research.[23] Lundquist, Misra, and O'Meara found that male faculty were far less likely to take advantage of parental leave policies, and those that did so usually had a spouse who returned to work full-time.[24] In addition, they found that both male and female faculty who had taken parental leave reported engaging in the tasks of caregiving as well as working on their research to some extent during their leave.

This raises two questions: Is keeping up with some of our ever-present work in academia while on parental leave really such a bad thing? What should parental leave really be used for? The obvious answer is that parental leave is primarily for caring for and bonding with a new child, which is important for both mothers and fathers. Research suggests that fathers who take parental leave are more likely to share childcare responsibilities.[25] Female faculty have the additional need to recover physically from childbirth while also often bearing the more physical demands of caregiving such as breastfeeding.

Lundquist, Misra, and O'Meara offer a new framework for how we view parental leave in the academy.[26] They suggest that the nature of work in the academy does not correspond with the expectation that all work must be suspended for the duration of parental leave. Tasks such as mentoring students or conducting research, especially those bound by grants and

---

[22]Gordon, *Maternity Leave*; Troeger, "Maternity Pay."
[23]Rhoads and Rhoads, "Gender Roles."
[24]Lundquist, Misra, and O'Meara, "Parental Leave," 337-63.
[25]Lundquist, Misra and O'Meara, "Parental Leave," 337-63.
[26]Lundquist, Misra and O'Meara, "Parental Leave," 337-63.

timelines, are very difficult to completely suspend for a period of time. Being able to choose to complete some elements of work, when convenient, should not be looked down upon. Troeger points out that maternity leave allows female faculty to take time off from non-research-related tasks such as teaching and administrative work and allows them to continue to conduct research that in turn helps them to avoid a gap in productivity that can impact promotion and tenure.[27] Lundquist, Misra, and O'Meara found that "parental leave enables parents to take extra time with their newborn while neutralizing any associated penalties by allowing them to retain some connection to their work" and that for faculty, "taking leave is what allowed their careers to stay afloat while being able to spend invaluable time with their child."[28]

CONCLUSION

So is it unfair that a female faculty member is eligible to be promoted despite being on leave for a portion of the promotion period? Hopefully this chapter has helped to dispel the myth that they have been given an unfair advantage of time. If anything, I would argue that it is more difficult for a female faculty member to accomplish the tasks necessary for promotion such as research and writing because they have significantly less time to devote to work-related tasks despite being on leave.

In conclusion, I would like to offer some parting advice to my fellow faculty who are preparing to grow their families. As wonderful as the blessing of having children is, there is no way to truly understand how much having a baby or adding another baby to your family will impact you physically and emotionally. Nor are you able beforehand to really understand how much it will impact how you spend your time. There are also so many unknowns that you cannot control that can alter your plan for your maternity leave.[29] Your baby might be premature, may have colic, may not be a good sleeper, or may have trouble learning to eat. I don't mean to give you more anxiety about having a baby than you probably

---

[27]Troeger, "Maternity Pay."
[28]Lundquist, Misra and O'Meara, "Parental Leave," 337-63.
[29]Gordon, *Maternity Leave*.

already have but simply to advise that your experience may differ from what you anticipate.

First, *take your maternity leave.* Don't think you don't need it. You will need it. In that same vein, do your research and know what your institutional and state policies are for maternity leave and utilize them to their fullest. Do not allow your decision to take your leave to be influenced by the negative perceptions of others. Male faculty, if you have the opportunity to take paternity leave, do it, and use it to support your wife and bond with your baby so you can be confident with caring for your child.

Second, *lower your expectations for what you think you will be able to accomplish during your maternity leave.* Do your best to take that pressure off of yourself. Your primary accomplishment during that time should simply be to bond with and get to know your baby and adapt to the new normal of your family. If you are able to keep up with some elements of your research, writing, or mentoring students while on your leave, that is great, but you will probably not be able to get as much done as you think.

Finally, *be gracious to yourself when you return to work.* Your life will be forever changed after growing your family. You will not be able to shift right into the person or the faculty member you were before simply because your maternity leave is over. This can actually be the hardest part as you juggle childcare, pumping if you are able to breastfeed, family life, and work-related responsibilities. Give yourself the freedom to say no to things that are not essential. Reach out to other faculty mothers on your campus. Practice self-care, even if it can only be in small ways.

A PRINCIPLED
DISCUSSION
FOR ADJUNCT
PROFESSOR MOTHERS

YIESHA L. THOMPSON, PhD

RECEIVING A PHONE CALL to teach at a four-year historically Black university in the District of Columbia was an exuberant moment for me. Even though I was working full time in a position I enjoyed, I was elated to accept a contingent position that enabled me to give back to students by providing practical- and theoretical-based instructional approaches and strategies in the social and behavioral sciences. I recall my own gracious professors whose advice led to life-changing internship and career opportunities. This contingent faculty position enabled me to mentor and help students matriculate through their undergraduate programs. I also found pleasure teaching in a discipline I love. But two semesters after signing my contingent contract, I soon learned the rigors of navigating adjunct[1] professorship and the necessity to lean on my faith as a compass while teaching in the academy.

---

[1]The terms adjunct and contingent faculty will be used interchangeably throughout this paper.

PRESSURES FOR ADJUNCT MOTHERS
TO FOREGO MATERNITY LEAVE

I returned to the classroom just two weeks after my daughter's birth. The decision to quickly return to academia was predicated on the timing of her birth. School began in the second week of January, and she was born a month later—two weeks prior to the midterm reporting period. I felt pressure to return to work to maintain the established trust with my students, knowing my return would ease their own concerns about their academic stability in the course. At the same time, the ability to exude compassion and help students can be onerous when you deliver instruction in a small department with only two full-time faculty members. In such cases, adjunct faculty may experience additional pressures and stressors to perform as if they are full-time. Dedication to the department and a strong desire to help students achieve academic and life success are the very tenets that led me to return to teaching just two weeks after giving birth to my daughter.

Subsequently, my bonding time with my daughter was cut short, leading to personal guilt. I adapted my time by pumping and producing extra breast milk so she could eat in my absence. I know four mother professors that opted not to breastfeed and initiate that additional form of bonding with their child because they were not certain they could sustain a concrete pumping schedule when they returned to the classroom. For these mother professors, it was better to start their children on formula and return to the classroom, versus allowing their children to breastfeed then stopping two weeks after the birth of the children. Every mother operates according to what is best for her family. Contingent faculty often make decisions that will lead to continued teaching contracts, choosing economic sustainability for their family.

According to research, "new mothers in the United States tend to return to work much more quickly after birth"[2] although the study did not yield

---

[2]Siv S. Gustafsson, Cecile M. M. P. Wetzels, Jan Dirk Vlasblom, and Shirley Dex, "Women's Labor Force Transitions in Connection with Childbirth: A Panel Data Comparison Between Germany, Sweden, and Great Britain," *Journal of Popular Economics* 9, no. 3 (August 1996): 223.

a conclusive rationale why women return to work sooner than the twelve weeks allowed by the Family Medical Leave Act.[3] For adjunct faculty, there are multiple reasons to return to the classroom quickly. Some adjunct faculty mothers may return to work because they cannot afford to take unpaid leave. Contingent faculty are not salaried employees and therefore only receive pay as contracted per semester. Within the District of Columbia and surrounding localities, like Northern Virginia and Southern Maryland, adjunct faculty make between $2,500 to $7,000 per course.[4] Full-time faculty, however, enter academia earning roughly $60,000.[5] This pay structure precludes benefits for adjunct faculty, as well as other supports for family sustainability. Furthermore, full-time faculty can take their desired parental leave with the benefits of continued pay and the assurance that they will receive a full class load the following semester. Adjuncts do not have this luxury. Many adjuncts who do not have full-time employment with benefits to take paid leave choose to return to the classroom as soon as possible.

While adjunct professors like me enter the academy with the intent of teaching part-time to supplement income and to apply practice to theory in the classroom, many adjunct professors teach because they have earned a doctoral degree but cannot attain a full-time teaching opportunity. This latter group may have to cobble together work at multiple institutions to acquire a full-time salary, albeit without medical, dental, or vision benefits. Adjunct mothers with multiple university contracts need to be paid in a timely manner to maintain their household bills and finances. As a result, if an adjunct professor elects to take a semester off to spend time with her child, she will not receive pay and will risk losing future employment at the institution. Institutions may prefer to pay another contingent faculty

---

[3]Lawrence M. Berger and Jane Waldfogel, "Maternity Leave and Employment Patterns: 1961–1995," *Journal of Population Economics* 17, no. 2 (June 2004): 331-49.

[4]Colleen Flaherty, "Barely Getting By," Inside Higher Ed, April 20, 2020, www.insidehighered.com/news/2020/04/20/new-report-says-many-adjuncts-make-less-3500-course-and-25000-year; Audrey Williams June, "3 Things a Faculty-Pay Survey Shows About Academic Jobs, *The Chronicle of Higher Education*, April 10, 2019, www.chronicle.com/article/3-things-a-faculty-pay-survey-shows-about-academic-jobs/.

[5]Annual salaries for professors differ geographically and based on the classification and endowments of the university or college.

member to instruct the course rather than appropriate additional funds to support contingent faculty members on maternity leave. If a new mother, in particular, has to go to the hospital or see a specialist, no benefits package is tied to the adjunct salary. Therefore, the adjunct mother needs to continue working to ensure she has money for an untimely illness, medical emergency, or hospitalization, should the need arise. Additionally, the cost of living in the Washington, DC, area is so high that professor mothers, even if married, cannot solely rely on their spouse's income.[6]

The prompt return of new mothers to the classroom is also initiated by the set schedules of collegiate life. Most institutions, regardless of the type—two or four-year colleges—operate on a fifteen-week schedule per semester.[7] If new mothers were to utilize the full twelve weeks allowed by the FMLA, students would only encounter the professor for a maximum of three weeks, which would not be advantageous to the students nor to the professor. This compounds the dilemma a mother professor makes when returning to academia immediately following the birth of her child. To avoid this conundrum of requesting time off altogether, many professors resolve to have children during the summer or winter breaks.

Even for adjuncts who have full-time jobs and are not obligated to return to their salaried position immediately, they may choose to return to the classroom early. This was my case. I was on maternity leave from my full-time job to bond with my daughter and enjoy time with my son so he wouldn't feel isolated with the birth of his baby sister. But I felt compelled to return to the classroom to minimize the pressure on my department chair and to make sure my students felt secure with their professor of record by providing equitable instruction commensurate with their other classes. I also wanted to avoid giving students any cause to file a grievance or request a grade change due to my prolonged absence from the classroom. This is because I had meaningful university experiences as a student.

---

[6]Sean Dennison, "The Salary You Need to Live in Washington, DC Skyrockets," GOBankingRates, April 5, 2019, https://www.gobankingrates.com/money/economy/rising-cost-live-comfortably-washington-dc/.

[7]Jennifer Weller, "The Length of a College Semester," Bright Hub, April 20, 2010, www.brighthub.com/education/college/articles/69143.aspx.

To this day, I vividly recall the impact my professors had on me—both full-time and contingent faculty. After attending a predominantly White institution (PWI) for my undergraduate degree and a historically Black college (HBCU) for my graduate degrees, I became cognizant of the various teaching practices and principled approaches used in the classroom. At the PWI, my advisor and Chair of Chicano Studies constantly reminded me to excel and pushed me to work hard "to gain opportunities of my privileged counterparts." Both adjunct faculty and deans alike at my HBCU, gave me the same encouragement. I recognize and am grateful that God allowed me to have mentors that were deeply committed to my advancement beyond the classroom and baccalaureate degree.

MAKING A DIFFERENCE FOR STUDENTS
WHILE BEING THERE FOR FAMILY

I was grateful to have professors at both institutions who cared and were committed to ensuring students thrived inside and outside of the classroom by encouraging field trips, assisting with internships and fellowships, and extending office hours to make sure the course material was fully understood. But as a student, I noticed differences between full-time and adjunct professors at both institutions. The adjunct faculty appeared to be younger, used relatable jargon and slang terminology, and were more willing to work with students; but these professors were scarce and appeared to have time constraints which limited their teaching duration at the university. I can recall a contingent faculty member students appreciated and respected because of his pedagogy and approach to student engagement. At the conclusion of the semester, numerous students elected to nominate him as professor of the year. But he was unable to receive the recognition because of his contingency status. These experiences gave me the desire to teach practical approaches to the theories learned and discussed in the classroom setting. I was motivated to show students that outstanding teaching can come from adjunct faculty members who are young, engaged, and reflect a similar upbringing as the students.

For me, teaching at a university with a large percentage of first-generation college students or a high percentage of economically disadvantaged students, or both, presents the unique challenge of developing trust with students and helping them understand that professors, such as myself, want them to acquire an advanced degree. My reason for teaching hinges on providing support and resources for students. But relationships are necessary for students to know that adjunct professors, in particular, have their best interest in mind. Being contingent faculty means not always being available on campus and rarely holding weekly office hours where students can create a safe space with the contingent faculty member. Yet once the relationship is established, students yearn for continued discussions and conversations with adjunct faculty to discuss their academic pursuits, challenges, and perils. The proverb "to whom much is given, much is required" resonates with me as an adjunct faculty member. Students have struggled to attend class because they are caregivers to a family member plagued with a terminal illness or were evicted and had to return home, which is out of the area. Another student had to return home in another country to check on her aging parents but could not return to the United States to finish the semester due to then president Trump's executive order banning individuals from seven countries. Coupled with the coronavirus, these very examples have crippled my students over the past three semesters. With the Covid-19 pandemic, more students dropped out of school in an effort to keep a roof over their heads and simply because they no longer had access to the university library, where they relied on the textbooks, computers, and printers to complete assignments.

At the same time, female professors with children must remain guarded in their faith amid the compounding university demands. Otherwise, the advising, meetings, and administrative tasks on the part of adjunct professor mothers can come at a sacrifice to the needs of their children, creating layers of separation rather than additional bonding time. To create balance, Christian professors must invest in a regular spiritual practice. This includes prayerfully conducting check-ins with God to center one's faith. In meeting with students, Christian professors can be prayerful in how they steer students in academic pursuits or in life lessons, while remaining cognizant of their own offspring and familial commitments and needs. Although contingent faculty do not have an obligation to produce scholarship, I believe we are also charged with helping those in need, as my professors helped me as I matriculated through my undergrad and graduate programs. God has positioned me not only to help my students academically but also to foster genuine relationships with students, host office hours, and discuss student support and services. While student conversations and support can extend well past office hours and cut into my family time, these responsibilities are a part of the contractual agreement at universities and colleges, where contingent faculty may carry heavy loads. This is exacerbated when a department only has two full-time faculty members and over one hundred student majors in a program of study.

Furthermore, as an adjunct professor working full-time in the discipline of social and behavioral science, students often hope that I am able to connect them with jobs, internships, and professional contacts from my network. Because I teach in the nation's capital, students constantly ask for assistance with career opportunities (federal employment) and request extensions on assignment submissions because they juggle multiple jobs to pay their excessive rent, which many times will interfere with them attending class on time. The desire to help students sometimes affects the attention a contingent faculty member provides to her own offspring. As professors, we do not want to see students struggle or drop out of college, so we research additional resources and support for students that often surpass class time and office hours and force us to return home after dinner or when our own children have gone to sleep. I give back and commit to student achievement because adjuncts are the nucleus of the department and because I hold a true conviction for my morals and values to lift others.

ADMINISTRATIVE DEMANDS ON CONTINGENT FACULTY

At small universities and programs, contingent faculty can also feel pressured to attend department meetings and assist with administrative tasks.

They are driven by the promise (which may appear exploitative) of office space, additional courses, or even full-time work. However, contingent faculty instructing in small departments are contractually bound to advise students and contribute to faculty discussions, which may lead to the secured space to convene before and after classes or provide future opportunities for the adjunct professor. As a result, the adjunct professor works additional hours to support and uphold the program above and beyond her contractual duties. In these scenarios, the adjunct professor may operate as a "visiting professor" because she carries the load of instructing three to four courses per semester and assists students, even if advising is not a part of their job description.[8] This feat is further complicated when adjuncts do not have access to university systems (Oracle, Banner, PeopleSoft) and therefore cannot fully assist students even though the adjunct is teaching multiple classes each semester and expected to attend department meetings.

I felt the weight of this responsibility, which often meant I was not at home during dinner, bath time, or story time. Even though my department chair was aware of how far I lived from campus (an approximately 45-minute commute) and my parental responsibilities, I was not encouraged to leave immediately following my evening classes to get home to my young kids. Instead, normalcy became me waiting for department faculty to respond to emails and complete last-minute paperwork so we could walk to the parking garage and ensure one another's safety. Those nights, I attempted to call my kids to hear their voices before they went to sleep because I knew I would not see them awake until the following afternoon. As I reflect on my time in the classroom, I still feel a sense of commitment and a strong desire to help my students. While I might change the time frame in which I assist students (so I can maintain my familial obligations), I know my purpose is to provide grace, compassion, and empathy to students attempting to navigate the collegiate life.

---

[8]Contingent faculty members' contracts will specify the additional responsibilities the adjunct must conduct in addition to teaching. Each college or university is different.

RECOMMENDATIONS FOR ADMINISTRATORS

To further assist and support contingent faculty mothers in the academy, I have a couple of recommendations. I strongly encourage department chairs to invite adjunct faculty to division meetings and to also create space for contingent faculty to collaborate among one another. Having an opportunity to connect and meet with other adjunct mothers within the department can greatly enhance camaraderie and contributions within the department. After I returned from maternity leave in 2013, divine intervention allowed me to meet an adjunct mother in the university's administration building. Meeting the contingent faculty mother, who also taught in Social and Behavioral Sciences, enabled us to discuss best practice models for implementing technology into instructional approaches, useful and up-to-date textbooks, and methods for balancing academic responsibilities with home life. The considerations we discussed allowed me to reconsider technological tools in the classroom and also enabled me to adjust how much time I provide to students during in-person office hours and when I am home with family.

Additionally, department chairs and academic deans should consider the burden of mandatory trainings and meetings on contingent faculty mothers. Teaching at a university that has multiple campuses means having various department trainings and orientation sessions at the beginning of each semester. While the trainings are useful and provide an opportunity for contingent faculty mothers to affiliate and collaborate with department faculty, my concern arises from times when campus coordinators or chairs have not communicated with one another about training dates. As a contingent faculty member who teaches on two campuses, I found myself contemplating which "mandatory" training session and orientation session to attend. Both training sessions for adjunct faculty were during the same date and time. While I received credit for attending one of the trainings, I also received an email communication stating I was not in attendance for the mandatory training that was held on the second campus. Adjunct mothers strive to meet academic obligations and ensure the department and students receive support and services. My colleague, who is also an adjunct mother, was able to attend mandatory training because her children are older, more independent, and understand how to access her via cellular phone when she is not home. Smaller children (aged birth to nine), however, need assistance, supervision, empathy, and attention, so they feel loved and supported. Department chairs and deans could greatly assist contingent mothers by thinking through the requirements and mandatory training for contingent faculty. Incorporating these recommendations into academic departments will enhance resources and provide helpful support to contingent mother professors in the academy.

NAVIGATING
MOTHERHOOD

THE "GOOD" MOTHER

CHRISTINA LEE KIM, PhD

WHAT DOES BEING A "GOOD MOTHER" MEAN TO YOU?
Describe her characteristics.

Are you a good mother?

I have this memory of something my mother said to me while I was pregnant with my first child. I married my husband during my last year of graduate school and became pregnant two years later while in my first year of a tenure-track faculty position at my current university. I remember struggling internally with the decision of whether I should continue working full time, cut down to part time, or quit working altogether while my daughter was a newborn baby and toddler. After all, that's what everyone around me seemed to be doing. So many of my female friends who had obtained law degrees, education degrees, or psychology degrees became stay-at-home moms after the birth of their children. Perhaps they also struggled internally with the decision, but if so, I couldn't tell. They seemed to love the decision they made, a "no-brainer." They were fulfilled embracing the role of "mom," but I had mixed feelings. I wanted to work, but I also wanted to stay at home. I wanted to do everything and be everything. Was I the only one who felt this way? It was actually my mother's comment that helped me make the decision to continue working. When I shared my dilemma with her, she said, in her sounds-like-she's-scolding-but-she's-really-being-supportive Korean (I'm translating here), "Of course you should keep working! I didn't raise you and see you through all your schooling so that you would just end up quitting your job to stay home and have babies!"

The strength and certainty of her response were striking to me. It contradicted all traditional and conservative gender ideologies that you might place upon my mother based on her social identities: Korean, Christian, stay-at-home mom, pastor's wife. Despite these social identities, my mother had strong beliefs about the value of women working and making a career and identity for themselves (and for their families). I'm positive that her beliefs shaped my own and my younger two sisters' attitudes around work and family. All three of us are mothers of two or more children with active professional careers. The Korean phrase that my mother would often use when hearing that a well-educated female friend of mine had stopped working to be a homemaker was "아깝다," which literally translates to "how regrettable, what a waste." This may sound harsh to some folks. Was she saying that to be a full-time mom was a waste? I didn't interpret it that way. In the context that she spoke it, I believe she meant that here was a woman who had invested in herself educationally and professionally. Within our cultural context, her parents and community had invested in her, too. Here was a woman who had something to offer her family and her community, something beyond the role of mothering her children. But by choosing to stay home, she was not exercising her full potential. That was how I interpreted that phrase.

I had always known that my mother was supportive of our education and careers, but until that moment, I had never given much thought to how her beliefs seemingly conflicted with the gender ideologies that were so prevalent in the culture around us as I was growing up. And honestly, I don't think she gave much thought to it either. To her, the "no-brainer" was that her three daughters would be educated and pursue the careers that they desired. Pursuing a desired career was something my mother had been unable to do after immigrating to the United States due to language barriers and the demands of raising three children with no extended family nearby to help. I suppose you could say that she intended for us to do all that she could not. As for family and children, of course we would have those too. There was no apology for that, no feelings of guilt, shame, or conflict (at least that I picked up at the time), and it didn't have to be one or the other. Yes, there was certainly the practical dilemma of childcare, etc., but those were merely problems to be solved when we got to that point. In fact, after she made that sounded-like-scolding-but-she-was-really-being-supportive statement, she followed with, "I will help watch the baby so that you can continue to work." To her, that was a problem solved. In that moment, upon hearing my mother's comment and subsequent offer to help, I found myself quite confused. Where along the way had I internalized these feelings of guilt, shame, tension, and conflict? Would I be considered selfish, a bad mother, for continuing to work after the birth of my child? Would I be considered selfish, a bad daughter, for choosing to stay home and not honor the investment made in me by my family? What did God desire of me? What would be honoring to him? And what did I believe about what it means to be a good mother?

This chapter documents some of my reflections on motherhood ideology, particularly as it relates to my experience in the Christian academy. I write it as I enter my fifteenth year of teaching at my current place of employment, a private, Christian university in Southern California that has been my "work-home" through the birth of my three children. I started work fifteen years ago as a bright-eyed, naive, fresh-off-the-grad-school-boat, newly married, no kids, post-doctoral fellow. Now, here I am, fifteen years later, a blurry-eyed (after forty, I now need glasses), not-so-naive, tenured, still married, mother of three kids, associate professor who loves her job but continues to find herself at the intersection of mixed messages when it comes to identifying as a mother and professor. I still want to do everything and be everything. But the ways I think about my identity as a mother and professor have morphed and evolved with the changing seasons that accompany family life, my professional identity development, a deepened understanding of my cultural background, and the ways God has so graciously been working in my personal and spiritual life.

The question of what it means to be a "good mother" is rife with meaning and implication. Over the years, I have discovered that while my fellow professor-mother colleagues in the Christian academy share many similar experiences related to balancing work and family, we have just as many differences when it comes to how we navigate and think about our role as professors and as mothers. I have often wondered about these differences. I have wondered whether they contribute, at least in part, to a hesitancy to engage a deeper level of support among female colleagues. This is not to suggest that I experience my female colleagues to be unsupportive. In fact, having fellow female colleagues who know the struggles of wanting to be both a good mother and a good professor has been life-giving to me. We support one another in our very existence, knowing that we are not alone and that the challenges we face in the academy are not unusual or due to personal shortcomings. We advocate for one another; we provide input on institutional policies—ideas that are born from experience and that will help make things easier for the next generation of professor mothers. This book was created with that very purpose in mind, that perhaps the collective experience of its contributors would offer support, encouragement, validation, ideas, and hope. It is in the spirit of that purpose that I write this chapter, with hope that the readers will engage in an exploration of their motherhood ideologies and consider their implications for how we relate to our fellow professor-mother colleagues.

GENDER AND MOTHERHOOD IDEOLOGY

Gender ideology is a term that refers to the attitudes and beliefs we hold about what is the right or appropriate role for men and women in our culture or society. It is a socially constructed concept which, at an individual level, is often shaped by messages, both explicit and implicit, that we internalize throughout our lives.[1] The messages we receive from our

---

[1]Candace West and Don H. Zimmerman, "Doing Gender," *Gender & Society* 1, no. 2 (June 1987): 125-51.

family of origin greatly influence the ways we individually think about gender, but other factors that shape our gender ideology include schooling, religion, media, and society or culture at large—not to mention that it is often these broader societal influences that shaped our parents' gender ideologies to begin with. In a graduate class that I teach, I have my students examine the messages they've received throughout the course of their life about what it means to be a man or a woman.

- What messages have you received about what it means to be a man or woman?
- Where did these messages come from?
- What messages do you readily accept?
- What messages do you resist or reject?
- What messages might you directly or indirectly pass on to your own children (should you have them), or to those you have influence over, in the future?

While it seems like a simple exercise, it is often quite illuminating for my students. You see, while gender ideology may have a tremendous impact on how we live our lives, play out our social roles, parent our children, or relate to our partners, it is not always conscious or explicit—that is, unless we make it so. Exploring what we, as individuals, believe about what it means to be male or female may help to explain why certain behaviors in ourselves and in others bother us, feel so natural or unnatural to us, and even help to explain why we don't see eye to eye with our partner or friends on certain issues.

It wasn't until graduate school that I learned that there was a subcategory of gender ideology: motherhood ideology. When I encountered the term during a research meeting with my dissertation committee members, my interest was piqued. What was "motherhood ideology"? My simple definition is "the beliefs and attitudes we hold about what it means to be a good (or bad) mother." A more academic definition might be that "motherhood ideologies" are sets of cultural beliefs, attitudes, and values that "define the status quo of motherhood and assign a cultural purpose and meaning to the role of a mother."[2]

Just as gender ideology is a social construct, motherhood ideology is also socially constructed.[3] All of our ideas about what constitutes a "good" mother are shaped by a complex collection of cultural, environmental, social, religious, family of origin, and personal factors, making each of us unique when it comes to our ideas about mothering.[4] But despite the tremendous diversity that these multiple factors may yield, much of the scholarly focus has understandably been on traditional and idealized motherhood ideologies that dominate US culture. In particular, traditional notions of ideal mothers involve expectations that a mother's primary responsibility is to raise children, while fathers take on the bread-winning role in the family. Such hegemonic ideologies persist despite the fact that, in reality, a substantial majority of mothers (70 percent) participate in the workforce.[5]

Ideal mothers are also often portrayed as having complete and utter self-sacrificing devotion to their children's physical, emotional, academic, social, and spiritual needs. Sharon Hays, in her research on the experience of motherhood in the United States, identified themes in her interviews with women that described a practice she calls "intensive mothering."[6] Intensive mothering suggests that the mother should be the primary caregiver for her children because mothers make the best caregivers. Mothers should also be fully present and fully giving, providing for every aspect of her child's needs by utilizing every aspect of her own resources, whether mental, emotional, physical, or financial. Furthermore, intensive mothering

---

[2]Terry Arendell, "Conceiving and Investigating Motherhood: The Decade's Scholarship," *Journal of Marriage and the Family* 62, no. 4 (November 2000): 1192-207; Sharon Hays, *The Cultural Contradictions of Motherhood* (New Haven, CT: Yale University Press, 1996); Tina Miller, *Making Sense of Motherhood* (Cambridge, UK: Cambridge University Press, 2005), cited in Grace Eun Lee, "The Role of Self-Compassion and Self-Acceptance in the Relationship Between Maternal Self-Discrepancy and Guilt and Shame," (master's thesis, Biola University, 2018), 4.
[3]Arendell, "Conceiving and Investigating Motherhood"; Hays, *Cultural Contradictions*; Miller, *Making Sense of Motherhood*.
[4]Hays, *Cultural Contradictions*, 21.
[5]US Department of Labor, "Working Mothers Issue Brief," June 13, 2016, https://digital.library .unt.edu/ark:/67531/metadc955340/m2/1/high_res_d/Working_Mothers_Issue_Brief.pdf.
[6]Hays, *Cultural Contradictions*, x.

suggests that the very act of being a mother should fulfill the mother's role as a woman and complete her identity.[7] It is fascinating to note that many middle- and working-class American women have adopted this intensive mothering style regardless of whether or not they work outside the home.[8]

Warner writes of the stress, anger, and guilt that consumes mothers as they strive to reach unrealistically high expectations of motherhood, describing the myth of the perfect mother as a "nationwide epidemic."[9] The research literature on the experience of motherhood documents feelings of guilt and shame among mothers all across the working to nonworking spectrum. Lee summarizes the literature well as she writes:

> Mothers who are employed experience guilt and shame due to difficulties with balancing both professional and domestic roles . . . , constant thoughts about what is not being done in other roles . . . , having to resort to childcare . . . , and trying to engage in intensive parenting to make up for time away from children . . . , while mothers who stay at home with their children experience guilt because of a sense of complete responsibility, sense of inadequacy and feeling like they are not doing enough for their child . . . . Mothers who are pursuing higher education experience guilt and shame for not being as present as they believe they should be . . . and mothers who have achieved higher education but choose to stay at home full-time experience guilt and shame from feeling as though they are not doing enough for their children and not living up to the potential of their educational achievement.[10]

The internalized expectations of being the "ideal mother" appear to contribute to a persistent experience of guilt, shame, and internal conflict and tension among mothers in American culture. Consequently, mothers

---

[7]Susan J. Douglas and Meredith W. Michaels, *The Mommy Myth: The Idealization of Motherhood* (New York, NY: Free Press, 2004); Hays, *Cultural Contradictions*; Glenda Wall, "Mothers' Experiences with Intensive Parenting and Brain Development Discourse," *Women's Studies International Forum* 33, no. 3 (May-June 2010): 253-63.

[8]Hays, *Cultural Contradictions*; Carol Vincent, Stephen J. Ball, and Soile Pietikainen, "Metropolitan Mothers: Mothers, Mothering and Paid Work," *Women's Studies International Forum* 27, no. 5-6 (November-December 2004): 571-87.

[9]Judith Warner, *Perfect Madness: Motherhood in the Age of Anxiety* (New York, NY: Riverhead Books, 2005).

[10]Lee, "The Role of Self-Compassion and Self-Acceptance."

engage various strategies to navigate such conflict. For example, multiple scholars have identified the meanings mothers attach to their decisions about work/family, the ways mothers reframe their decisions in order to reduce conflict,[11] or even the ways mothers actively resist hegemonic ideologies, rejecting core tenets of "intensive" mothering and adopting alternative ideologies such as "integrated" mothering[12] or "extensive" mothering,[13] which involves delegating caregiving tasks while remaining ultimately responsible for their child's needs.

Further, it is interesting to note that much of the research done on intensive mothering and the motherhood experience in the United States has neglected the collective experiences of ethnic minority mothers. Studies including more diverse samples of mothers in the US suggest that perceptions of what constitutes the "ideal mother" vary crossculturally and that such cultural variance may, on the one hand, buffer some of the negative impact of "intensive mothering" demands, but on the other hand, raise other kinds of conflict and tension that remain underreported in the predominant literature.[14] Such findings resonate with my own experience. While I identify with much of what is written about motherhood ideology in the US, the intersection of my Korean American cultural background, the experience of growing up among immigrant parents, my class background, my faith identity, the experience of growing up in a Korean immigrant church—all of these factors (and more) make the ways that I think

---

[11]Mary Blair-Loy, *Competing Devotions: Career and Family Among Women Executives* (Cambridge, MA: Harvard University Press, 2003); Karen Christopher, "Extensive Mothering: Employed Mothers' Constructions of the Good Mother," *Gender & Society* 26, no. 1 (January 2012): 73-96; Dawn Marie Dow, "Integrated Motherhood: Beyond Hegemonic Ideologies of Motherhood," *Journal of Marriage and Family* 78, no. 1 (October 2015): 180-96; Kathleen Gerson, *The Unfinished Revolution: How a New Generation is Reshaping Family, Work, and Gender in America* (Oxford, UK: Oxford University Press, 2010); Hays, *Cultural Contradictions*; Arlie Hochschild and Anne Machung, *The Second Shift: Working Families and the Revolution at Home* (New York, NY: Viking, 1989).

[12]Dow, "Integrated Motherhood."

[13]Christopher, "Extensive Mothering."

[14]Dow, "Integrated Motherhood" 188, 194; Christopher, "Extensive Mothering" 77-78, 92; Seung-sook Moon, "Immigration and Mothering: Case Studies from Two Generations of Korean Immigrant Women," *Gender & Society* 17, no. 6 (December 2003): 857; Pratyusha Tummala-Nara, "Contemporary Impingements on Mothering," *The American Journal of Psychoanalysis* 69, no. 1 (March 2009): 7, 12.

about motherhood unique. As I mentioned earlier, we all have unique experiences and beliefs about what it means to be a good mother. The articulation of shared experience surely carries many benefits, but I also believe that the articulation and understanding of our differences can provide us many opportunities for deeper levels of supportive interactions among colleagues. In the next section, I will articulate my own experiences and how this has fostered, but at times also hindered, deeper levels of supportive interactions among my colleagues.

AT THE INTERSECTION OF MIXED MESSAGES

Despite the pro-"work plus family" environment in my family of origin, as I prepared to give birth to my first child, it was clear that I had indeed adopted a form of intensive mothering ideology. As a second-generation Asian American, conservative Christian female with a doctorate in clinical psychology, my motherhood ideology had been shaped by a mixture of factors beyond my family of origin, including, but not limited to, religion, formal education, my discipline, media, and the culture at large. It was a form of intensive mothering ideology with a professional and cultural twist. I identified with many of the expectations that mothers should be fully present and fully giving and must meet their child's every need. The professional twist was that, being a psychologist, it seemed the stakes were even higher as I "knew too much" about the impact of motherhood and parenting on a child's attachment and cognitive, psychosocial, and emotional development.

The cultural twist was that, consistent with my Asian cultural values, I gravitated toward a desire to foster interdependence in my children alongside, and sometimes much more than, independence. For example, my husband and I were quite comfortable cosleeping with our children and saw the benefits that it brought the whole family. I had a strong desire to be accessible and available to my children at every turn. Consequently, I wanted to utilize the least amount of childcare possible. What was interesting was that with every occasion that I accepted help with childcare from my mother (aside from formal educational settings, I can count on one hand the times I have ever left my children with nonfamily caregivers), I felt guilt not only toward my children, but also toward my mother. I appreciated her help, but I often resisted her help. I interpreted this mix of emotions as stemming from a desire to do things on my own (and even a feeling that I should be doing things on my own), but also from a feeling of not wanting to burden someone who had already sacrificed so much for me. Reflecting on this, I find it quite interesting how much of a push and pull I often feel between the values of independence and interdependence. In any case, the cultural twist was that with the added help and support I received from my family, I often raised the expectations that I placed on myself. I felt that I had no excuse not to be a "good" mother and no excuse not to be a "good" professor. I felt this way even as I was fully aware that in its extreme manifestations, these were completely unreasonable standards that stemmed from my own perfectionistic and neurotic tendencies. They did not come from my parents, my place of employment, or even from God.

Becoming a mother while working at a private, predominantly White Christian university added another cultural layer to the mix. I had never really given much thought to this prior to beginning my job, but for most of my life, my experience of my faith and God had been in the context of other Asians and Asian Americans. Growing up, I attended my father's church. It was small and made up of mostly working-class Korean immigrants and their families. In college, I was heavily involved in a discipleship-focused campus ministry that also was made up of mostly Korean Americans. While in graduate school, I attended a large nondenominational church made up of mostly Asian Americans. All my life, I had gone to church and was involved in ministry, so I naturally assumed that coming to work at a Christian university would be a familiar experience and a smooth transition. But it wasn't long before I realized that I was experiencing a bit of culture shock, especially when it came to the topic of gender.

In the first few years after starting my job, I remember listening in on many conversations among my female colleagues about their experiences with men and the debates over the roles of men and women in church leadership and in the home. Complementarianism and egalitarianism were words that everyone seemed to know much about. Despite having been a Christian all my life and growing up in the church, it was the first time I encountered so much hubbub around these labels and around the issue of gender. Such debate had simply not been a very important part of my religious or spiritual experience. So when I encountered these debates at every corner in my predominantly White evangelical Christian academic workplace, I felt a mixture of amusement, bewilderment, and culture shock. The debates were not just about leadership roles in the church. They spilled over into the realm of motherhood. Was it possible to be a good Christian mother if you chose to pursue a career outside of the home?

The culture shock came from the dawning realization that in contrast to my cultural and religious upbringing, the beliefs I held about being able to pursue both career and family seemed to violate what appeared to me to be some sort of White conservative Christian standard that said that women (especially if they were mothers) should not work. In the Asian American immigrant circles where I grew up, working mothers were a common phenomenon, a necessary and valuable source of financial contribution to households trying to establish a life in the United States. Of course, I was not naive. I knew that there were people who felt that the best Christian mothers were the ones who stayed home with their children. But I had never encountered them in person, and certainly not in groups of peers and colleagues. The debate over gender roles was a cultural dimension of influence on motherhood ideology that I never really had to engage. But for some of my professor-mother colleagues, this was an all-too-familiar debate in their cultural experience, a powerful influence on the messages they internalized about what it meant to be a good mother. The gender debate explained some of the behavior of my male and female colleagues—the significance of certain workplace decisions, the strange gender-specific comments, and the anger, frustration, and emotional reactivity that several of my female colleagues had over incidents that I didn't even notice until they were pointed out. The lack of experience I had in relation to religious debates over gender, and the relative insignificance of such debates in my own family and community, buffered much of the negative impact of such debates on my sense of self and identity. But this lack of experience also resulted in a naiveté and insensitivity on my part to the experiences of my fellow professor mothers.

I share this story as an example of the ways our unique experiences impact our ability (or inability) to understand and support our fellow colleagues. It reminds me of five words that a pastor friend of mine shared with me many years ago. He said that if I wanted to be successful in life, I must remember that "everyone is not like you." I confess that the life experiences that have shaped my motherhood ideology have, at times, limited my ability to understand and support my fellow professor-mother peers. Motherhood ideology is so intensely personal and comes with such a strong sense of rightness or wrongness that unless we intentionally remind ourselves that there are stories and experiences that have contributed to that other person's view of what a "good mother" is, we will be tempted to make assumptions about, invalidate, or even judge and condemn the actions of our fellow professor mothers. (We will be tempted to do this with all mothers, actually.)

I was recently involved in helping to collect data for a gender climate study at a Christian university. While interviewing female faculty for this study, a theme that kept arising among the small subset of participants that I interviewed was the difficulties and conflicts that female faculty experienced with other female faculty. I am certain that my sociology peers are much better equipped to explain this phenomenon at a societal, systemic, and institutional level than I am. There is a context for why we women sometimes fail to uplift other women despite our feminist labels and our professed care and commitment toward advancing women's issues. We definitely need those explanations. But we also need to take an honest and deep look inward. The discipline I was trained in suggests that how we treat or react to others can sometimes reflect attempts to protect ourselves or "defend" against feelings of anxiety, threat, guilt, and pain.[15] If it is true,

---

[15]Anna Freud, *The Ego and the Mechanisms of Defence* (London: Hogarth Press and Institute of Psycho-Analysis, 1937).

as the research suggests, that mothers in American culture experience persistent feelings of guilt, shame, and internal conflict, it is only natural that we would also be engaging in persistent efforts to cope with, manage, or defend against these negative feelings, whether we are aware of it or not. What impact might a state of persistent defensiveness have on our ability to come alongside and engage our fellow professor-mother peers? The word *defensiveness* can carry such negative connotations that I hesitate to use it here. What if I were to rephrase the question to ask, what impact might a constant state of wanting to protect ourselves from being thought of as a less-than-ideal mother have on our ability to come alongside and engage our fellow professor-mother peers?

LOVING GOD MOST

Earlier, I described the incredible pressure I placed on myself due to the adoption of an intensive mothering ideology "with a professional and cultural twist." It has been an ongoing process and journey for me to willingly let go of some of these pressures I place on myself to do everything and be everything. As my children have moved past the baby and toddler years and into the middle school years, some anxieties have naturally lessened. But different kinds of anxieties and pressures have emerged. Feeling more established in my work and having attained tenure has also reduced much of the anxiety and work-related pressures that colored those initial years in the academy. But academia continually brings new challenges, opportunities, and expectations. I do not know that I will ever *not* feel pressured to keep producing, keep improving, keep contributing to the field and to society. Such is the nature and privilege of our work and I love it as much as it also stresses me out.

The journey of letting go, or surrendering, some of my intensive mothering expectations has been intertwined with the lessons God has been teaching me about learning to depend on him more, and on myself less. In this journey, I have become increasingly aware of the enormous amount of pride that I have. Pride is a tricky word, especially for Christians. We must discern between a pride that is healthy and appropriate (Ecclesiastes 3:22;

2 Corinthians 5:12; 7:4) versus the sinful pride that God hates and opposes (Proverbs 8:13; James 4:6). Most of what is written about pride in the Bible refers to the latter. Sinful pride causes us to be boastful, arrogant, and self-centered. It also leads us to self-sufficiency rather than Spirit-dependence. We place ourselves at the center, we take control, and in the pride of our heart, we think we are as wise as a god (Ezekiel 28:2). I have come to think of professor mothers as an extremely competent group. We have educational and scholarly attainment that many folks do not have. We are extremely hard workers. In addition to the time and effort we put toward our profession, we strive to be good mothers. Many of us volunteer in our children's schools, we lead their scout troops, we plan those playdates or those educational family outings, we craft, we clean, we cook, we shuttle, we tackle those household chores. And even if none of those things are on your list of mothering activities, you have your own list of things you do as you strive to be a good mom to your children.

A huge temptation that I have, and that I know other mothers share, is the temptation that results from such competence: the temptation toward pride and control and self-sufficiency. When I know I "can" do what I need to do, I depend on myself more and on God less. The opposite of this is humility, having a right view of who I am in relation to God, my Creator and Lord. If I am honest with myself, the intensive mothering expectations I have adopted are largely void of humility and the daily practice of Spirit-dependence. Even in moments where I might rationalize or provide some sort of religious justification for why I need to do things in accordance with those ideal-mother expectations, the truth is that I am often still placing myself (or my children) at the center, rather than God.

I'm convinced that self-sufficiency also perpetuates the guilt, shame, and internal conflict that we tend to feel as mothers because, in the end, we always come face-to-face with our limitations. Without the help of his Spirit, it is impossible for me to love my children the way I desire, much less the way God desires. As much as I try to be that perfect (or even just "good") mother, as much as I try to provide the best environment for my child's development, I fall short. My sinful nature messes it up. In addition, there are so many things that are simply outside of my control, so many things where I am utterly helpless and at God's mercy when it comes to desiring the best for my kids.

My father passed away from cancer almost six years ago, just two weeks after the birth of my third child. In one of the last real conversations I had with him, he said to me, "Remember to always love God most, even more than your kids." I have been pondering over those words ever since that conversation. Does loving God more than my kids fit into my motherhood ideology? At that time, looking deep into my heart, it did not. And since that time, I have been on a slow journey of learning what it means to love God most, more than my work, more than my family, more than myself. At the start of this past year, something my pastor said really struck a chord in me. He said, "The best way to love others is to be healthy, spiritually vital, fully alive, and fighting for joy in God." It was an encouragement to our congregation to prioritize our relationship with God over other relationships, and that out of that spiritual vitality, we will be able to love.

What this meant for me was that the best way to love my kids, my husband, my colleagues, my students was for me to tend to my relationship with God, to "fight for joy," and maintain my spiritual health and vitality even in the crazy busy schedule that has come to define my professor-mommy life. God is the source of all love, of perfect love. He is life. He is the Vine, we are the branches (John 15:4-5). Apart from him, we can do nothing. Humility and Spirit-dependence are acknowledging that we need him in order to thrive, to bear fruit, to be effective in all the roles he has given us. But what does this look like at a practical level? The answer to this question may look different for each of us. For me, in order to be intentional about Spirit-dependence, I have had to daily confess and *kill* my default gravitation toward self-sufficiency. It sounds violent, but I use that word because many times it truly feels like "dying to self." It is interesting to me that intensive mothering ideology suggests that mothers will utilize all their available resources, essentially emptying themselves, for the sake of their children. I have engaged in many conversations with mothers who share that having children has forced them to be less selfish, has forced them to consider someone else more important than themselves. But the object for whom we empty ourselves is of supreme significance. According to the Scriptures, such devotion and selflessness for the sake of our children can also lead to idolatry.

Such knowledge ultimately raises several questions for me. As a professor mommy, every day, I am faced with competing demands for my attention. I work hard. I have multiple spinning plates in the air at any moment. I am on the road to perfecting the art of multitasking. I can pick up toys with my feet while checking emails on my phone. Yes, I love and need my downtime too, but give me fifteen minutes anywhere (waiting in my car at the school drop-off zone, standing in line at a coffee shop) and I can be productive. But the question this raises for me is, *For whom do I work so hard?* What does it look like to empty myself for the sake of Christ versus for the sake of my children? Or for the sake of my career? How do I honor God and place him at the center? What does it look like to love God with all my heart, soul, mind, and strength as I live out my identity (and my calling) both as a professor and as a mother? What does it mean for me to "fight for joy" in my relationship with God and prioritize him over other relationships? Over my kids? Over my work? Again, the answers to these questions may look different for each of us, but I believe they are important questions to ask.

And let's be honest. Many of us professor mommies are exhausted. Working hard understandably leads to fatigue, exhaustion, and the need for rest. Several years ago, my routine of working late into the night after the kids went to sleep did a number on my health. I spent more days sick that semester than healthy. During that time, I remember coming across Matthew 11:28-30 which says, "Come to me, all you who are weary and burdened, and I will give you rest. Take my yoke upon you and learn from me, for I am gentle and humble in heart, and you will find rest for your souls. For my yoke is easy and my burden is light." This was a familiar passage to me, and I have always loved the first part of those verses. Come to me, all you who labor, and I will give you rest. Rest. That sounded wonderful. But then as I spent more time poring over those verses, I had to admit that the next few lines were confusing. Take my yoke upon you. A yoke? Isn't that like a shackle? Yokes look heavy, uncomfortable, restricting. They do not look easy; rather, they look like they restrict freedom. When I think of rest, I do not think of a yoke.

Perhaps you understood this passage much earlier than I did, but it was only as I reflected upon those verses several years ago that I became aware of a major blind spot in how I was reading that passage. I was reading it as if I wasn't carrying any burdens at all. As if I was this free bird flying about with not a care in the world. And so, the thought of a yoke (even to Jesus) seemed restricting. I had completely neglected that my day-to-day striving—striving for perfection, striving for control, striving to perform, striving to juggle all the different roles and responsibilities I had, striving to love and do good to others, to be a good mom (and much of this striving coming from a place of sheer determination and self-originating strength), that all of these were actually a huge burdensome yoke I was carrying, stubbornly and blindly, on my own. I had gotten so accustomed to my default of self-sufficiency.

To be yoked to Jesus is restful because it means first, that we surrender our burdens to him. In yoking ourselves to Jesus, it does not mean that we have no burdens, but his promise is that his burden is light. Now there's an aspect to this that I'm still trying to wrap my head around, much more that I have yet to understand. But what I have come to realize is that in being yoked to Jesus, in staying ever so close to his side, I can experience his burden as light because he carries so much more of it than I do. There is humility in this realization, this image of Spirit-dependence. Will we yoke ourselves to Jesus and allow ourselves to experience that rest? Again, I imagine that each of us will have different reflections, responses, experiences that come to mind as we consider the call to come to Jesus and take his yoke upon us. And I am so curious to know, What is God speaking to you?

RECATEGORIZATION

A GRACE FOR WORKING MOMS

JI Y. SON, PhD

CATEGORIES ARE INCREDIBLY IMPORTANT to the human experience of the world because we group things in the world all the time. Even though no cat is *exactly* like another cat (different fur, different sizes, different personalities, different behaviors), we have no problem calling them *cats* and ignoring what makes them dissimilar. Every act of categorization, identifying a vehicle as a *bus*, diagnosing some sniffles and fever as a *cold*, and calling a drink a *latte* involves some interpretation: highlighting certain features as important and relevant and disregarding some dissimilarities.

As a Christian, I engage in this abstract activity of categorization all the time. I see God's grace in a variety of ways and categorize all of the following situations as *grace*: my husband's willingness to forgive me after an argument, an answered prayer in the form of a friend's healing, and a stranger's helping hand while I struggle to get a stroller onto a bus. These situations are, on the surface, quite dissimilar. But I see the grace in these situations as the same grace the father extends to his son in the parable of the prodigal son (Luke 15:11-32)—not because the parable contains information about strollers nor the details of my spat with my husband, but because the critical feature I see is God's extension of favor to me that I did not earn and did not deserve.

Thinking with categories is rampant and unconscious. This way of experiencing the world in categories has consequences. Our use of categories (a subset of these being "stereotypes") shapes our expectations. For instance, people assume professors are some baseline level of smart. As a professor, even when I do something incredibly stupid, I am not perceived as a total dummy. The human reliance on categories, although it can let us down (for evidence, see America's long history of racial discrimination), also helps us get lots of things right. Even though I may have never interacted with a particular instance of a cat or bus or latte, I can generally figure out what to do with it based on my past experience with members of the same category.

Expectations have real world consequences for a category that I am a card-carrying member of: *working moms*. There is a double disadvantage for working moms documented in a number of domains including psychology, economics, law, and sociology: they are "damned" if at work and "damned" if at home. Mothers are assumed to prioritize home and family, and this assumption follows them at work and home. At work, working moms suffer well-documented costs including a wage penalty, discrimination, and blame for the lack of women in top leadership positions. At home, working moms are judged more harshly both in comparison to fathers and nonworking moms. Dads are held to a lower standard regarding parenting practices, so they can subjectively receive more praise even while objectively doing less. Thus, being a working mom entails *doing more for less credit* both at home and at work.

DISADVANTAGED AT WORK

Women without children earn eighty-seven cents for every dollar a child-less man earns, but moms earn seventy-five cents on the dad's dollar.[1] Working mothers account for most of the pay gap seen between men and women[2] and mothers with lower socioeconomic (SES) status (either in education or type of job) experience an even greater wage penalty than higher SES mothers.[3]

As humans, we naturally make up just-so stories on the fly to account for any data we may be confronted with. We naturally ask, "Why?" and then immediately answer that question with whatever we want. Many possible stories come to mind. Perhaps mothers are paid less because of some true pattern of traits, skills, and behaviors. Maybe mothers really are worse workers in some way, shape, or form. Researchers have tried to account for these possibilities by statistically controlling for interruptions in work (e.g., maternity leave), less experience (because they took a maternity leave), lower seniority (after all they have less experience), "mother-friendly" job characteristics (e.g., flexible time, part-time), spousal income (maybe her job is secondary to her husband's), and many other controls. Even taking all these possibilities into account, there is still a significant motherhood wage gap.[4]

Perhaps there are differences in the ways that mothers work that are not measured by these (and many other) variables. The limitations of research and statistics are real after all. *Clean* experimental setups, however, have revealed that even when a woman is the same in every other way except

[1]US Bureau of Labor Statistics, *Highlights of Women's Earnings in 2016, Report 1069*, August 2017, 63, www.bls.gov/opub/reports/womens-earnings/2016/pdf/home.pdf.
[2]Jennifer Glass, "Blessing or Curse? Work-Family Policies and Mother's Wage Growth Over Time," *Work and Occupations* 31, no. 3 (2004): 367-94; Ann Crittenden, *The Price of Motherhood: Why the Most Important Job in the World Is Still the Least Valued* (New York: Macmillan, 2002).
[3]Michelle J. Budig and Melissa J. Hodges, "Differences in Disadvantage: Variation in the Mother-hood Penalty Across White Women's Earnings Distribution," *American Sociological Review* 75, no. 5 (2010): 705-28; Deborah J. Anderson, Melissa Binder, and Kate Krause, "The Motherhood Wage Penalty Revisited: Experience, Heterogeneity, Work Effort, and Work-Schedule Flexibility," *ILR Review* 56, no. 2 (2003): 273-94.
[4]Anderson, Binder, and Krause, "Motherhood Wage Penalty," 355-357; Margaret Gough and Mary Noonan, "A Review of the Motherhood Wage Penalty in the United States," *Sociology Compass* 7, no. 4 (2013): 328-42.

that she is a mom, discrimination ensues. For example, merely describing someone in a paragraph as a mother (everything else in the paragraph was the same) led to lower competence ratings by evaluators.[5] Undergraduates who watched a video of a female manager who was visibly pregnant rated her as less committed, dependable, and authoritative than one that was not pregnant.[6] Unbeknownst to them, the videos were scripted and both the pregnant (not even a mother yet!) and nonpregnant woman were played by the same actress.

The motherhood penalty not only starts before the woman is a mother, it also starts before a woman starts working. Job applications that only differed by one line in a resume, participation in the Parent-Teacher Association, were perceived as less competent and less promotable if these candidates were women.[7] Importantly, they were offered lower starting salaries: mother applicants were offered on average $11,000 less than childless women and $13,000 less than fathers.

Not only are mothers devalued and underappreciated at work, but fathers, in contrast, are seen as more competent and deserving of more pay for being a parent.[8] In particular, high-income men get the biggest fatherhood bonus and low-income women pay the largest motherhood penalty. The conventional story is that fathers are the main "breadwinners," so they are more devoted to their work, where mothers are "caregivers," so when push comes to shove, a mother will always choose home over work.

From the world's perspective, being a mom goes against the very idea of being a good worker. But the double disadvantage is tragic in that this harsh judgment follows working mothers home. Not only are they deemed

---

[5]Amy J. C. Cuddy, Susan T. Fiske, and Peter Glick, "When Professionals Become Mothers, Warmth Doesn't Cut the Ice," *Journal of Social Issues* 60, no. 4 (2004): 701-18.

[6]Jane A. Halpert, Midge L. Wilson, and Julia L. Hickman, "Pregnancy as a Source of Bias in Performance Appraisals," *Journal of Organizational Behavior* 14, no. 7 (1993): 649-63; Sara J. Corse, "Pregnant Managers and Their Subordinates: The Effects of Gender Expectations on Hierarchical Relationships," *The Journal of Applied Behavioral Science* 26, no. 1 (1990): 25-47.

[7]Shelley J. Correll, Stephen Benard, and In Paik, "Getting a Job: Is There a Motherhood Penalty?" *American Journal of Sociology* 112, no. 5 (2007): 1297-338.

[8]Michelle J. Budig, "The Fatherhood Bonus and the Motherhood Penalty: Parenthood and the Gender gap in pay," Report, Third Way, Washington, DC, September 2014, www.thirdway.org/report /the-fatherhood-bonus-and-the-motherhood-penalty-parenthood-and-the-gender-gap-in-pay.

as inadequate and deserving of less in the workplace, they are also held to a higher bar at home.

DISADVANTAGED AT HOME

Imagine this scenario: On a bright California summer day, a parent left a four-year-old boy reading a book in a car while dropping off his brother at day camp about a block away. Should this action be "illegal"? In California, there is a law called the Unattended Child in Motor Vehicle Act that says a parent may not leave a child younger than six in a motor vehicle unattended if "there are conditions that present a significant risk to the child's health or safety."[9] This law rests on some subjective judgment about what a "significant risk" is.

Research by cognitive psychologists Thomas, Stanford, and Sarnecka demonstrates that judgments of risk about leaving a child unattended vary with a number of factors including the reason why the child was left unattended and who left the child there.[10] If a parent is involuntarily separated (e.g., hit by a car while returning a library book), a separation of thirty minutes is seen as minimally risky compared to leaving a child for thirty minutes because a parent needed to work, relax, or engage in a romantic affair. The more "immoral" the reason is, the risk to the child is perceived to be higher. This tells us that our judgments of "risk" are influenced by factors other than risk.

If the parent in the story is a father, the level of risk is judged to be lower than when a mother leaves a child unattended. Even though an unattended child is an unattended child, we blame the mother more. What about a working mother versus a working father? If a father needs to leave a child briefly to attend to work, the risk is judged to be similar to an unintentional absence! But if a mother leaves a child unattended because of work, that was judged to be as "morally unacceptable" as a mother leaving the child to find time to relax.[11]

---

[9] California Vehicle Code § 15620, 15630, 1563215620.

[10] Ashley Thomas, P. Stanford, and Barbara Sarnecka, "No Child Left Alone: Moral Judgments About Parents Affect Estimates of Risk to Children," *Collabra: Psychology* 2, no. 1 (2016): article 10, http://doi.org/10.1525/collabra.33.

[11] Thomas, Stanford, and Sarnecka, "No Child Left Alone."

On some level, we equate "working" mothers as making a choice that is detrimental to the child's well-being and safety, simply by choosing to work. We do not frame it the same way for fathers. We do not talk about a father's choice to work; we simply assume that dads will have to work.

Many of us who are working moms, even ones who are married to truly amazing dads, are the *default parent*, the one juggling, coordinating, and managing all the bits so that there are no holes in the family net. A Pew Research Center survey in 2015 found that mothers report doing the majority of childcare, housework, and management while fathers were more likely to report that they share equally in the responsibilities. When I think about my amazing husband, I always think he is a great dad. But I come to that conclusion because I instinctively compare him to other men (as many other women report doing[12]). If I took the time to consciously compare him to parents of both genders, he "loses" to a lot of mothers I know.

This tendency to cut men some slack when judging their parenting has even been made into policy in Japan. In 2010, Japan's Minister of Health, Labour, and Welfare formalized the idea of a hunky dad into a national program. *Ikumen* is a combination of the words *ikuji* (childcare) and *ikemen* (hunk) and the Ikumen Project was launched to encourage men to be more involved in daily life. By changing the image of a dad from a rigid salaryman to be feared to a hunky hero saving Japan by nurturing their children, this marketing campaign has been credited for the uptick in paternity leave taken by Japanese men and a gradual shift in expectations about gender norms. Even though women welcome the idea of *ikumen*, there is a worry that men are getting a hero level of recognition for merely wiping the table after dinner.[13]

---

[12]Barbara J. Risman, *Gender Vertigo: American Families in Transition* (New Haven, CT: Yale University Press, 1999).

[13]Kosuke Mizukoshi, Florian Kohlbacher, and Christoph Schimkowsky, "Japan's *Ikumen* Discourse: Macro and Micro Perspectives on Modern Fatherhood," *Japan Forum*, vol. 28, no. 2 (2016): 212-32.

BRINGING THE DOUBLE DISADVANTAGE
TO THE FEET OF CHRIST

Combating the negative effects of these expectations requires real world policy and social solutions. As a Christian, it is my responsibility to engage with local policies that affect parents of all kinds but especially policies that can ameliorate the double disadvantage for the mothers who are subject to the greatest social penalties: low income, low education, single mothers. The truth is that the double disadvantage interacts with race, class, and ultimately power in the United States, and Christians are charged to act justly, love mercy, and walk humbly with our God (Micah 6:8). Throughout the Scriptures, we are called to stand with the marginalized. I can almost hear the voice of God over someone who defends the cause of the poor and the needy—"Is that not what it means to know me?" (Jeremiah 22:16).

I know policy is boring. Local policy is even more dry. Sometimes we only want to *actually* feed the hungry, clothe the poor, and hobnob with prisoners (Matthew 25:31-40; and let me be the first to say, "Yikes, I should be doing more of this too!"). But we as Christians must bring the fire of the prophet Amos to boring policies like taxes, property rights, and labor laws that afflict the needy. Our righteous God calls out these policies as "evil" and charges us to instead "love good" (Amos 5:15). We who are privileged to live in a democracy have a greater responsibility because as Paul points out in Galatians 6:10, "*As we have opportunity*, let us do good to all people, especially to those who belong to the family of believers" (emphasis mine). Enacting policies that disproportionately impact the "least of these" (Matthew 25:40) would be a collective act of worship to "establish justice in the gate" (Amos 5:15 ESV).

Coming down a level of engagement to the personal, as a cognitive scientist and a Christian, my hope is that every member of a family—moms and dads, grandparents, uncles, aunts, and children—would be "rooted and grounded in . . . the love of Christ . . . that surpasses knowledge" (Ephesians 3:17-19). So I have a personal solution that is temporary and facetious yet genuinely allows me to experience a little bit of the grace afforded to almost half the working parents currently operating in the world.

At the heart of my solution is this: a working mom actually functions as a traditional dad. If I think of myself as a working mom, I do not feel rooted in grace. But if I think of myself parenting as a dad, even a "female dad," I feel the grace given to dads!

As I reflect on Ephesians 3, "That you, being rooted and established in love, may have power, together with all the Lord's holy people, to grasp how wide and long and high and deep is the love of Christ, and to know this love that surpasses knowledge—that you may be filled to the measure of all the fullness of God," there are moments when I realize how great this promise is. But sometimes I find myself wanting to trade in some of that glory for some help with childcare during the seemingly interminable three-week winter vacation from school: the working mom's version of giving up my birthright for a bowl of lentil stew (Genesis 25:29-34). Why am I so easily willing to give up on the power and glory of God? Part of it is that I just do not connect with the grace of God as I play my role on earth as a working mother.

"Feeling" God's grace is *not* the most important part of a relationship with God, but the fact that many mothers cannot access grace in their role as a mother psychologically separates us from the love that God has for us. Unlocking the grace that is already apportioned for us as members of God's family is an access issue that goes hand in hand with seeing the power of God. Ultimately, connecting with that grace is a way that mothers can more truly worship God.

LIVING OUT GRACE

So how does thinking of myself as a "female dad" help me to plumb the depths of Christ's love? I think it's somewhat akin to a discipline of grace:[14] it releases me from playing the impossible game of being the ideal mom because of the unmerited favor granted to me through the power of Jesus Christ. I remember a moment when visiting my brother-in-law, a professor in vision science at a prestigious university, and his incredible wife, who is a stay-at-home mom for their four lovable kids. Early in the morning,

[14]Jerry Bridges, *The Discipline of Grace* (Colorado Springs: NavPress, 2018).

she was cooling a cake she had baked from scratch, whipping cream with a whisk, and creating a melted chocolate face of a Japanese cartoon character (Anpan man) on waxed paper. I stood there dumbfounded as she delicately made an Anpan man cake for one of her son's birthdays and thought, "Wow, I could never do that." All of a sudden, I felt simultaneous wonder for her and disappointment in myself. Somehow in that moment, because we belong to the same basic category of "mom," I had implicitly compared myself to her and in that comparison, I lost.

I wish at that moment I could have thought of myself as a female dad and accessed the grace God has for me. The good news of the gospel of Christ is that I am not saved from sin because I am a great mom or a great cognitive scientist or a great anything. And even if I were, my own greatness would never be enough. I wish I could have experienced that freedom from having to be an ideal mom to just be a female dad, secure in playing a different kind of role and walking in my own path of obedience to Christ. Then I could have taken joy in her skills and expressed love in a way that could be untainted by my self-judgment. I could have realized that in a lot of ways, I am professionally quite similar to her husband—and that it's reasonable for me to buy a birthday cake from Costco! Praise be to God!

Recategorizing myself briefly as a female dad helps set me free from the judgments of the world, and myself, that I have to be better at home and at work; I recognize that even on my so-called "good days," I cannot meet an impossible superficial standard. I can be free to be held to the standard of God, where moms and dads alike get the same offer, the same help, and the same promises: an unattainably high standard of righteousness that is met solely by faith in the work done through the incarnation, crucifixion, and resurrection of Jesus Christ. The kingdom offers a better impossible standard to strive for and a better means of arriving at it.

Beyond escaping the comparison to other moms, part of the grace that dads get in life is that they are not culturally expected to bear the full parenting brunt. Thinking of myself as a female dad helps me realize how much I rely on my amazing husband, one of the best dads I know. The demands on my career as a tenured professor, researcher, author, speaker, etc., force me to give my husband space to be the best parent he can be to our boys. Would I do things differently than he does? For sure! He feels fine to let them drink out of their water bottles without any clue as to when those bottles were last washed. But as a female dad, I need to trust and lean on him. Part of the skill of being a mom develops from spending a lot of time with kids, making a lot of mistakes, and figuring things out. My husband is such a great dad because he has had the space to increase his own capacity to parent. This in turn allows me to trust him more and be more grateful for him.

On days that my husband is the exclusive parent to our boys, they have their own routines and rhythms. They might eat six mangoes for breakfast or hang out at the library's graphic novel section for two hours. But there are things that are the same no matter who is the primary parent that day: the boys are probably going to fight with each other, we'll all make mistakes, and a snack will be had along the way. When I play the role of female dad, I can do my work out in the world with the peace of mind that comes from having another really capable parent in our family. Whatever happens, my husband and my boys will figure it out. Ultimately, both my husband and I are able to invite Jesus into our family and together, as followers of Christ, take in his gift of grace. We can live the fullness of God we have been called to live not just as individuals but as a family unit.

All of this is not to say that I am actually good at practicing this discipline of grace. I have a cycle where at least once a week, I might yell at one or more of my children, feel incredibly guilty, and label myself as a failure in parenting. I have days when I find myself judging my husband's way of doing things as a possible public health hazard. I might see a curated social media post and think, "How does that mom have time to curl her hair? How are *both* of her kids looking at the camera?" Even though it's a bit of a joke, saying to myself, "Hey, just think of yourself as a female dad!" reminds me that I *ain't about that game*. I can escape the vortex of shame and comparison that moms, especially working moms, can get trapped in. My ambition as a female dad is to not lose out on the grace set aside for me in Jesus Christ.

IMPOSTER BLUES
AND FINDING
REST IN GOD

JEAN NEELY, PhD

*The good news is that God has such low standards,
and reaches out to those of us who are often not
lovable and offers us a chance to come back in
from the storm of drama and toxic thoughts.*

ANNE LAMOTT, *HALLELUJAH ANYWAY*

A FEW MONTHS AGO I was feeling rather depressed, thoroughly beaten by life and some discouraging circumstances. I had plans to meet some friends at a local garden after church and arrived early to give myself time to brood and pray about the awful week I'd had.

I walked around for a bit and eventually planted myself on a bench in the shade. Then came the all-too-familiar spiel of my dominant inner narrator. *What have I done with my life?! (Nothing!) I'm not a* real *professor.* (Not tenured or on a tenure track.) *I'm not a good wife or mom.* (Always failures there—on an hourly basis!) *I'm not a writer. I'm not anything! I haven't had a full-time job in years—and I don't even know if that one counts as a proper job. I'm so useless!*

Now, I don't think such things about other people who don't have jobs, or who aren't professors, or writers, or perfect parents. I can see lots of ways *other* people are lovely just for being who they are. It's more difficult to feel that way about myself; and when I'm severely depressed, it's nearly impossible to see myself in any positive light.

As I sat there on the bench, I prayed, "Well, Lord . . . I feel awful! Sinking again! Back in the pit. I'm just not good at being a grownup. I'm not made like other people. I'm not tough enough for any of this. You know that! I'm a delicate flower!" (In the back of my mind also lingered the thought, *You're the one who made me like this, so this is all really your fault!*)

Several groups of people walked by, including a couple of families with kids. Most seemed headed to the fountain on the far side of the lawn. After a while, a woman with a baby came and laid a blanket down just a few feet away from me.

Inwardly, I rolled my eyes. *Oh, come on!* was my first thought. *There's this whole acre of lawn, and you need to sit* right *there? There's shade on that side too!*

I sighed, closed my eyes, and tried to get back to prayer. "Well, God? Anything? What say you? I need . . . something. Put me back together."

Stillness. Silence.

Then I heard the mom's warm and adoring voice as she cooed over her baby, "Ohhh, you're doing *so* well! . . . Good job! I see you! I seeee you!"

!?! My inner ears perked up. *—Is that . . . ?!* Sigh. *Wishful thinking! Get real. I can't claim that. I haven't done anything praiseworthy. I'm living my cushy little life and moping over my stupid little projects. . . . Me and my silly first-world problems! There are kids in cages out there, and people dying at the border, and I'm sitting here whining in this obscenely lush garden! I'm so spoiled! There's no way God would say anything like that to me right now.*

"But . . . still, God, I would *love* for you to say that to me!! That would just be so great. Is that possible? Do you see me? Is that from you? For me? . . . Is that you, Jesus??"

I wondered what the baby was doing when the woman spoke. Perhaps taking tentative steps? Or maybe just exploring at a playful crawl?

I didn't want to read too much into the moment, so I held it loosely. Just in case, I wrote the woman's words down in my journal while they were fresh in my mind.

Whatever those words might have been, whether meant for me or not, what I took away from the experience was that I need to trust God's love is as much for me as for anyone, and that the familiar inner voice that calls me useless is *not* true.

That encounter highlighted for me how even after all I've received of grace over the years, one of the hardest, most counterintuitive things for me to imagine is that *I* might be beloved of God, that God's love for me could approach anything involving delight.

IMPOSTER SYNDROME

Imposter syndrome is common among all academics, but some of us have particularly severe cases of it. Regardless of our accomplishments and abilities, we tend to think we've somehow duped others into thinking we're way more competent than we actually are. We suffer from constant performance anxiety. We tend to beat ourselves up for not being as stellar as others in our fields. We've internalized those committees of experts who got to decide whether we were qualified to join their ranks, and we now walk around with numerous inner committees that scrutinize every aspect of our lives and feed us endless play-by-play critique.

Like many working moms, I'm also very aware that the list of my shortcomings as a mother is potentially endless. I don't play enough with my child. I lack patience. I'm too often preoccupied with work and other concerns. I often feel like I'm doing none of it well.

Many of us are constitutionally incapable of having low standards—at least when it comes to our own work. We aim for outstanding; that's how we got through all those years of school. We're good at pushing ourselves to our upper limits. Whatever we do, we want to do it exceptionally well.

Generally, this aiming for excellence is a great thing. It can serve us and our communities for good. But our desire for excellence also has a shadow side: the harsh inner critic. We tend to hold ourselves up to punishingly high standards for "scholarly rigor," service, contribution to new knowledge and human flourishing, and the rest. If we don't keep it in its place, sometimes the inner critic can wear significantly on our souls and our mental health.

For me, imposter syndrome showed up early on and then decisively grabbed the reins of my inner life in my midteens when I was diagnosed with bipolar disorder.

From then on, it didn't matter how well I did in school or what I was able to accomplish. "Whatever!" I'd tell myself. "Probably a fluke. Just because I did it once doesn't mean I'd be able to do that sort of thing again. Plus, I did such an embarrassingly *shoddy* job!"

My family, friends, therapists, and professors could tell me until they were blue in the face that I wasn't "slow," or "stupid," or "incompetent" (which was how I tended to see myself for roughly twenty years). I always dismissed their comments, assuming I knew myself best and that others had no idea how truly messed up or "stupid" I really was. They couldn't see the full extent of the wreck inside, after all.

Nothing could heal this wound of feeling mentally defective and not smart enough. It remained when I got a Fulbright teaching assistantship, after I wrote a master's thesis in French and got a degree at the Sorbonne, and even after I finished my PhD—which I had hoped for years might do the trick.

It took me longer than the average graduate student to get my PhD, partly because of repeated depressive episodes and other bipolar-related symptoms. While I loved the concentrated intellectual vitality of graduate school and found it delightful to be around people who got as excited as I did about literature, I also got easily overwhelmed. My meltdown from anxiety around qualifying exams was *not* pretty, and the stress of dissertation-writing coupled with severe postpartum depression at the time resulted in my having to take a medical leave from my program. I was able to finish my degree thanks to fantastic care from my psychiatrist; a dissertation advisor who believed in me more than I believed in myself; and phenomenal support from my husband, mom, and other family—but I just barely avoided hospitalization.

Even after getting my PhD, I continued to see myself and the world through my stubbornly depressed filter on reality.

MENTAL HEALTH

My circumstances and particular condition are somewhat atypical, but I see myself as a sort of canary in the mine, an extra sensitive gauge of harmful elements that eventually affect everyone. I may be more vulnerable to stress than others, but anxiety and depression are increasingly common, and mental health is a serious concern for a lot of academics.

There are plenty of issues that need to be addressed regarding adverse work conditions on the institutional level, perhaps especially for those of us who are contingent faculty. This part of the battle will be ongoing and will require collective action. That said, even if we can't change or leave our work environments right away, there may be steps we can take for ourselves that could make our work more sustainable for us.

I believe that many of us as academics sabotage our mental health in various ways by giving too much authority to those inner critics and the esteem of others in our fields. I used to exacerbate depression and anxiety symptoms by constantly comparing myself to my favorite professors from the past and colleagues who seemed able to do and have it all. Some of my friends who already had tenured positions were pushing out their second and third books. Many of them won research and teaching awards. Some had full teaching loads while also raising multiple kids and being activists in their communities. I, on the other hand, struggled at times to stay sane while teaching one or two classes per semester and helping to raise one child.

Sometimes it feels like most of my friends are able to tolerate much more stress and handle more work in their schedules than I can. If I compare myself to them, misery ensues. So I try to keep my eyes on my own path and steps. I wrestle so much in this area, comparing myself to friends who hold it all together gracefully—the house, the parenting, the flourishing career in scholarship and teaching. I'm just slowly beginning to accept my limitations and feel peace about a vocation that might not look like the typical academic career.

I've finally stopped comparing myself to the best professors I've had—because I'm simply not them. Nothing I do will change that! It may well be true that my past professors and current colleagues are smarter than I am. It might also be true that most of them are more gifted at teaching. (Most of my academic friends are not only cutting-edge experts in their fields, they're also amazingly witty, sparkling human beings who just *kill it* every time they're in front of a crowd.) Whatever the case, I have to remind myself that my purpose in life probably does not involve having to measure up to all my peers in academia.

When I started out teaching, I feared I had little to offer my students apart from the fact that I really cared. I used to overprepare and stress out so much about students' needs, expectations, and evaluations. I was often overwhelmed with trying to make sure that all my students were doing okay and getting what they needed.

For the sake of survival, I've had to learn to adjust my expectations of myself in the classroom. I've found that even if I aim lower than my own inner standards, the work I do is still more than enough. And it turns out that caring goes such a long way. Students happen to appreciate the fact that I'm fully present in the classroom and do obviously care about them.

In my days as a newbie literature and writing instructor, I used to spend hours and hours (and *hours*!!) on end poring over students' papers and writing long, detailed letters of feedback to each student. That was not sustainable. With the help of my colleagues, I've learned over time to streamline my process. I now read with greater focus on global issues in students' essays and offer brief feedback with points of appreciation and just a few actionable comments on the most significant issues in their papers. I let them know that I'd be happy to offer additional feedback if they'd like to make appointments with me to discuss their work further. And I mean it. I want them to engage.

Many of us may be pushing our bodies and brains beyond reasonable limits. I know from experience that I personally require a buffer of some free, unscheduled time in my days. I know that this can be difficult for many contingent faculty and others with heavy departmental responsibilities to manage, but for me, the consequences of my not maintaining healthy work-life-play balance can be debilitating. Out of necessity, I limit myself to a light workload and teach only one or two courses per semester as adjunct faculty. Thankfully, our family can afford my working part time. I realize that not everyone has this privilege.

Some of us who love our work intensely may feel that we're being "selfish" for giving it an important place in our lives. The whole time I was in grad school, there was a part of me that felt guilty for pursuing interests that might never serve my family, the church, or the common good. It'd be one thing if I were studying how to transform global economic policy or if I could contribute to cancer research or something like that, but I was spending all my time ruminating on *literature* and reading philosophy. How was my reading poetry and novels going to help anyone?

But I also know that "poetry is not a luxury," as Audre Lorde wrote.[1] Poetry saves lives. It has helped me to survive some of the toughest seasons in my life and has fed me in the most vibrant seasons as well. When I'm depressed, I can find concrete comfort in words that disrupt the grim thoughts on replay in my mind. I can focus instead on the pleasant rhythms of "pied beauty" in "dappled things."[2] Poetry can help to draw my attention away from my personal despair and remind me of my connection to others. As Palestinian poet Mahmoud Darwish put it, "Poetry is blood in the heart, salt in bread, moisture in eyes."[3] When I'm feeling crushed by

---

[1] Audre Lorde, "Poetry is Not a Luxury," *Sister Outsider: Essays & Speeches* (Freedom, CA: The Crossing Press, 1984), 37.

[2] Gerard Manley Hopkins, "Pied Beauty," *Selected Poetry* (New York: Oxford University Press, 1998), 117.

[3] Mahmoud Darwish, "Defiance," PoemHunter.com, April 15, 2014, https://www.poemhunter.com /poem/defiance-7/.

powers that seem greater than me, poetry helps me draw strength from the "fighting songs" of my people.

Over time, I've gained a better perspective on how reading beautiful literature and doing work that I love help me to be a much happier and healthier version of myself than I'd be without those things—which *does* benefit my family and community in the long run.

I've also learned to enforce strict boundaries around a self-care regimen that includes regular exercise, a decent amount of rest, creative activities, and restorative time with people I love who spark some serious joy. I've stopped telling myself that my routines are "selfish" or proof of my being "spoiled." I figure that if there's something that can help me stay out of the hospital and also become more whole, then it's not purely selfish. Rather than feel guilty about every nice thing and privilege I have in life (which is my tendency), I try to see my collecting yarn and good books, treating myself to coffee, going to my favorite barre class at our local Y, playing piano, and even taking a nap as investments not just in my own health but in the greater good.

Those of us grappling with depression, other mental illness, or any serious trauma in our histories may have trouble breaking out of the most destructive stories we've had ingrained in us. We need to give ourselves more credit for what we *have* done and can do, and we've got to stop cultivating misery by always comparing ourselves to the intellectual 1 percent, the rock stars within our fields. If we have harsh inner committees who have been filtering our realities into damaging narratives over a long time and blind us to everything but our deficiencies, we may need outside help to rewrite our core inner narratives.

Since our stories about ourselves often feel so objectively true, loosening their grip can be difficult and even take a lifetime. It took me over *twenty years* of dealing with bipolar to just begin to dismantle my most crippling inner narratives. A good therapist can be helpful for this sort of work. If we don't have the desire or wherewithal to go see a therapist, talking to even one or two close friends about our struggles can relieve some of the suffering.

Those of us who repeatedly find ourselves in acute distress need to seek out help and may want to explore the possibility of taking medication. Modern medicine is a *gift from God*, and there's no shame in needing something more than prayer or heavy doses of Bible reading for one's mental health. Effective medication can be literally lifesaving, especially for those of us with chronic or serious conditions.

That's not to say that medication will fix everything, but for some of us, it could be an important part of moving toward deeper wholeness. Medication, for me, helps to maintain a basic ground of mental balance and stability that then enables my capacity to address issues in other important areas of my life—emotional, cognitive, spiritual, and relational.

Staying connected to friends and community is essential. I've also found it helpful to connect to the broader fellowship of saints outside my own circles. Reading about how other people of faith have navigated inner distress has been a source of comfort and inspiration. In recent years, I've been encouraged to see that an increasing number of writers have tackled the challenging topic of mental health. There are more and more thoughtful books out there now by people of faith on their experiences with mental illness. A few I've appreciated and recommend include *Bipolar Faith* and *Not Alone* by Monica Coleman, *Glorious Weakness* by Alia Joy, and *Darkness Is My Only Companion* by Kathryn Greene-McCreight.[4]

My view of myself and my fears of how God might view me exacerbated depression, anxiety, and mental unwellness for over two decades. Seeing my spiritual director regularly has been a huge help in this area. A spiritual director is someone who helps us to notice how God is present and speaking in our daily lives. A good spiritual director listens with us and helps us to discern God's voice amid the cacophony of all our inner voices. This sort of spiritual companion can open up our perspectives on God and bring to light damaging core beliefs.

I've been seeing my spiritual director for several years now, and she has helped me to experience greater freedom to be who I am in Christ. I now

---

[4]Monica Coleman, *Bipolar Faith* (Minneapolis: Fortress, 2016) and *Not Alone* (Culver City, CA: Inner Prizes, 2012); Alia Joy, *Glorious Weakness* (Grand Rapids, MI: Baker Books, 2019); Kathryn Greene-McCreight, *Darkness Is My Only Companion* (2006; Grand Rapids, MI: Brazos, 2015).

feel much less burdened by everything that I feel I *should* be doing but don't have the energy or the ability to do. Over the years, I've learned that the voice of Christ-in-me may clash not only with that of my inner task-master but also, often, with the loudest and most dominant voices in the church. I've been learning that God might be much gentler and more welcoming than I used to imagine was possible. For someone like me, to hear that *God* might have "low standards" is both a surprise and an immense relief.

GOD'S MOTHERLY LOVE

Our inner images of God can significantly impact our emotional and mental conditions, for ill or good. A few years ago, because of specific is-sues I was wrestling with at the time, my spiritual director asked me whether I had ever tried praying to God as *Mother*.

I hadn't.

Beginning to consider God not merely as Father but as Loving Mother has helped to transform my inner life and dislodge deep spiritual anxiety I used to carry around. Giving myself permission to relate to God as Mother, together with the experience of actually being a mom, has been remarkably healing.

After my son was born, I knew *in my body* what it was to experience immeasurable, immovable delight in another person's very existence—in the existence of someone who was totally helpless. I didn't get upset with our child for not pulling his weight in the family. He didn't have to *do* anything! I loved watching him at play, at rest. Just watching him sleep was a source of joy and wonder. Nothing he could do (or fail to do) in life could ever make a dent in my core delight in him, even if I might in the moment lose my patience and get angry over something. I just wanted him to be, and to be *himself*. He was adorable even in the ways he threw tantrums. I loved all his expressions and little scowls. Even when, as a toddler, he slapped me hard on my face once, my love for him was not the least bit shaken. (I did make it clear that that was totally unacceptable behavior.) And if my son has major health issues later in life, whether of mind or body, I'm confident that they will not diminish my love for him in the slightest.

Being a mother has helped me to finally conceive of the possibility of an all-embracing love that accepts me as I am—warts and all, with my short list of accomplishments, my great capacity for wickedness, and my complicity in evil on a planetary scale. I figure that if my tiny little heart can do that, then perhaps God's love is big enough to include me.

Thinking of the love I have received from my own earthly mother in this light has also been helpful. In my family of origin, my own mother was the primary nurturer in the family. While she worked more than full-time as a nurse, she ran the household, carted us around to various activities, and always made sure there were things we liked to eat at home. After my diagnosis, when depression became a chronic problem, she scrambled to do *anything* that might shed a little light in my darkness. When I mentioned that I was unhappy and bored at my school, she was the one who went out of her way to set up my piano audition for a local performing arts high school. Knowing how much I loved flowers, she'd often buy little bouquets for my room, though our family was always on a tight budget. When I was out of the house during college, she called nearly every day to ask if I was eating okay and taking my medication. When she felt out of her depths in being able to encourage me through my grad school woes, she urged me to connect with my Aunt Miyoung, who is a kindred spirit and speaks my heart's languages.

During my postpartum crisis, my mom led the charge in caring for both me and the baby. She practically lived with us for the first six months, shuttling frequently between her home (which is about an hour's drive away) and ours. She cooked endless batches of traditional Korean seaweed soup and brought over DVDs of K-dramas for us to watch, hoping they'd help cheer me up and keep my mind off despairing thoughts. She stayed over often and insisted that she would get up on some nights with the baby so that both my husband and I could sleep.

I think that imagining God with this sort of visceral, aching mother-love for me has more substantially helped in my long fight against imposter syndrome than any single other practice or form of therapy. I used to fear that God just barely tolerated me, and then only because of Christ's great sacrifice. This new lens allows me to hope that God's essential posture toward me is one of tender nurture, not holy disgust.

We all need people in our lives who offer us incarnated forms of God's mother-love. Such love often does come through the love of our families and the body of Christ, but if we can't find it at church or in our families, we may have to look for it in other spheres or try to piece a patchwork support network together for ourselves.

It's okay to shield ourselves from people who might make things feel worse, even if unwittingly so. Some of us, for instance, may need to spend less time with people who believe that "strong Christians" who are "right with God" never get depressed. They may mean well, but when I'm in the swamp of severe depression, I have to steer clear of this lot. And if certain family members happen to spark much more distress than joy, it's totally acceptable—and at times necessary—to establish strict boundaries to protect our own mental health.

I've personally found that church is not always where I'm going to find what my soul needs most to weather the worst of depression or anxiety. I need people who can view the kind of suffering I experience with clear-seeing compassion rather than pity or judgment, people who will hope for me when I'm feeling hopeless and help me rest in God, rather than add to my spiritual to-do list. In my life, these tend to be my closest girlfriends and my family. They're people who don't demand that I do anything for them in order to be accepted. They've walked with me through many a dark abyss and have seen God rescue me and work good in my life, so they're not easily alarmed by my existential crises and disasters.

In recent years, Jesuit and Benedictine monastics have also played a large part in creating this sort of communal space for me. I go on an annual silent retreat at a local monastery, and this one weekend is always so profoundly refreshing that it recalibrates my inner settings for the entire year. There's something special about simple, quiet, prayerful time in community that seems very conducive to encounters with the living Christ.

I think Julian of Norwich knew this. If any typical North American churchgoer were to tell me something like "all shall be well, and all shall be well, and all manner of things shall be well" when I'm feeling low, I'd want to tell them to go mind their own business. But when I hear these words of Mother Julian, I sense that she really knows the One of whom she speaks, and I'm able to grasp toward hope.

This saint also wrote, in her *Revelations of Divine Love*, that "our Savior is our true mother, in whom we are endlessly born, and out of whom we shall never come to birth."[5] As I encounter more and more of Christ in my weakness, I've been learning that these words are truth.

This Christ-love is the only thing that can make it all okay for me. It's the only thing that helps me to accept that I'll be okay even if I never become a "real" professor, never amount to anything in the eyes of the world.

We all need to remind ourselves daily that God is the most loving Mother to us—whether we feel it or not—and the academy is not the true measure of the universe or of our worth. Each of us is intrinsically sacred and beautiful in God's eyes.

I no longer believe that God sounds anything like my very broken inner critics, who often claim to speak for God. God is the One who gazes on us adoringly and coos with delight over our feeble and wobbly little steps. It doesn't matter how others see or may never clearly see us. We don't belong first and foremost to all these others—to the university, to our students, to the fallen church, or even to our families. We belong to Christ. *I* belong to Christ—the lover of my soul, the One who gives me rest, who knows and loves me through and through and through. *That* is good news.

---

[5]Julian of Norwich, *Revelations of Divine Love* (Penguin Books, 1998), 136.

PART THREE

NAVIGATING
MULTIPLE
CALLINGS

JUGGLING MULTIPLE ROLES

NARRATIVE OF A KOREAN PASTOR'S WIFE, A MOTHER, AND A PSYCHOLOGY PROFESSOR

JENNY H. PAK, PhD

STUDENTS FREQUENTLY ASK ME how I am able to juggle so many different roles—wife, mother, pastor's wife, psychologist, and professor. In my twenties and thirties, I too would have asked myself the same question. Starting in my forties, however, something shifted for me as I began to think of them not as multiple roles but one. On the surface, these roles appear to be different and many, but over the years I have come to see that they share one common purpose: facilitating growth and the transformation of self and others to be more like Christ. This was a profound realization for me. Knowing that I am seeking to fulfill the same goal—whether I work inside or outside the home, or inside or outside the church—set me free from tension and guilt. In short, a lifelong journey toward a more unified self has led me to integrate the multiple roles in my life.

Looking back, I see God's hand in placing me on this path early in my life as I immigrated to the United States with my family at age ten. As a 1.5-generation (referring to individuals who immigrated to the US as children) Korean American Christian woman, I had to deal with conflicting values on a daily basis. Over the years, God has helped me see that the conflicted, divided self is not unique to bicultural individuals but is a shared human condition needing to be reconciled and in union with him in order for us to recover from our brokenness and become whole. In this way, I have come to see that regardless of whatever activities (e.g., child-rearing, teaching, counseling, researching, mentoring) we engage in the church or the world, God's goal for us as his children is to be transformed, sanctified, and complete in him.

IMPORTANCE OF NARRATIVES

We are not simply academics, researchers, or administrators. The stories we possess, consciously and unconsciously, shape the way we are formed and the way we live our lives. Over the years, as I have mentored and taught many graduate students narrative analysis, I have come to see that life stories are powerful tools in promoting self-understanding as well as illustrating the complexity of lived experiences at the intersections of race, culture, gender, and religion.[1] Stories implicitly carry the primary images, metaphors, and paradigms of a culture. Stories are one way a culture creates a common worldview, an acceptable ethos, an ethic worth striving toward, and a sense of personal identity.[2] Narrative research shows that at all points in development, individuals interact with local social narratives and in turn, their lives are structured and mediated by the available cultural tools.[3]

---

[1]Jenny Pak, *Korean American Women: Stories of Acculturation and Changing Selves* (New York: Routledge, 2006).

[2]Dan McAdams, *The Stories We Live By: Personal Myths and the Making of the Self* (New York: Morrow, 1993).

[3]Qi Wang and Jens Brockmeier, "Autobiographical Remembering as Cultural Practice: Understanding the Interplay between Memory, Self, and Culture," *Culture & Psychology* 8, no. 1 (March 2002): 45-64.

MY LIFE STORY: OVERCOMING
GENDER AND RACIAL REJECTION

Reflecting on my own multicultural history, I will share how I stumbled into psychology and came to be both a pastor's wife and a professor in Christian higher education. The first part of my life journey involves meeting Christ and learning to deconstruct the inferiority society had attached to my identity as a woman and a racial minority. After coming to accept my identity, my life journey moved on to integrating and reconciling its contradictions: East versus West, mother and pastor's wife versus professor. Most importantly, throughout all stages of my development, my individual growth occurred alongside the growth of others in my life (e.g., my children, students, clients, Korean congregation). Hence, I have come to see that, unlike the world's hierarchical power structures, God desires mutual empowerment of self and others toward growth and maturity.

Childhood. I am the oldest child born to Korean parents, who both came from families with strong Confucian roots. I grew up hearing the story that I was rejected at birth because I was a girl and my paternal grandmother had expected a boy. My mother had three more girls consecutively. But she was not recognized as a legitimate daughter-in-law by my paternal grandmother until she finally produced a son, even after ten years of marriage to my father. These stories of woe had a powerful impact on me growing up. When I was old enough to enter elementary school, I remember promising myself that I would strive to achieve academically in order to be worth more than three sons.

Unfortunately, my story of rejection and devaluation did not end in elementary school. When I was ten years old, my family immigrated to the United States and settled in Modesto, California. In the seventies, we were one of the few Asian families living in the small, rural town. As my sisters and I were walking home after school, we would often hear children from the sidewalk calling us "chinks" and yelling at us "go home," meaning we should go back to Korea where our family came from because we did not belong in America. Similar to my early childhood, I fought back tears and feelings of rejection and devaluation with a stronger determination to succeed academically—the only control I had belonging to a small ethnic minority group.

College. I graduated as valedictorian in both middle and high school and was able to attend UCLA with a full scholarship. Rather than feeling victorious, at seventeen years old I felt burned-out and empty, wondering what the purpose and meaning of life was. I realized then that no amount of achievement in the world would change the unfairness and shame I experienced growing up. It was around this time that I was finally able to surrender my powerlessness and my life to Jesus as my Lord. I fought for a just world all my life, and Jesus was the true equalizer—all have sinned and all were in need of the Savior.

This marked the first major turning point in my life. I was actively involved with the Navigators on campus and participated in their discipleship training. I was determined not to strive for things in this world that had no eternal value. I thought this meant I needed to give up everything of this world—marriage, education, and even myself—and only live for Jesus. I imagined handing my diploma from UCLA to my parents, selling all my books, and heading off to serve as a missionary in a remote, obscure place on the other side of the globe. I didn't know then that God had a completely different plan for me.

Marriage, ministry, and therapy in the early years. My life took off in the opposite direction shortly after I graduated from UCLA. At the time, I was told by my family and Korean church leaders that the seminary was no place for a woman. They also said I should not continue to pursue my graduate studies in psychology as a Christian. I spent a year working an odd job and wondering what God was calling me to do.

While I was praying for his direction in my life, I unexpectedly met a young man named David with the same Korean background, except he came from a fourth-generation Christian home whereas I was the first Christian in my family. As we dated and our relationship became more serious, David warned me of his calling as a minister, even though he didn't know when it might be. I thought for sure God had mistaken my desire to serve him fully as a missionary with someone else who wanted to be a pastor's wife, which was far from my mind! Earlier in my junior year in college, I had prayed for the gift of singlehood to be a missionary, only to discover deep in my heart that what I was asking God was why I needed to serve any man when I only needed to serve him. God confronted my attempt to escape with my promise to follow him in singlehood or marriage. I reminded God I had never, however, agreed to be a pastor's wife. If I had an option, I told him, I would take the quick death of a martyr over a slow one as a Korean pastor's wife. Besides, I warned both God and David, I wouldn't make a good pastor's wife because I didn't even play piano or the organ. God dealt with all my fears and promised to take care of me if I would follow him; David convincingly said he wasn't looking for someone who would make a good Korean pastor's wife, but a partner in life. I thought for sure I would scare David away when I shared my dilemma about graduate school in counseling or seminary. Without any hesitation, he told me I should do both. Long story short, I married him!

After our wedding, we began our graduate studies together at Fuller Theological Seminary (David working on his master of divinity and I on a master's in marriage and family therapy). David also began as a youth pastor in inner city Los Angeles. This is how I became a pastor's wife in the Korean immigrant community, and strangely enough, I have not been able to leave Southern California ever since. The community God had placed me in happened to be first-generation Korean American churches in the Greater Los Angeles area.

To be completely honest, like Jonah, I had told God I would go and serve any people anywhere, except Koreans. I didn't realize then that the "mission" he had in mind were the people in my own backyard. I was thinking far away, and he was looking near me. Of course, this is precisely the reason I was trying to escape; it was too close to home. It was easier to love strangers than the people I knew well. Ironically, as I was working on separation-individuation from my family of origin during the early years of marriage, God sent me right back to work with Koreans who were just like my family. In the early years of our ministry, I was working on my master's degree at Fuller Theological Seminary. I thought my new mission was to learn all the clinical theories and techniques and "fix" all the dysfunctional people in the church.

Of course, I immediately hit a wall. In the early years of my ministry and training as a therapist, my husband would patiently listen to all my struggles dealing with people's dysfunction and resistance; eventually, he wisely suggested that it would be better for me to love them rather than impatiently try to change them. This was the hardest thing for me to do, but I knew he was right. I had to surrender what I had learned about psychology and let it sit in the back of my mind. There were pathologies to be sure; but using psychology as a weapon to judge everyone would not only have been a misuse and dangerous—more importantly, it would have been spiritually poisonous, much like seeing the speck in others' eyes and not seeing the log in our own.

As I have helped various families in crisis, I realized over the years that the church never could nor should become a professional counseling center. While confidentiality is the most essential aspect of the therapeutic relationship, which creates safety and trust, the church is called to be a loving, caring community. Trained pastoral staff, like first emergency responders, could respond quickly to crises and help connect individuals or families to appropriate, competent professionals; the church could serve best, however, by continuing to be a supportive community as members go through the recovery process. Psychotherapy often involves working through deep personal issues, which requires vulnerability and would be unethical to attempt without privacy. As I train doctoral clinical psychology students, I explain the collaborative relationship between professional psychotherapists and pastoral care using the following metaphor: While brain surgeons operate on the brain as a physical organ, psychotherapists operate on the mind (also referred to as the "psyche," "soul," or "self"), especially in the long-term growth-oriented work. The therapy office is a sacred space like the "surgical" room; although the emergency team in the war zone, for example, may provide the first aid, wounded patients who require professional attention are brought to the hospital. For this reason, though I hold two professional licenses (psychologist as well as marriage and family therapist), I intentionally restrain from doing psycho-therapy in the church not because I don't care, but more for the congregant's sake. Also, I learned over the years serving in the Korean immigrant church context that it is better for congregants who need professional care to find help outside the church than risk losing the community one belongs because a member feels ashamed or emotionally "naked" after disclosing too much. The way psychology can be most helpful in the church is by facilitating relationships that provide support, encouragement, and caring community (e.g., groups for young mothers, elderly, widows, etc.).

Motherhood and doctoral studies. After obtaining my MFT license, I was codirecting an early childhood program at a local clinic while building my private practice. As I was settling in my professional career, my husband and I thought it was time for us to plan a family. After seven years of marriage, I was pregnant with our first and we were both excited. I was eagerly preparing the nest and gearing up for the next chapter in my life as a mother, but something else was stirring inside me. While I was earning my master's degree, my husband and some professors encouraged me to consider applying for doctoral studies. Because I pursued MFT training primarily to help with ministry, I ignored various recommendations. While I enjoyed gaining clinical experiences out in the real world, I felt uneasy that psychology had not addressed more deeply how cultural and religious values impacted human development at the core. My husband David would listen to my searching questions and urged me to apply to doctoral studies even though I was pregnant. I thought he was preposterous, but I applied to a doctoral program in counseling psychology at University of Southern California (USC), which was local. Knowing how competitive the program was, I expected to receive a rejection letter and hoped it would stop my husband's nagging. To my surprise, I was accepted, and my long journey into motherhood and academia unfolded.

During my first semester at USC, my mother was diagnosed with cancer and was given three months to live. I immediately withdrew from school and took my one-year-old daughter to Northern California to be with my mother. As my mother was facing death, my attempt to earn a doctoral degree and research culture and self all seemed futile. Although my mother's dying wish was for me to continue with my studies, I seriously considered dropping out, recognizing the brevity of life. After she passed away, I spent that summer in prayer, seeking guidance from God about whether I should return to USC or not. Whether I had one day or a thousand, God reminded me that what he always desired from me was my first fruit, not my last. Though I may not know how long I had to live, I needed to remain faithful with everything he had entrusted to me. Whether I was a wife or mother, God reminded me my relationship with him and his calling for me had not changed. Hence, I pressed forward.

Going back to school after a long hiatus was not easy, especially with a toddler. In a competitive doctoral program with mostly young singles coming directly from undergraduate, I felt like the odd one out. Moreover, being a pastor's wife in a secular school was like being in a desert. I felt all alone, but strangely, looking back, I did the deepest work on integrating psychology with theology and culture as I lived out my life, which was much more dynamic and complex than the artificial insulation of disciplinary boundaries. God was forming me out in the wilderness.

Somehow, I managed to get through the course work in three years with a child, but to be quite frank, much of it was a blur. My husband, who was incredibly supportive and understanding throughout, felt it was time we needed to plan for our second child because it was important for my daughter to have a sibling close in age. Although I thought it would be impossible to finish the remaining requirements if I gave birth to another child in the middle of the doctoral program, I did just that—and I was right. Everything came to a screeching halt! It was exponentially more challenging even to get out the door with two little ones, let alone study. Because of God's goodness and faithfulness, I somehow thought he would provide the perfect nanny for me to finish my doctoral degree. Unfortunately, Mary Poppins never knocked on my front door. Instead, I sat in the nest for four years and waited for my second daughter to enter preschool. Waiting in limbo felt like an eternity, not knowing when I would ever finish the program. Altogether, it took nine years for me to complete my doctoral degree. But looking back, my deepest personal transformation occurred during the four years I waited and came to terms with conflicting cultural messages and multiple roles in my life. I will share in the following section how God was doing deeper work in me.

NOTIONS OF MOTHERHOOD, "MOMMY MYTH," AND MOTHER WARS

The post–World War II American middle-class ideal of the attentive, stay-at-home mom is a psychological standard for promoting the health of children all over the world.[4] Though weary of this ideal, I knew the first three years was critical developmentally and could not neglect my maternal duty—especially without reliable, consistent help with childcare during graduate school. What I knew from psychology and my clinical training only induced guilt from the thought of abandoning two young children when they needed me the most. It was not coincidental that I was caught in the middle of the "new momism," a set of norms and practices represented in the media at the turn of the twenty-first century, which held contradictory tension; it seemingly celebrated motherhood while upholding impossible standards of perfection.[5] It fueled "mommy wars" between stay-at-home mothers and mothers who work outside of the home.

Needless to say, I was tormented every day. I asked myself more than a thousand times, *Is it going to be me or my children?* I even sought therapy for myself, hoping it would resolve the tension. But predictably, the psychologist I saw was steeped in Western theory and assumptions stressing it was "my choice." The rhetoric of choice, which focused on maintaining the feeling of being an independent and liberated free agent, however, missed the point that my private choices did not occur in isolation. This strategy did not situate the historical, cultural, and gendered constraints nor the inequity I faced as an ethnic minority woman.

---

[4]Gilda Morelli, Naomi Quinn, and Nandita Chaudhary, "Ethical Challenges of Parenting Intervention in Low- to Middle-Income Countries," *Journal of Cross-Cultural Psychology* 49, no. 1 (Dec 2017): 5-24.

[5]Susan Douglas and Meredith Michaels, *The Mommy Myth: The Idealization of Motherhood and How It Has Undermined All Women* (New York: Free Press, 2004).

My therapist also could not grasp why I was so divided and stuck inter-nally. Living in the United States since I was ten had indoctrinated me to uphold the American ideals of individual freedom and autonomy. But this modern view of self was in direct contradiction with the traditional Korean cultural image of the selfless, "virtuous" woman embodied by my mother and my maternal grandmother who both raised me. The traditional expectations of women and the rhetoric of sacrifice, which lay dormant in me, were awakened when I became a mother.

Trying to integrate East and West was like mixing oil and water. Tradi-tional Asian cultural values and spirituality encouraged what Sampson calls "ensemble individualism" (i.e., putting the family, community, and others above self), while all my Western education and training in psychology pointed to self-contained individualism (i.e., putting needs of self before others) as a model of health and maturity.[6] Perhaps in my twenties I could flip back and forth, adapting my behavior depending on the context of the group. But as I was approaching midlife, I was questioning more than adjusting, searching for meaning and coherence. I was seeking to integrate not only psychology and theology, but also culture at a deeper level, and I wondered which side Jesus would be on—East or West, traditional or modern? Would he be on the side of the traditional family and tell me I should sacrifice myself for my children and give up my doctoral studies as a mother? Or would he be on the side of the modern woman and tell me I had the right to pursue my individual desires and a fulfilling career?

For four years, this was the burning question I put before God every day in my prayers. He was strangely silent until two weeks after the 9/11 ter-rorist attack in 2001. One morning, I broke down in tears wondering what would have happened if the tragedy had occurred in Los Angeles and I were to stand before his throne to give an account of my life. As I went through discipleship training with Navigators in college, I was inspired to live for Christ and bear much fruit for his kingdom. But if my life were to be cut short at that point, all I could present before him was that I went

---

[6]Edward Sampson, "The Debate on Individualism: Indigenous Psychologies of the Individual and Their Role in Personal and Societal Functioning," *American Psychologist* 43, no. 1 (Jan 1988): 15-22.

to school all my life and tried to raise my two daughters. I was certain God would be disappointed with me as I had yet to save lives or accomplish anything substantial for his kingdom. To my surprise, he did not scold me but affirmed my obedience and perseverance in not giving up on myself or my children. He reminded me with passages from John 15: "remain in me . . . remain in me . . . remain in me. . . . If you remain in me, you will bear much fruit; apart from me you can do nothing." I had read this chapter many times before, but strangely that morning, I heard it with new meaning and understanding. Foremost, his commandment for me was to stay attached to him, just as my young children had to stay attached to me to survive. Second, I did not make or produce the fruit, but he did; my job was to simply stay attached to the Vine.

What God revealed to me that morning melted away the dual cultural wall and conflicting values I was grappling with for so long. Until that morning, I was divided. Faced with plurality, would Jesus say all cultural narratives are truly equal? After many years of struggling with this question in clinical practice, research, and ministry, I realized Jesus was not inclined to take either side. East or West, traditional or modern, both sides contained sin or pathology—especially at their extremes—and needed transformation. The reign of God offered his people an alternative, new culture where the right way was not fighting over either self *or* other but embracing both self *and* other into wholeness. Only in God's kingdom can both individual uniqueness and unity of the community coexist harmoniously and grow together at the same time. His desire was not only for my children, but also for me to grow. It was not either/or, but both/and. This was an important turning point in my life story. In short, the realization that I was on a lifelong journey toward a more unified self put me on a path to integrate the multiple roles in my life.

MOTHERHOOD AND ACADEMIA: THE ONGOING STRUGGLE OF WORK-LIFE BALANCE

After that morning, the question was no longer whether or not I should continue with my doctoral studies, but when I should finish. Once my second child was old enough to start preschool, I was able to move forward and complete the remaining degree requirements. I did not anticipate being offered a tenure-track faculty position immediately following graduation. Hence motherhood, academia, and internal conflict continued. After reconciling the tension between East and West, I was soon confronted by the tension between work and family.

For my first full-time position in Christian higher education, my main negotiation for the contract was to finish teaching classes by 2 p.m. in order to pick up my children after school. Like many, I incorrectly assumed that flexible schedules and extended summer breaks would make the academic setting compatible with the demands of parenting. When I worked full-time at the community mental health clinic, I used to work four long days and never brought work home; it was nice to have three days off to take care of things around the house and help my husband with church on the weekends. For the last ten years I have been teaching, the work has always been with me. During winter and summer breaks, church members would comment how nice it must be that I could slow down and not go to work. Hidden in the comment, I sensed the message that perhaps I could help with church more, even if it was just during the breaks. Little did the congregation know that the demand for high productivity and the environment of "publish or perish" in academia made it impossible to maintain a forty-hour work schedule even during the summer. My work, in fact, never stopped whether I was at school or home, and I felt more pressured to get things done during the breaks. More work was waiting for me with tight deadlines, including turning in grades, preparing new courses, completing research projects, presentations, and publications—all on top of endless emails that could take up to several hours each day.

The truth was that I always felt guilty for not doing more to help out with church. I was well aware that I was doing the bare minimum to get by as a senior pastor's wife, especially for a Korean congregation. I could not have survived thirty years as a pastor's wife juggling motherhood and academia if not for my husband's conviction and loving affirmation that I needed to be who God created me to be. He was the one who recognized my gifts when we were first taking theology courses together at Fuller by encouraging me to pursue my doctoral studies. Even when the traditional Korean image of the virtuous wife and sacrificial mother was awakened and I wanted to give up my personal dreams for ministry and my family, he fought for me to continue. I owe much to my husband for not only believing in me, but also encouraging me to focus on my own formation and developing my identity separate from his role as a pastor. This was not a small feat, given that traditionally, a Korean woman's identity was defined by her relationship to three men in her life—father, husband, and son. This Confucian, patriarchal family ideology is still alive and well in everyday practice even today. I am referred to as "so and so's wife" or "mother," not by my first name. In encouraging me to find my own voice, my husband would humorously tell me to "go find my own audience"—to develop my own professional identity as a professor and a psychologist apart from him, outside the church.

Despite having an incredibly supportive husband, internal conflict between my professional career and ministry persisted, although the tension between East and West, family and self, had resolved earlier. The false dichotomy surrounding what separates work and ministry partially contributed to this tension. Although I was following my calling by working in Christian academia, the twinge of guilt lingered, especially given the disproportionate amount of time and energy I dedicated to being a professor.

I was constantly juggling academia, church, and home. Pulled in a million different directions, on a good day I felt like I could barely breathe. During holidays (e.g., Thanksgiving, Christmas, New Year) everything would intensify and collide—a perfect storm would hit. Somehow I learned to just put one foot in front of the other and ride through the unmanageable chaos each year. One year, I was at my breaking point and thought I could not possibly survive another holiday balancing multiple roles, which included cooking the annual, traditional New Year's lunch for the entire congregation. In my prayer during the New Year's Eve service, I wept to the Lord about how impossible it was for me to fulfill all the different expectations and roles. But I was reminded that they were not multiple roles but one. Whether I was preparing a meal for my family, the church, or a new course for my students, the heart or intent behind all three were one of the same: to nourish, strengthen, and grow. This was a profound realization for me. Knowing that I was seeking to fulfill the same goal—whether I worked inside or outside the home, or inside or outside the church—set me free from tension and guilt. On the surface, these roles appeared to be different and many; but in that moment, I realized that they shared one common purpose: to facilitate the growth and transformation of self and others to be more like Christ. But achieving this ideal of integration is definitely challenging in the current reality of the academic environment.

CHRISTIAN HIGHER EDUCATION

Despite these realizations and personal formation, several years into teaching full time, I recognized my work hours sadly resembled that of my mother's—every waking moment dedicated to the multiple roles I juggled. I watched my mother pass away at fifty-five after living like superwoman, and so I had no intention of being a supermom or super–pastor's wife. I was simply attempting to do my work faithfully. But like many women in academia trying to balance heavy workloads and family, I similarly found the occupational stress of higher learning was neither affirming nor conducive to a healthy lifestyle.[7] As I faced my midfifties, my body started to show the years of neglect—deadline-driven, overscheduled (sixty-to eighty-hour weeks), chronically lacking sleep, and sedentary. Taxed to capacity, it was sending the signal that something had to change.

Needless to say, juggling multiple roles as a mother, professor, and pastor's wife has been riddled with conflicts and challenges, but the entrenched power structure and culture of academia does not help. Castaneda and Isgro remind us that the struggles mothers face in academia are not just personal, but largely stem from an outdated educational model based on the legacy of an era when students and faculty were all men and were either single or had wives and servants to take care of parental and household

---

[7]Maria P. Michailidis, "Gender-Related Work Stressors in Tertiary Education," *Journal of Human Behavior in the Social Environment* 17, no. 1-2 (Oct 2008): 195-211.

responsibilities.[8] Interestingly, at the turn of the twenty-first century, feminist scholars have come to recognize that academia is an important site for analysis,[9] as there is still systematic failure despite the fact that women make up more than 38 percent of faculty members in the United States.[10] These experts point out that a fundamental structural and cultural shift needs to be made in higher education in order to correct existing inequities in how resources and power are managed (e.g., expanding family-friendly policies, providing more flexibility in hiring and promotion policies, ensuring that women have a voice in the workplace), which can profoundly alter female academics' careers and management of stress, family, and self-care. Unfortunately, fueled by the increasing commercialization of higher education and declining US economy, such initiatives addressing work-family concerns have raised heated debates with little improvement.[11]

Sadly, race and class complicate the experience of being an academic mother. For women of color, the reality of exclusion, devaluation, and marginalization in the academic setting is compounded by an Anglocentric paradigm that shapes the landscape of American universities and privileges Western, masculine frameworks for learning, teaching, and research.[12] Minority women are often recruited as tokens to improve institutional image and satisfy the organizational need to meet the diversity quota, but they are frequently dumped before they can become tenured. Women in general, but minority female faculties in particular, are also susceptible to getting stuck in the "second tier" system (low pay, low security part-time or adjunct positions) where they are expected to provide instruction as well as fill a stereotyped nurturing and caring role on campus. Students increasingly come to the classroom with a

---

[8]Mari Castaneda and Kirsten Isgro, *Mothers in Academia* (New York: Columbia University Press, 2013).

[9]Andrea O'Reilly, *Twenty-First-Century Motherhood: Experience, Identity, Policy, Agency* (New York: Columbia University Press, 2010).

[10]American Association of University Professors, *AAUP Faculty Gender Equity Indicators*, Washington, DC, 2006.

[11]Gaye Tuchman, *Wannabe U: Inside the Corporate University* (Chicago: University of Chicago Press, 2009).

[12]Gabriella Gutierrez y Muhs et al., ed., *Presumed Incompetent: The Intersections of Race and Class for Women in Academia* (Boulder, CO: University Press of Colorado, 2012).

consumerist mentality and become hostile when their expectations are not met as the culture of American higher education has shifted to a corporatized and outcome-driven climate.[13]

Having to battle challenging biases, being a woman of color in an academic setting can easily feel like a tiring job. Female faculty of color are vulnerable and forced to do more than what is expected of others in order to advance their careers. Scholars warn that unless the cycle of unequal power structure and male-dominated academic culture is transformed, it will continue to have detrimental physical, psychological, and spiritual consequences—especially for women of color, who must constantly fight chronic stress and microaggressions.

CONCLUSION

Women are pulled in a million different directions today with unrealistic expectations. Between taking care of children, marriage, and caring for elderly parents, most of us don't have the luxury to think about this elusive idea of "balancing" between work and family. Amid this productivity-driven culture, more and more women are finding it challenging to fulfill their roles both at home and work. Trying to find balance between family and academy is a daunting process, often resulting in strained familial relationships, stress and burnout at work, and even poor physical and mental health. One of the biggest problems today is that as a culture we have framed work and family as opposite, competing ideals (i.e., career woman vs. family caregiver), which often leads to a no-win situation where many of us are feeling torn, stressed, and guilty. We need to let go of the unrealistic societal and cultural expectations and renew what God has called us to be as image bearers, even as we live in tension—juggling family and career. In the last two decades, I have negotiated my identity in the intersections of race, gender, culture, and religion within the context of higher learning. I hope that my personal narrative as a 1.5-generation, Korean American pastor's wife could add texture and nuance to the larger discourse around motherhood and academia.

---

[13]Gutierrez y Muhs et al., ed., *Presumed Incompetent.*

ANSWERING A
THREEFOLD CALLING

MOTHERHOOD, THE ACADEMY,
AND THE PASTORATE

JENNIFER POWELL MCNUTT, PhD, FRHistS

THE YEAR I GRADUATED WITH MY PHD, I did what you should never do all at once: I defended my dissertation while pregnant, gave birth to my first child, moved internationally, and started my first full-time teaching job within a matter of months. My husband and I were living in England at the time. When Wheaton College came calling, we packed up our tiny flat, managed to get our newborn a passport, and moved to Illinois to begin the next chapter of our lives as a family of three. There was little to no room to manage an additional milestone, but I was also in the final stages of the highly intricate ordination process of the Presbyterian Church (USA). Ordination exams and field education requirements had long been completed during my studies at Princeton Theological Seminary, but a final examination on the floor of Presbytery still awaited me as a candidate for ordination. I was awash in the firsts of teaching and motherhood, and my husband was also finishing his PhD and pursuing ordination. It was enough to stay one day ahead of the demands, and I was stalled.

I remember the moment distinctly when things shifted. My dean sought me out in the hallway to ask about how my ordination process was coming along. I fumbled with explaining that teaching and the new baby were occupying my attention. Travel was required to finish up, and I was not at all sure how we could manage the cost or the time. She looked at me with understanding, and then she said firmly, without any equivocation, "We want you to finish the ordination process."[1] That verbal confirmation was exactly what I needed.

Soon after, Chicago Presbytery ordained me to the church office of Teaching Elder (*presbyter*) or Minister of Word and Sacrament in the Presbyterian Church (USA). Coming from a family filled with generations of pastors, my ordination was a family affair in every possible way. My father preached the sermon, my mother delivered the charge, my brother served on the clerical commission, and my husband offered the presentation of the candidate. Local and out-of-town friends and family sat in the pews of First Presbyterian Church of Glen Ellyn and witnessed the moment I took vows before the assembly to serve and honor the Triune God and the Body of Christ with all faithfulness and devotion to the Word of God to the very best of my abilities. For the first time, all three of my callings converged as I raised my hand to deliver the benediction to the congregation. I was a mother, a professor, and a Presbyterian minister. How was this going to work?

ACKNOWLEDGING THE COMPLEXITY

This book is a collective testament to the enormous amount of effort, resolve, endurance, and support that is required to manage the demands of both motherhood and academics. More often than not, the seasons of motherhood clash with the timelines for professional advancement. Motherhood

---

[1] I am grateful for the mentoring and support that I received from Dr. Jill Peláez Baumgaertner, retired dean of Humanities and Biblical and Theological Studies and Professor of English Emerita. She encouraged me in ordination, guided me through the tenure process, and has continued to be a sounding board of wisdom in my life.

does not easily align with the life of the mind, which requires space and time for sustained reflection, concentration, and output. The physical toll of pregnancy, labor, and recovery impacts everything—teaching, research, and publishing—with far reaching effects. The situation is further compounded when paid maternity leave is unavailable and the cost of full-time childcare is out-of-reach.[2] A motherhood penalty can bear out in academics when the frequency of publishing is key to promotion and promotion is key to salary advancements—even within institutions that aspire to a level of equal pay between male and female professors.[3] Meanwhile, promotion and tenure are to an extent dependent on student evaluations, which have frequently been shown to disadvantage women and minorities.[4] These reasons and more have been identified in the scholarly literature as the cause of a persisting "gender gap" in academia with fewer women, particularly women of color, advancing to full professor and holding endowed chairs. Although women have earned more than 50 percent of all doctoral degrees since 2006, a "leaky pipeline" has meant that, as one ascends to the highest academic rankings, fewer and fewer women are found.[5] In my case, as a European historian who works on rare manuscripts and books in foreign languages, research trips to national and international archives have proven to be the most difficult aspect of my academic work to negotiate with my motherly responsibilities.

---

[2]Pamela Stone's book, *Opting Out?: Why Women Really Quit Careers and Head Home* (Berkeley: University of California Press, 2007) explored the way in which inflexible career expectations do not align with the reality of women's lives and end up discouraging the pursuit of work outside the home. At that time, statistics indicated that nearly half of women were leaving their jobs after becoming mothers rather than staying in the workforce to advance their careers. Stone's book was written before the 2008 economic crisis saw women enter the US workforce in droves, and in fact, I was among them as a first-time mother. By 2013, a record 40 percent of women were functioning as the sole or primary breadwinners of their families according to a Pew Research Report. Pew Research Center, *Breadwinner Moms*, Pew Social and Demographic Trends, May 29, 2013, www .pewsocialtrends.org/wp-content/uploads/sites/3/2013/05/Breadwinner_moms_final.pdf.

[3]Beth Z. Schneider et al., "Women 'Opting Out' of Academia: At What Cost?" *Forum on Public Policy* 2011, no. 2 (August 2011): 8.

[4]Shauna W. Joye and Janie H. Wilson, "Professor Age and Gender Affect Student Perceptions and Grades," *Journal of Scholarship of Teaching and Learning* 15, no. 14 (August 2015): 126-38.

[5]Heather L. Johnson, *Pipelines, Pathways, and Institutional Leadership: An Update on the Status of Women in Higher Education* (Washington, DC: American Council on Education, 2017): "As of 2015, women held 32% of the full professor positions at degree-granting postsecondary institutions" (5).

When I was a bit more than three months pregnant with my third child, I began a research fellowship in order to consult a collection of university archives. The college had offered me a spacious apartment to live in for the month. I needed to bring my two daughters with me due to the length of the trip, but my husband was working full time and unable to get away. Without my parents willing and able to join me, the kids and I could not have embarked on our journey. Gratefully, we arrived eager to rest and settle in, but nothing started out as planned. Rather than receiving a welcome, I was unexpectedly told that my children could not stay in the apartment. Negotiations followed to allow me and the children on the premises. I was battling nausea from a combination of pregnancy and jet lag, but this was another level of discomfort entirely. The entire conversation was embarrassing, but I was also concerned that we would have no place to stay that was affordable or available at this late a point. In the end, we were shown to our apartment and given a map that included marked-out spaces where my children were not allowed to be seen or heard. In no uncertain terms, it was made clear to me that being a mother was beyond the pale of their expectation for suitable scholars and in every way a burden. The axiom—"We expect women to work like they don't have children and raise children as if they don't work"[6]—had never rung so true. My entire experience there was undercut by their profound lack of hospitality, and sadly, for the duration of my stay, I was never able to shake the feeling of being unwelcome simply because my family was with me. Yet despite that difficult experience, I have nevertheless managed to bring my children on research trips with me, and I would never trade those moments with them despite the added financial costs (since grants are typically restricted from covering living costs that academic mothers manage), energy, and logistics required. In the end, to be able to show them the world through these opportunities has been a joy and a privilege rather than a burden.[7]

---

[6]A version of this quote is attributed to Amy Westervelt's *Forget 'Having It All': How America Messed Up Motherhood—and How to Fix it* (New York: Seal Press, 2018).

[7]I have benefited from the support of my husband and parents in making these trips possible, but this has required managing the added costs outside of grant support.

Meanwhile, pastoral ministry as a woman adds its own complexities to life particularly when living and working in evangelical circles, though it was not always that way. Historic evangelicalism since the eighteenth century pioneered the advancement of women as public pastors before other Christian traditions. As historian Timothy Larsen writes, "This is a distinctive because no other large branch of the Christian family has demonstrated as long and deep a commitment to affirming the public ministries of women—not theologically liberal traditions, not Roman Catholicism or Eastern Orthodox traditions, not Anglicanism or other mainline Protestant traditions."[8] Wheaton College's own story reflects these dynamics at its establishment in 1860 by Jonathan Blanchard when it became the first college in America to permit female students to enroll in the full curriculum offered, including homiletics.[9] Wheaton's student newspaper, *The Record*, even expressed affirmations for women in public ministry by printing ordination news and pastoral appointments of female students in the following manner:

> Wheaton College has had for some time three lady students in the ministry. Mrs. Caldwell, formerly Miss Hewes has labored with great success as an evangelist among the Methodist churches of the United States and Great Britain. Mrs. Fannie Townsly was ordained as pastor of the Baptist church in Nebraska. She also has been an evangelist highly spoken of for her works' sake. Miss Juanita Breckenridge is now the ordained pastor of the Congregational church in Brookton. N. Y., as noticed recently in these columns. Another of our young ladies has just been ordained as pastor of the Congregational church in Gustavo, Ohio. In this church our brother C. W. Hiatt, now of Kalamazoo, Mich., preached while in the seminary and had a blessed revival and numbers were converted. Miss Jeanette Olmstead has just been ordained as pastor in this church. She was with us some while since and commended herself to her comrades in the College and to the

---

[8]Larsen defines "public ministry" in terms of preaching, teaching, pastoring, administering the sacraments, and providing spiritual oversight to adult believers. Timothy Larsen, "Women in Public Ministry: A Historic Evangelical Distinctive" in *Women, Ministry and the Gospel: Exploring New Paradigms*, ed. Mark Husbands and Timothy Larsen (Downers Grove, IL: IVP Academic, 2007), 213.
[9]Larsen, "Women in Public Ministry," 222.

teachers as a Christian woman and a good student. We congratulate her on the service to which she has been called.[10]

It was not until the mid-twentieth century in the post–World War II context that a shift in outlook and practice became commonplace. According to Larsen's work, women's public ministry grew problematic with the emergence of the sexual revolution and its links with the feminist movement.[11] As mainline denominations opened their doors to female pastors for the very first time, evangelical churches became more oppositional. I grew up navigating those waters in culturally conservative contexts, always uncertain whether my pastoral calling would be received or would be something of a liability. I have experienced both.

In some cases, I have been invited to speak on my area of academic expertise at a seminary or church where my ordination and pastoral ministry roles were acknowledged and celebrated, and in other cases, only my academic credentials were recognized due to the institution's restrictions on women in ministry.[12] In the latter case, I have experienced a mix of emotions. On the one hand, my academic expertise has provided opportunities to speak into spaces where female professors in my discipline or female pastors would never be hired. In those situations, my goal has been to offer a winsome spirit, sharp mind, and an earnest heart for building bridges in the most gracious way possible. On the other hand, a lack of acknowledgment of the pastoral dimensions of my work and expertise can also feel like a vocational fracturing. The academic mother and pastor is all too frequently put in the position of navigating, in multiple spaces, others' reception of her vocational callings as legitimate or not, and the act of accommodating can take a toll.

In truth, anyone pursuing both academics and the pastoral office faces a complex landscape today. After my first monograph was published on

---

[10]*Wheaton College Record*, November 5, 1892, 3. Available at College Archives, Buswell Library Special Collections, Wheaton College (IL).

[11]Larsen, "Women in Public Ministry," 231-35. Larsen writes, "Women in public ministry has not been a historic commitment of those branches of Christianity marked by theological liberalism" (230).

[12]I was once invited by faculty to speak at an institution on an academic topic and then uninvited by their dean because of my ordination.

the history of Geneva's clergy during the age of Enlightenment, the hard-back dust jacket included details about my ordination. Much to my surprise, a book review from a journal published abroad unfairly highlighted that dimension of my identity as the basis for critiquing the book's conclusions without supplying counterevidence; insinuation was apparently sufficient. Nevertheless, the book won the American Society of Church History's Brewer Prize for the best book written by a first-time author,[13] and I was elected to the Royal Historical Society for the groundbreaking archival research I conducted. The quality of the work had the last word, though apparently, my ordination was a bump in the road. There was a time when the church and the academy more easily intersected in outlook and purpose.[14] The Presbyterian tradition, reaching back to its roots in John Calvin's Geneva, valued the overlap between clergy and professors well into the twentieth century. Today, those spaces are harder to come by. My husband (the Rev. Dr. David McNutt) and I established "McNuttshell Ministries" in 2016 with a vision for bridging the church and the academy through teaching, writing, and speaking on Christian faith in a nutshell.[15] We have also been grateful for the fellowship provided by the Center for Pastor Theologians where speaking, writing, and gathering has offered respite for a shared vision of ministry. A proactive approach has been required.

At no point has drawing these three paths together been simple or clear. Maintaining vocational commitments through different seasons of motherhood has required tremendous focus, energy, support, and encouragement from my faith in Christ. A threefold calling is certainly not celebrated in every context, and that reality has meant that I have had to learn to be highly adept at navigating different spheres of the church and the academy. This chapter will explore three significant ways that I have flourished in my journey.

---

[13]Jennifer Powell McNutt, *Calvin Meets Voltaire: The Clergy of Geneva in the Age of Enlightenment, 1685–1798*, An Ashgate Book (Ashgate, 2013; New York: Routledge, 2019).

[14]See Gerald Hiestand and Todd Wilson, *The Pastor Theologian: Resurrecting an Ancient Vision* (Grand Rapids, MI: Zondervan, 2015).

[15]Our cowritten book *Know the Theologians* for Zondervan Academic is forthcoming. The Center for Pastor Theologians has been another important avenue for exploring this aspect of my ministry.

YOU NEED A SUPPORT SYSTEM TO FLOURISH

Since my ordination, hardly a day has gone by without someone asking me honestly and with a hint of bewilderment, "How do you do it all?" The truth is that every part of my story has involved a support system of people who have been critical to my flourishing. If the pandemic has taught our society anything, it has shown us how easily and quickly women can drop out of the workforce.[16] We already know what can happen when mothers do not have suitable support systems. In my case, support and mentoring have consistently come from my family (though not exclusively), even as that too is proving harder as I move into the "sandwich generation."

My third child was born in 2017 just days before the five hundredth anniversary year of the Reformation began. Since I am a Reformation historian, this meant that I entered maternity leave at the most critical moment of my academic career. Invitations to speak and write had never been so generous and copious, and this opportunity would not come around again in my lifetime. I was committed to juggling it all, and so, my son flew with me all over the country. When he could not travel with me, I struggled with the discomfort of needing to pump at the most inopportune moments and places. While I was still exclusively nursing him just months after his birth, I faced the reality of an inflexible writing deadline. I had been slowly researching the chapter for weeks but had not reached the point of weaving together my ideas. My son had been diagnosed with acid reflux, so the incessant crying left me more frazzled than inspired. Strapping him to me while I typed proved to be essential to the task even as I was beginning to face the hard truth that interruptions would have to become my friend in order to get this chapter completed. It was the timing of my daughters' spring ballet performance rehearsals that put me over the edge. I reached out to my recently retired parents for help. Soon we were in the car, my dad driving us to dance rehearsal while I sat in the passenger's seat typing furiously. Not everyone

---

[16]Alisha Haridasani Gupta, "Why Did Hundreds of Thousands of Women Drop Out of the Work-force," *New York Times*, October 3, 2020, www.nytimes.com/2020/10/03/us/jobs-women-dropping-out-workforce-wage-gap-gender.html.

has family around or family willing to help in these kinds of moments, but it is critical to the threefold calling to have those who can be called upon in the direst moments of juggling.

Part of fostering a support system requires seeking out mentoring from those who inspire you forward. More and more studies show that female modeling and representation in ministry and in academics can have a notable impact on the next generation of female leaders. According to a groundbreaking study by Benjamin R. Knoll and Cammie Jo Bolin on clergywomen in modern America, females who directly observe clergywomen during their childhood tend to grow up with higher self-esteem, better employment, and more education.[17] Similarly, "having female instructors is a predictor of success for female students."[18] Knoll and Bolin also claim a correlation between the underrepresentation of women in America's pulpits and the persisting gender gap in the wider economic, social, and political spheres. A woman in leadership—whether in the pulpit or in the lectern—is an empowering model for encouraging girls to advance. In my own life, that representation primarily came from my mother.[19]

My parents, the Rev. Drs. John and Pamela Powell, met and married at Fuller Theological Seminary in the 1970s. Soon after their ordinations, they copastored a Presbyterian church in Sherman Oaks through most of my elementary school days. They were committed to the evangelicalism of the 1980s while living out an egalitarian dynamic in the family and at work.[20] I grew up at the nexus of female ordination and the evangelical world, and so, for much of my childhood, I watched my mom preach one Sunday and my dad the next. Eventually, my mother would go on to pastor her own

---

[17]Benjamin R. Knoll and Cammie Jo Bolin, *She Preached the Word: Women's Ordination in Modern America* (Oxford University Press, 2018). Reported by Jana Reiss, "It's good for girls to have clergywomen, study shows," *Religion News Service*, July 17, 2018, https://religionnews.com/2018/07/17/its-good-for-girls-to-have-clergywomen-study-shows/.

[18]Schneider, et al. "Women 'Opting Out' of Academia," 9.

[19]I am also grateful to my aunt of the heart, Rev. Karen Berns, who has supported me throughout my life every step of the way. Numerous female professors have provided encouragement and guidance over the years including Dr. Erlyne Whiteman, Dr. Karen Jobes, and Dr. Lynn Cohick.

[20]Among egalitarian evangelicals, Ephesians 5:21's affirmation of "mutual submission" has been foundational.

churches,[21] complete a doctor of ministry degree, and teach on the faculty at two seminaries. I watched her successes and challenges unfold as she persisted within various contexts that either celebrated her gifts or challenged her calling to ministry as a woman. Because of her determined faithfulness and resilience, she achieved more than what was expected of her at the time. There is a lot to admire and appreciate about the woman who gave me life, but the inheritance that I most value from her is the faithful, vocational representation as a mother, professor, and pastor before I ever took up the mantle. Although our journeys have been different in notable ways, and my call is certainly my own, I hope that I can navigate this threefold calling with half the grace that she has shown.

Discerning the threefold calling is not an easy undertaking, but a support system makes flourishing possible. Prioritizing friend networks with other women who are walking the same path has been an added source of encouragement and inspiration to me each step of the way. Most of all, having a spouse who supports, encourages, collaborates, celebrates, and prays for me day in and day out has been crucial to my flourishing. I'll never forget those first moments when I met my husband and he asked me what I wanted to do with my life. Inside I cringed because of how my answer to that question had so often stifled my previous relationships, but I took a deep breath and shared my vision. When he responded, "That's great!" I knew that I would never let him go. To be sure, the ideal support system includes family and friends who know and understand you (mistakes and all!), believe in your calling, and are quick to encourage—and even quicker to lift you up in prayer to the Lord. This is nonnegotiable.

MANAGING YOUR TIME

The threefold calling requires an immense amount of doing to keep all three callings thriving, and one can easily be overloaded. In academia, women and particularly women of color are disproportionately asked to

---

[21]See her chapter about her ministry, which was presented at the Wheaton Theology Conference. Pamela Baker Powell, "Meeting Messiah," in *The Gospel in Black and White: Theological Resources for Racial Reconciliation*, ed. Dennis Okholm (IVP Academic, 1997), 151-65.

volunteer their time on faculty committees to the disadvantage of their research and writing. Meanwhile, when others are focusing on paper presentations at conferences and building their professional networks, we may be nursing between sessions and juggling childcare. Even the relational expectations from students differ in contrast with male counterparts: "Students expect male professors to be effective in their work but expect female professors to spend time building supportive relationships with students."[22] These gender dynamics can also play out in the church. Even as an evangelical in a progressive denomination, there is still a disconnect between the affirmation of women in ministry and the hiring of women to pastoral positions. According to the *Gender & Leadership in the PC (USA) Report* of 2016, though seminary enrollment has been seeing parity between male and female students, only one third of women were serving as active teaching elders in the church at that time.[23] Women were found more likely to participate in voluntary leadership roles without pay than men. Moreover, when women did hold a pastoral office, their time was demanded more often and disproportionately toward offering workshops, planning activities, serving in childcare, and engaging in kitchen duties.[24] A woman's time is rarely her own to shape.

My firstborn daughter was born just weeks before I graduated with my PhD from the University of St. Andrews. I wore the blue doctoral gown and held our six-week-old baby proudly at graduation, basking in the festivities and wondering how I could break away to nurse her. I was new to the juggling act and nursing had not been easy; nevertheless, I was brimming with the wonder of celebration with family and dear friends. I did not fully recognize it then, but a complete paradigm shift was at work in my life, reprioritizing my focus while also physically tethering me to the needs of another person to an extent that I had never experienced before. True to form, I had over-researched the start of parenting, trying

---

[22]Joye and Wilson, "Professor Age and Gender," 133.

[23]The report predicts that parity would not be reached at that rate until 2027.

[24]See Presbyterian Church (USA), *Gender & Leadership in the PC(USA)*, Research Services of the PC(USA), Summer 2016, www.presbyterianmission.org/wp-content/uploads/Final-Report-Gender-Leadership-101916.pdf.

to anticipate every challenge in advance. Yet nothing I read prepared me for what it felt like to turn down an invitation to meet renowned theologian Jürgen Moltmann because we could not find a babysitter. That was when the realization set in that I was really no longer in charge of my own schedule.

This dilemma of conflicting demands is a constant with no easy solutions except that every moment of the day must be put to good use. In my case, I discovered that it was nearly impossible to manage teaching adult education or preaching at my church when my responsibilities at the college required a Monday-Wednesday-Friday teaching schedule. At that rate, there was never a night free from teaching preparation, and I still needed to find time for my own research and writing. Under my original schedule, preaching quickly became a burden even when I was repeating sermons at different churches through pulpit supply. A decade filled with three pregnancies and the publication of two books required me to step back from church leadership for a season though I felt the loss. As it turns out, shifting my teaching schedule to Tuesday and Thursday has proven to be key in allowing me to expand my work as a parish associate at my church, to offer more pulpit supply and adult education, and to develop a joint ministry with my husband.

There is always more to do, and the challenge I face today is learning to respect my limits and the multiplicity of demands in order to say "no" when necessary. If every moment counts and the load is immense, then we must discern how best to direct our energies. We must weigh opportunities and create boundaries to protect our emotional well-being and the needs of our families for the sake of longevity and thriving. From that standpoint, we are able to accept that sometimes our callings are reordered in different seasons of life. Sometimes our families will sacrifice for our work, and other times our work will sacrifice for our families.

KNOW THE "WHY" BEHIND YOUR WORK

Above all, I have found that the ability to manage academics, motherhood, and pastoral ministry has required anchoring my commitment in the "why" rather than the "how." *Why* do all these things? Why bridge motherhood, academics, and ordination, when clearly women cannot "have it all"?[25] Time and energy are precious. The race is relentless, so why run?

Before I had ever aspired to complete a PhD, I received my calling to pastoral ministry as a child while attending the church camp of a cherished friend. An open invitation at the fireside on the last evening compelled me to share my testimony with the camp, and what happened afterward set the trajectory of my life. As the pastor read out the Great Commission (Matthew 28:18-20), I also heard the Lord calling me to pastoral ministry. "Be a pastor," said a still, small voice (1 Kings 19:12), and a deep gratitude washed over me as I relinquished my future to God's plan. Since then, I have resonated with John Calvin's description of the "secret call" to ministry in the *Institutes of the Christian Religion* as reflective of my own experience:

> I pass over that secret call, of which each minister is conscious before God, and which does not have the church as witness. But there is the good witness of our heart that we receive the proffered office not with ambition or avarice, not with any other selfish desire, but with a sincere fear of God and desire to build up the church. That is indeed necessary for each one of us (as I have said) if we would have our ministry approved by God.[26]

A clarity of conviction was fostered in my life that night years ago, and it has continued to generate much-needed resilience and courage like an anchor during times of weariness and discouragement. That "yes" offered to God as a child at overnight camp has expanded like the ripples from a pebble dropped into a pond, bringing me from one stage to the next.

And yet, there is nothing like managing a threefold calling to feel in your bones that life is truly a race. Each of us runs at our own pace and ability, though none of us knows the actual length of the race set before us. According to the apostle Paul, we are running for the prize: "Do you not

---

[25]The New York Times bestseller by Ada Calhoun, *Why We Can't Sleep: Women's New Midlife Crisis* (New York: Grove Press, 2020), highlights the struggles of Gen-X women coming to terms with this realization.

[26]John Calvin, *Institutes of the Christian Religion*, ed. John T. McNeill, trans. Ford Lewis Battles, Library of Christian Classics XX (Philadelphia: Westminster Press, 1960): IV.3.11.

know that in a race all the runners run, but only one gets the prize? Run in such a way as to get the prize" (1 Corinthians 9:24). Here Paul likens the follower of Christ to an Olympic athlete, and in the process, he reinterprets the very nature of the race and the prize itself. The training, the endurance, the hardship of the race are all in pursuit of an imperishable wreath rather than a perishable one. For Christians, the race is run not for fleeting glory but for the sake of the gospel with each movement directed toward that end (1 Corinthians 9:25-27).

This image is also echoed in Hebrews 12 as an analogy for the Christian life. Believers are encouraged by the news that we do not run alone or even by our own strength. We benefit from a cheering section filled with the "heroes of the faith" who spur us ahead:

> Therefore we also, since we are surrounded by so great a cloud of witnesses, let us lay aside every weight, and the sin which so easily ensnares us, and let us run with endurance the race that is set before us, looking unto Jesus, the author and finisher of our faith, who for the joy that was set before Him endured the cross, despising the shame, and has sat down at the right hand of the throne of God. (Hebrews 12:1-2 NKJV)

As we run, we are actually fixing our eyes ahead on Christ, who has already won the race on our behalf. We are, in a sense, called to run in his footsteps and keep to his lane—yet not by our strength alone.

Again and again we are reminded in Scripture that there is no endurance apart from the indwelling of the Holy Spirit (Romans 8:11). No matter how much I love my work, my family, and my church to the best of my abilities, my inner drive alone cannot meet the demands required to do all these things all the time. Prayer, friendship, rest, accepting failure, and celebrating the victories of others has been key to enduring the struggle. Meanwhile, none of this endangers the race to "have it all" if what we ultimately mean by that is seeking the imperishable prize already won for us through Jesus Christ.[27] Framing my work as the outworking of the faithful

---

[27]The parables of the hidden treasure and of the pearl merchant in Matthew 13:44-46 both convey that upon discovering God's kingdom, people give everything they have to possess it, such as buying the most valuable pearl or a treasure hidden in a field.

stewardship of God's gifts and calling is the core inspiration of my commitment to my family, the academy, and the pastorate.

CONCLUSION

No matter where your church tradition stands on the issue of women's ordination, the Protestant tradition has always emphasized from day one that all believers are counted as part of the priesthood of believers by virtue of their baptism (1 Peter 2:9).[28] A vocational lens for the work that we do as mothers, academics, and pastors (or church members) is crucial.

In his book *Called: The Crisis and Promise of Following Jesus Today*, Mark Labberton explores how following Christ is our essential, primary vocation and the way in which that unfolds in our lives is our secondary vocation:

> The vocation of every Christian is to live as a follower of Jesus today. In every aspect of life, in small and large acts . . . we are to seek to live out the grace and truth of Jesus. This is our vocation, our calling. Today. In relation to this primary calling, all the rest is secondary. It matters, but not as much as this vocation. Gifts, context, challenges, personality—these affect how we embody and enact our following of Jesus. Such things have all kinds of impact on how we live out our imitation of Jesus. But they are not the call itself. . . . Following Jesus this day, in the life we are living right now—this is the vocation we must grasp and exercise.[29]

According to this understanding, our vocations as mothers and academics are the outworking of our primary vocation to follow Christ, and following Christ means functioning as a member of his body, the church. Although not everyone is called to serve as ordained ministers, all Christians are called to participate in the ministry of the body of Christ in different ways. To that end, each person is equipped with different gifts from the Holy

---

[28]For how the proclamation of this concept impacted women during the Protestant Reformation, see Rebecca A. Giselbrecht, "Women from Then to Now: A Commitment to Mutuality and Literacy," in *The Protestant Reformation and World Christianity: Global Perspectives*, ed. Dale T. Irvin (Grand Rapids, MI: Eerdmans, 2017), 65-95.

[29]Mark Labberton, *Called: The Crisis and Promise of Following Jesus Today* (Downers Grove, IL: IVP Academic, 2014), 45, 48.

Spirit bestowed according to God's will and purpose (1 Corinthians 12:4-11) for the good functioning of Christ's body (1 Corinthians 12:27-30).[30]

In the midst of hectic schedules and overloaded lives, there is a primary commitment to Christ and to his church. From this standpoint then, as Christians who are both mothers and academics, we are all answering a threefold calling. Through it, we are united to Christ and made a member of his body so that there is no living in Christ apart from the care of his church and the ministry of the church, though fulfilling that commitment will look differently for different people. This should not require us to run ourselves ragged with commitments and busyness. Let us not run "aimlessly," Paul says (1 Corinthians 9:26). Rather, we work with intentionality to bring glory to the Three-in-One who has made, saved, and equipped us and who sends us into the world.

---

[30]Carolyn Custis James, *Half the Church: Recapturing God's Global Vision for Women* (Grand Rapids, MI: Zondervan, 2015).

BALANCING UNIVERSITY TEACHING AND HOMESCHOOLING

YVANA URANGA-HERNANDEZ, PhD

I BEGAN TO PONDER HOMESCHOOLING even before God gifted us with our firstborn. My husband and I were attending a local church with a large population of homeschoolers. According to research, approximately "3% of American K-12 students are homeschooled at a single point in time."[1] Getting to know these families and listening to their stories, I decided to explore homeschooling as an option if God ever sent us children. At that time, I was working at a school district as a program specialist (in the special education administration office), an all-day and many-evenings consuming job. The idea of homeschooling with that type of schedule seemed impossible, and although homeschooling appealed to me, it was definitely not appealing to my husband. His disapproval of

---

[1] Angela R. Watson. "Is Homeschool Cool? Current Trends in American Homeschooling," *Journal of School Choice* 12, no. 3 (2018): 406.

homeschooling resounded with many common misconceptions. He did not want his children to be isolated from their peers; he did not want them to be antisocial or fall behind academically. Interestingly enough, ten years after starting this journey of homeschooling, he is the first to say that we must continue regardless of the challenges that often arise. So how did we go from disagreeing about homeschooling to now being ten years into it? This chapter will detail our adventures in homeschooling, including how we manage it while working full time. A question I often get is, "Where are your children when you are at work?" The answer to this question has changed over the years. At times they were at home and other times at drop-off classes. Furthermore, I will show how working at a university actually opened the door to many opportunities for both my children and my education. In addition, I reveal how asking for help and support from others is essential to making this work. The saying "it takes a village to raise a child" truly describes how we managed to homeschool all of these years. The discussion and reflection questions provided (226) will help guide your thinking about homeschooling. Last, I hope to paint a picture in the following pages that acknowledges God's hand in this journey.

THE EARLY YEARS

In 2004, God opened the door to a new career opportunity when I was offered a job at a Christian university in Southern California. I clearly remember signing a full-time contract in May only to find out in June that I was expecting our first child, a baby boy. As I look back on those events now, I know that it was all part of God's plan, as it was never my intention to be a working mother. But I was 100 percent sure that God had opened the door to my new career opportunity and 100 percent sure that he had answered my prayers and sent us a baby and that somehow the two gifts had to coexist. Twenty-one months after the first baby boy was born, another baby arrived, this time a beautiful little girl. By the time she was about two years old, I knew that I had to ask for a 75 percent contract. I had heard at the new faculty orientation early on that this was possible, yet it was a lot more challenging to actually obtain that contract than I initially had been told. The benefit of obtaining a 75 percent contract was that I would only have to teach nine units a semester instead of twelve, but I would continue to receive medical benefits along with the tuition waiver our university offers. The pay, of course, would also be at 75 percent of my original contract. This new contract would allow me more flexibility to be at home and care for my two babies. After a challenging time, I obtained a 75 percent contract. I was able to enjoy this benefit for eight years, returning to a 100 percent contract in fall 2016.

When our little boy turned four years old, I convinced my husband that I wanted to homeschool. I believed in my heart that this was what God wanted for our family. I had researched the subject of homeschooling extensively, I read about homeschooling methods, researched various curricula, and looked into different homeschooling programs. I knew that homeschooling was the school option I wanted for my very inquisitive and quiet child. He was a quick learner with an amazing memory. Having had the opportunity to work in the public school system, I understood it from the inside. I knew that I could teach my children at home. We would homeschool for a trial year to see if we could actually get all the required days in and to see if I could manage to do it while working. The majority of states (California included) require 180 school days. That year our little boy learned to read and his love of learning flourished.

For an entire year, I had been having an ongoing conversation with a homeschool mom whose little boy attended the speech-language clinic that I both directed and supervised at as part of our undergraduate program. Her two boys were part of a homeschooling co-op,[2] and I knew simply from what I had heard about it that I wanted to enroll my little boy in this program. I had researched this community and liked the fact

---

[2]"A homeschool co-op is a group of families who meet together and work cooperatively to achieve common goals. Co-ops can be organized around academics, social time, the arts, activities, crafts, service work, or projects—or some combination of these. Activities and classes that are part of a co-op may be led by parents, or the parents may chip in to pay all or some of the teachers and activity leaders. There may be as few as three families in a small co-op or as many as several hundred children in the largest co-ops." Jeanne Faulconer, "What Is a Homeschool Co-op?" *The Homeschool Mom* (blog), last updated February 4, 2019, www.thehomeschoolmom.com/what -is-homeschool-co-op/.

that they met on Fridays, had a drop-off option, and that they fostered community by creating small groups of children with like ages that would meet outside of school time. They also offered extracurricular activities like choir and school plays. Along with all of this, they offered field trips, and most importantly, it was a Christian homeschool community. I thought this would be a good complement to our homeschooling. My child would have the opportunity to get the classroom experience one day a week as well as other activities, and the rest of the week I would be able to homeschool him at home. After persuading my husband that we could not send our little boy to kindergarten because he already knew all that he had to learn that year (I knew this because I had followed the kindergarten state standards at the time), we decided to tour this program right before our little guy was supposed to enter kindergarten. I had heard about this program for an entire year, and I knew it was perfect for us, or so I thought. The day we toured it, my husband waited in the car with our baby girl. When our son and I returned, he said, "Are we all signed up?" I looked at him, and he was quite surprised to hear me say, "Nope, this is not the program for us." "You talked about this program for an entire year," he said. "What happened and now what?" I told him that I simply knew as I walked that campus that God was calling us elsewhere. The atmosphere was not friendly (at least not to us). The questions I asked were answered with responses that did not fit our family values and the homeschool style we were wanting to follow. For example, one of the reasons we were homeschooling was because I wanted to be with my child as it pertained to his education. I quickly learned that this program did not permit parents who were not already teaching a class to stick around during the day to support their child. Although it had all the aspects I had learned about that brought me there, God made it very clear that we were not to join this program. To further elaborate on the point, as a Mexican American woman I felt that there were enough cultural and parenting differences to tell me that we did not belong there. I took this as a sign from God because this was the one issue I had not taken into account when researching this program. All of the while, I had made my own plans and God had a very different and wonderful plan for us. Finding a homeschooling program that works for your family can take time, and it might not be the first option that you are led to.

The option we found for my son's kindergarten year was a nationally recognized homeschooling program that provides support for parents wanting to educate their children with a Christian classical education. The classical method of education involves the "trivium" in which children are educated in three stages: grammar, rhetoric, and dialectic; add to this the idea that all knowledge comes from God and points to him, and you have a "Christian classical education." Throughout the nation and now across the world, there are different homeschooling communities that come together one day a week to follow this specific program. We joined a local community that had been together for only one year. It was a diverse group of families who welcomed us to their program. The program offered a day when the families came together to teach our children, and parents are required to stay with their children as well as with a specific curriculum. We have used this curriculum as our spine for many years, and other years it served as a supplemental curriculum in addition to others we were using.

Our typical schedule with this group was attending community on Mondays. I worked long days Tuesdays and Thursdays and then we home-schooled Wednesday, Friday, and Saturday. While I was at work, I would leave assignments for my children to complete on their own or with the help of their caregiver (their maternal grandmother). I have not always worked two days a week, so we have had to adapt our homeschooling schedule with a commitment to participate in this Christian classical education program one day a week. I recently commented to a friend that my two older children were not aware that other children did not go to school on Saturdays (at least not at that age). Later on, as my schedule changed to three days a week, we made adjustments but continued using Saturday for school. To this day, we still use Saturdays several times a month. When children are in their primary years, schooling can be very flexible.

After joining this homeschool group, I learned that homeschooling was going to be about God's plan, not mine. Still, throughout the years I have had to be reminded of this many, many times. Just as God had opened the door for me to leave my job in special education, he now had opened the door to the homeschooling program that would work for our family. My oldest son is now a freshman in high school and my oldest daughter is in middle school, and we continue to homeschool now four children as we also have a younger son and a younger daughter. Our weekly schedule has changed over the years as we have added other outside classes. My oldest currently attends classes that are part of another homeschooling program offered by the outreach ministry at my university. In this program, my son attends classes twice a week; he also takes an online language class as part of his schedule. He is given a syllabus for work throughout the week. He no longer participates in the program we joined all those many years ago. My other three children still do, along with taking other classes through a different homeschool program that is actually a drop-off program. (In our area, a Christian private school has allowed a homeschool group to use its campus. Because this is a drop-off program, I can homeschool them and work.) Unlike when we first started, our current school choice is now a hybrid with on-campus classes as well as homeschooling at home. Homeschooling has many different options, and taking outside classes is definitely one of them. We have participated in classes where parents were required to stay on campus as well as classes where parents were allowed to drop off children and have someone else be responsible for their teaching for a few hours. The reason it is considered homeschooling is that you are provided with a lesson plan for the week that will need to be followed when the children are not at their drop-off class. In some situations, parents (when working in co-ops) are the ones who write the lesson plans even if they pay a teacher to implement it. During our homeschool journey, we have benefited from many different options. My prayer is that God will continue to allow us to homeschool until they all graduate.

HOMESCHOOL OPTIONS AND
FACTORS TO CONSIDER

With the growth and popularity of homeschooling, there are many options for homeschooling families. These options can be broadly broken up into two different styles, structured and unstructured.[3] But it appears that most families do not adhere to simply one or the other option and really do a mix of options throughout their children's educational careers. This has also been the case for our family. Although we have always had some structure such as schedules, lesson plans, and set curriculum, there have been times when there was much more flexibility. One of those times happened in 2014 when I was sick for more than half the year. Although we continued schooling, we held our plans loosely, not knowing exactly where life would lead us. I am so grateful that God in his mercy allowed us to continue to see our children grow and to continue to homeschool.

Another option that people consider when homeschooling is the method they will follow. For us, the method we have used primarily is the Christian classical education. We have focused on the trivium and on the idea that all knowledge is from and points us back to God. Other methods that we have researched along the way are Charlotte Mason, unit studies, unschooling, school at home, and, of course, the eclectic method. After researching other methods, we decided on Christian classical education because we knew we wanted to continue to teach our children about God, we liked how memorizing bits of information in the grammar years truly worked for our oldest, and we liked the progression that this method takes as the children grow.

A third factor that parents need to consider is who will keep their school records. In California there are three main options for doing this. The first is to file your own affidavit with the state, basically saying that you are your own private school and that you keep all of your records. We followed this option for one year. The second option is to pay a Private School Satellite

---

[3]Oz Guterman and Ari Neuman, "Personality, Socioeconomic Status, and Education: Factors that Contribute to the Degree of Structure in Homeschooling," *Social Psychology of Education: An International Journal* 21, no. 1 (2018): 76.

Program (PSP) to keep your records. In the years we have homeschooled, we have been with two main PSPs; the most recent one is also part of the university I work at. The third option is to sign up with a charter school. One of the main reasons people sign up with charter schools is that it makes homeschooling more affordable because charter schools provide money that can be used for extracurricular activities and classes. We have looked at charter schools on several occasions but have chosen not to participate in them.

Last, the decision that is probably the most time consuming is selecting what curriculum you will use. There are so many possibilities that sometimes parents are quite overwhelmed when choosing one. Many times, the choices can be decreased depending on the method one chooses, as many methods will point you to the curriculum they feel works best. There are also books you can research that can help with curriculum choices. Two of the books we used when first looking for a curriculum were Cathy Duffy's *100 Top Picks for Homeschoolers Curriculum* (2005), which has since been revised. I also read *The Well-Trained Mind* (now on its 4th edition, published 2016) by Susan Wise Bauer and Jessie Wise and still reference this book on occasion.[4] The most important factor to remember when making curriculum choices is that not all choices will work with every child or with every family. Even if you do start a curriculum and figure out halfway through the year that it is not working, it is acceptable to change it midyear.

DIFFERENT SUPPORT SYSTEMS

When my first two started homeschooling, I was able to work two very long days. But that schedule changed as the years went by to an average of three days a week, depending on the semester (and really, on the week of each semester). Sometimes my children are at a drop-off homeschool program, and sometimes they are at home with my parents. Except for three years of my oldest child's life, we have always shared a house with

---

[4]Cathy Duffy, *102 Top Picks for Homeschoolers Curriculum* (Westminster, CA: Grove Publishing, 2014); Susan Wise Bauer and Jessie Wise, *The Well-Trained Mind* (New York: W. W. Norton, 2016).

my parents. This has allowed my husband and me to work while my parents watched our children and assisted in transporting them to different activities. It took both of us a very long time to get over the fact that we could not do this simply on our own accord and that we needed the help extended family so willingly offered. For those of you that are reading this and thinking, *I could never live in the same house as my parents!* (a comment I have often heard), I have this response: Like in any relationship, living with other people takes a lot of work. It takes people willing to listen to each other, be flexible, and have boundaries. Some years we have done this much better than other years. Long ago, my husband and I made choices that took us down a specific path of life, but as I look at how God has allowed us to raise our children, including the strong relationship they have with my parents, I am extremely grateful for his provision. Having support from extended family is one way that we have been able to homeschool. Now that there are four children, not only do I teach at home, but my mother has stepped into the role as well, taking time out of her already busy day to work on lessons with our two youngest. My parents' support was particularly important during two major life events for our family. The first was in 2014, the year I had a health crisis, and the second was from 2015 to 2016 during which I completed my dissertation for my doctorate degree.[5] Both times they stepped up to fill in the gaps that were left so that we were able to continue our homeschooling journey.

Another support that I find to be invaluable is that of other homeschooling mothers. The ability to discuss what you are doing with other homeschooling mothers is so essential to success. Homeschooling is not easy, but it is worth it. At times, sharing with another person the specific struggle that is occurring and hearing how they have handled it helps you continue on this track. For many years, we have been part of the same homeschooling group. This has allowed us to develop deep friendships

---

[5]The terminal degree for my profession (speech-language pathology) is a master's degree, which I possessed when I was hired to teach undergraduates at my university. But in 2008 I decided to start the journey toward my PhD in Educational Studies. I completed it in the spring of 2016 right before our first cohort of graduate students enrolled for our new master's of speech pathology program (fall 2016).

and, most importantly, a community of other homeschooling mothers with whom I can discuss all things related to our homeschooling experiences. Although many of those families have moved on to other communities, I can still pick up the phone and call them to simply share or ask a question. I believe that at some level, having homeschool dads to talk to is also important to husbands and fathers. In our case, my husband and I have been blessed to have both in our sphere of friends and acquaintances.

The third support system is that of the tutors or teachers that may be part of your homeschooling journey. For many years, I have been my children's only teacher. But as we have grown as a family and they have grown in their learning, we incorporate outside classes with the mindset that we (their parents) continue to be their primary teachers. My advice to those seeking to homeschool is to have open communication with those who are teaching your children. For us, knowing that they are also Christians has been very important. While all parents have to think about this regularly, homeschooling moms are the principals (so to speak) of their child's educational experience.

Last, my department chair's understanding of our schooling choice has made scheduling creativity a much easier process in that he is usually willing to allow those of us with more restrictions to schedule our classes first. He tends to schedule his classes around everyone else's. In my department, there is only one other faculty member who homeschooled her children up until they entered high school; having her understanding has also been helpful. The fact that my university focuses on the importance of family has also been beneficial, especially on those occasions when I have needed to bring children to work with me. All of these support systems have had a positive influence on our homeschooling journey, and this last one was definitely in place because I worked in academia.

THE JOURNEY CONTINUES

Ten years after starting this homeschooling journey, I can honestly say it is one of the best decisions we have ever made. It has not come without its challenges, and some years have been more difficult than others. But for the most part it has worked for our family, and I pray that God will continue to lead us in this direction. My oldest is currently in ninth grade. Our youngest is in first grade this year, so for us the journey is far from over.

As I reflect on what I have learned so far, I can see that my thinking has changed in some areas and stayed the same in others. I continue to believe that, when possible, parents should be the primary educators in their children's lives and for us that has also included being their academic instructors! The charge given to the Israelites in Deuteronomy 6:5-9 guides my thinking. I want to be the one imparting my faith, ideas, and teaching to my children. I want to be able to talk about God and our faith throughout the day. I want to direct them to Jesus and teach them what it means to walk with him. This does not mean that I have always done this correctly, so they have also seen when I have wavered and how we get back on the path and continue our Christian walk. I truly believe that one of the benefits of homeschooling is that it strengthens the relationship between siblings and parents, and, in our case, grandparents. If I were to summarize why it is that we chose to homeschool, I believe that it comes down to three main ideas: (1) faith, (2) family ties, and (3) strong academics.

As a side note, I do not think that homeschooling parents need to overly stress about our children's education, especially in the early years. Bible, reading, math, and writing are the most important academic areas. After these, adding others when possible is a benefit. Building relationships, trust, and character traits should also be a focus. As I look back, I know that I focused much more on academics when my two older children were very young. I hope that with the two younger I am able to provide a more well-rounded education.

SYNERGY OF PROFESSOR AND HOMESCHOOLING MOM

For me, one of the extra unexpected benefits is that there is a synergy between my role as a professor and a homeschooling mom. If I go to a workshop for my profession (speech-language pathology), I often leave with information to teach my students, improve my clinical practice, and information to assist me in educating my children. In my university classes, I often share how my children learn and communicate as a teaching illustration for my students. My children have often been part of my teaching; they have allowed my students to apply their theoretical knowledge by practicing their clinical skills on them. My children have been assessed by university students as well as been given therapy for speech difficulties. Not only have I used their assistance in my classes, but another colleague of mine has also used one of my children as a model in her classroom. In that situation, she administered a speech assessment to my child while her students practiced taking data. The fact that my children are homeschooled and their schedule is flexible has allowed for these experiences. Working in academia and in my specific discipline has made it possible for my children to be very much a part of my daily work as well as allowed me to be part of their daily learning. My role as mother and professor regularly intertwine. In walking this journey, you may also discover unexpected and wonderful synergies. I can clearly see God's hand in my journey as a professor and as a homeschooling mom. He meant for me to do both even when I was not sure that both were possible.

I have often been asked if I had to start all over, would I still homeschool, and the answer is a definite yes. There is so much value that I see in doing so. As I look at my children and the people they are becoming, I know that it is partly due to the choices we have made for their education. They are caring, compassionate individuals who enjoy learning. They have strong sibling bonds, and they are confident individuals who understand that God needs to be the center of their lives. They are also still young and have more learning to do, but this educational option we have chosen for them seems to be one that will continue to help their academic, personal, and spiritual growth. Whether you are teaching at a university or if you are working in another setting, know that with some creativity, it is still possible to make this choice for your children and for your family. I am not saying it will be easy to do, but it is definitely possible.

PART FOUR

NAVIGATING SUPPORT

IT TAKES A VILLAGE

RAISING CHILDREN WITH SUPPORT

DESHONNA COLLIER-GOUBIL, PhD
AND NANCY WANG YUEN, PhD

IT TAKES A VILLAGE TO RAISE A CHILD. Some of us have relatives and friends who can help out with childcare. Others rely on childcare providers at home, at daycare centers, or both. If in a dual-parent household, we lean on our partners to share childcare and house-hold tasks, along with emotional and spiritual support. If in a single-parent household, we lean on an extended network of family and friends. In this chapter, we review the role that men play as husbands and fathers, par-ticularly those in partnerships with Christian academic mothers. We will end with how one Christian faculty mom relies on a true village while dealing with loss.

HUSBANDS SPEAK OUT

Fathers are much more involved in childcare now than they were more than fifty years ago. In 2016, fathers reported spending an average of eight hours a week on childcare—about triple the time they provided in 1965.[1] This is partly due to the changing economic pressures on families to have dual incomes. In addition, societal attitudes surrounding men participating in childcare and household chores have evolved. This is even the case among Christian men who were raised with more traditional gendered ideals in which women shoulder the bulk of household duties including childcare. One Christian man describes how he was initially hesitant when considering marriage to an academic but changed his mind after praying to God:

> When I was considering marrying her, I remember having reservations about her working in a field that would demand her being away from home and any future mothering as her work would likely require. But as I prayed about it, I sensed God telling me: "I have gifted her uniquely to be a blessing in the work she does; free her up to do that." Since then, I've felt peace about her work and career. Indeed, I see how God has given her favor with powers to affect greater change beyond a classroom.[2]

Christian men also report contributing more to household chores. One husband of an academic told us, "I try to support my wife by helping with housework and childcare so she can focus on her career," while another shared, "I think it only fitting that I step in when I can as she does the same so much for me." Besides household and childcare duties, Christian men also support their academic wives by making sure she "gets her rest," and making "space to check in with each other at least once a week to know how to better support and pray for her." One academic Christian mom shared how her husband, over time, became supportive:

> In the early years of kids and marriage, it was not always smooth in terms of me feeling supported by my husband. I think it took us both a little while to figure out the best ways to support one another in our careers and in our roles as parents. Now, I am so thankful for the ways my husband has stepped

---

[1]Gretchen Livingston and Kim Parker, "8 Facts About American Dads," *Fact Tank* (blog), Pew Research Center, June 12, 2019, www.pewresearch.org/fact-tank/2019/06/12/fathers-day -facts/.

[2]All of the quotes in this chapter are from a survey we conducted with spouses of Christian academic mothers in June 2019. All sources wish to remain anonymous.

up to support me. He usually picks the kids up from school so that I can catch some extra work hours at the office before heading home. He is very involved in my daughters' lives, especially involved at their school serving on one of the parent boards. He doesn't mind that we eat take-out a lot, often offers to pick up food or do the grocery shopping. He is definitely an "acts of service" (five love languages) guy, and the only reason I can do this work/family thing is because of his partnership.

At the same time, husbands of Christian academics also lament not "spending enough time together at times" or how "her work never stops." There are compromises that dual-earning households must make for both partners to thrive.

Increasingly, more dads are staying home to care for their kids. The share of fathers who are stay-at-home dads rose from 4 percent in 1989 to 7 percent in 2016. As a result, dads made up 17 percent of all stay-at-home parents in 2016, up from 10 percent in 1989.[3] As more dads stay at home, many more mothers are working. In 1970, nearly half of families (47 percent) with children younger than eighteen had fathers as the sole breadwinner. That number has significantly diminished, only 27 percent of couples in 2016 have families where only the dad works.[4] Furthermore, more families have mothers as breadwinners.[5]

Men also report benefiting from having an academic partner who not only stimulates them intellectually, but also provides financially for their educational and philanthropic pursuits. One minister describes the perks of an academic partner:

> She is the smartest person I know (with a voracious appetite for knowledge about the world), so I constantly learn new things from her and, though it challenges me at times, I am made better by her feedback. I also appreciate the flexibility of her schedule as needed. Plus, she's my sugar mama who allows for me to do ministry full-time and still be sustainable!

---

[3]Livingston and Parker, "8 Facts About American Dads."
[4]Livingston and Parker, "8 Facts About American Dads."
[5]A. W. Geiger, Gretchen Livingston, and Kristen Bialik, "6 Facts about US Moms," *Fact Tank* (blog), Pew Research Center, May 8, 2019, www.pewresearch.org/fact-tank/2019/05/08/facts -about-u-s-mothers/.

EXTENDED NETWORKS AND SOLO PARENTING

Christian academic mothers also rely on extended family. One described the blessing of having her mother live nearby:

> My mom lives next door to me, literally two doors down. I try not to rely on her too much for childcare (she has her own life and especially after my father passed away, I want her to pursue the things she loves and build an identity for herself), but I know she is there and willing to help when I need it . . . and just having that knowledge is such a source of comfort for me.

Extended family help is even more essential for solo Christian academic mothers. In 2017, nearly one in four children in the United States were living with a solo mother.[6] The pressures of being a breadwinner and sole caregiver is immense for mothers. Statistically, the financial burdens are extremely high, with 30 percent of solo mothers and their families living in poverty compared with 17 percent of solo father families, 16 percent of families headed by a cohabiting couple, and 8 percent of married-couple families.[7] Deshonna Goubil-Collier shares her own story (below) of assembling a team-based village approach to parenting as a solo academic mom.

When I began this volume, I had planned to share my experience of birthing multiples. One year after beginning a dream job as the founding chair of a new academic department at my university, I learned that I was pregnant with twins. Life for me at that time was stressful. Leading a new program, driving recruitment during a time of enrollment decline, re-cruiting (and retaining) diverse faculty, being a woman of color in an academic leadership role in which there are not many, and then adding becoming a new mom to two darling infants was definitely a much fuller plate than I had ever imagined. I was sleep deprived, exhausted, joy filled, happy, busy, overwhelmed, and successful—all at the same time!

Two and a half short years into my new role as mom and breadwinner, I would experience yet another change, this one devastating. On the first

---

[6]Geiger, Livingston, and Bialik, "6 Facts about US Moms."

[7]Gretchen Livingston, "About One-Third of US Children are Living with an Unmarried Parent," April 27, 2018, *Fact Tank* (blog), Pew Research Center, www.pewresearch.org/fact-tank/2018/04/27 /about-one-third-of-u-s-children-are-living-with-an-unmarried-parent/.

day of spring break 2019, I became a widow. My husband died suddenly and unexpectedly due to a heart attack. My world shattered. While things had been challenging before, I had no marker, no guideposts, and no way to know how to move forward in this new and awful twist of life. During the first few weeks, I survived on autopilot. My sister, a dear friend from seminary, my best friend, my cousin, and my parents all immediately came to my aid—picking up children from school, feeding them, ensuring they bathed, ensuring I ate food (or some semblance of food). They escorted me to the mortuary, held my hand as I cried through making the final arrangements for my love. My pastors, friends, sorority sisters, church family, and university community extended themselves to me greatly. One dear friend set up a meal service for me, another created a video montage of family photos for the service, another introduced me to online grocery delivery services, and several others sent flowers, cards, notes of encouragement, and even helped me pack up my home (thank you Lord!). I have never in my life felt so enveloped by the everlasting love of God. That love has not stopped, extending to me today. Today it shows up in the village (team) that God has given me, which enables me to survive as a solo parent. (Some widows or widowers refer to ourselves as solo parents rather than single parents as it better describes our role as the sole surviving parent of children.)

Solo parenting with a support team. Seven months after my husband's death, I am getting used to my role as a solo parent. My children are happy and thriving due to my amazing team. I now feel as if I am a quarterback managing a team of star players to ensure that the joy of our lives (my children) are protected, safe, and continuing to learn and grow. The very first change I made was to move in with my parents. I am blessed and privileged to have parents who own a home with enough room for my twins and me to move in with them unexpectedly with no set move-out date in mind. Moving in with my parents in the early weeks and months after my husband's death provided me the peace of mind that someone would feed and clothe my children and get them to daycare even on my most grief-stricken days. Now, seven months later, living with my parents provides me extra help getting the children ready for school in the morning and someone else to assist with household tasks: cooking, cleaning, grocery shopping, and another set of eyes on nights when my workday has run long.

Childcare was the next large feat. Now that the grandparents' home has become our home, I needed to hire a babysitter who could provide my mom and me regular breaks throughout the week so that we do not burn out. The youth director at my church (and my really good friend) offered to step into this role for me. This was amazing! Someone I love and trust immensely and who has extensive experience with children (she is a teacher by profession) cares for my children two days a week, one weekday evening, and several hours on the weekend. This provides my mom and me a regular break and the ability for us to catch our breath, go see a movie, take a nap, or any other tasks that one would accomplish while their partner spent time with their children.

As a solo parent, time to yourself, sleeping in, or help with making even the most mundane decisions are all on you. After working a full day grading papers, preparing exams, running or attending administrative meetings, and working on research, I have to also show up for parent-teacher night, run to the store to pick up last-minute items on the school shopping list or toothpaste, keep children's schedules and important dates straight, plan birthday parties and outings, take children to those parties and outings alone (did I mention I have three-year-old twins?). Every so often, you need a bit more than a babysitter to provide you respite. In my village, my loving sister and best friend alternate flying into town one weekend a month to provide me help. Specifically, they help in making decisions, taking my kids on outings, cleaning up and organizing the mountain of paperwork affiliated with my husband's estate that stacks up on my mom's dining room table because I am just too tired most days to deal with it, or anything else the children and I need.[8]

---

[8]Dealing with the endless paperwork that comes with the death of a spouse can be overwhelming and grief inducing. I have managed to work on it in bursts. I might work on closing out accounts and making death notifications for a month, then I take a break for two months. It also depends on what else is going on at my job, the kids' school, and whether or not I am managing anxiety for a "special day" (anniversary, birthday, holiday, notable day for my children, etc.).

Walking through grief is a journey, and that journey has valleys, peaks, and deserts. My own mental health care includes attending a grief support group meeting weekly, one-on-one counseling with a licensed therapist who has had experience working with young widows, and occasional meetings with a family therapist who helps me to address grief-related issues manifesting in my children's behaviors. Being a young widow, I have to manage my grief, my children's grief, and my husband's estate, and I have to ensure that my husband's family still feels connected to my children and me—all on top of the regular responsibilities of any parent. I can burn out quickly if I am not watchful of my time, my energy, and "special" days. For widows, "special days" are those days in which the waves of grief might just take you out as you can never fully estimate what emotions will show up for you on certain dates. On my first Mother's Day without my spouse, for example, I thought I would be just fine. After all, it's Mother's Day. It's not a day for my husband (e.g., a birthday, Father's Day, or our anniversary); it's a day for moms! I usually spend Mother's Day cooking brunch for my mom, so I expected everything would be fine. I was so, so wrong. I failed to make a plan for myself that day and ended up in a very deep depression for the whole weekend. The thoughts of having to parent my children alone and no longer having a husband who will celebrate what an awesome mom I am on that day were more than I could bear. I have learned that I have to make plans for special days. I try to take a weekend out of town if I am able. In order for me to do this, my village, in the form of my cousins, will keep my children for me for the whole weekend! It works out wonderfully as my cousin is a "supermom" and my children love playing and spending time with her children. These are also days that I can let go and not worry at all about my children. I know they are safe, cared for, and loved.

I have become a master planner! A quarterback figuring out plays well in advance. I look months ahead on the calendar and coordinate with different members of my village to ensure that I have proper coverage for all of my children and my self-care needs. While we sometimes have hiccups and bumps along the road (like the time I drove two hours away for a work trip with all of the car seats in my car and I had to call my cousin last minute to go purchase new ones—that's a funnier story today than the two-hour panicked drive home was for me), God provided me with a village of people who are dedicated and committed to my children being surrounded in love, in spite of the ashes of having to grow up in a world without their dad.

Resources for solo academic mothers. I have come to find a few resources and good advice as a young widow that have helped me immensely. I will share some information here.[9] If you ever find yourself in shoes similar to mine (and I pray that you do not), get yourself connected to other widows! My "wisters" (widow sisters) have literally pulled me out of depression and anxiety, and they have provided clarity, great ideas, reassurance, and advice along my journey. One helped me to think through my financial decisions, another helped me prepare for widow life with children (e.g., that I will need to always keep copies of my husband's death certificate on hand throughout my children's lives since one never knows when I will be asked for it—did you know that you need a death certificate for each child when applying for a passport? I had no clue!). Yet another widow sister meets with me for coffee from time to time to check in and chat about all the things going on in life (e.g., returning to work, going on an outing with married friends for the first time, surviving my first Father's Day without hubby, etc.). This widow sister gave me information on "camp widow" (yes, there is a camp for widows!) and counseling, therapy, and camp recommendations for my children as they grow up (there are camps specifically for children who have lost a parent). Another widow sister sent me flowers and text messages, and she checked in with me regularly especially during those early weeks as she understands the depth of grief that I experience on this journey.

Next, I would highly recommend getting yourself into some form of counseling, whether it is a group counseling session similar to Grief

---

[9]I have chosen not to mention specific names of organizations as I have not personally tried out every resource mentioned. I hope that discussing some of the resources I am sharing will encourage you to seek out information and resources in your area.

Share[10] or individual therapy (or both). You will really need a space to express and process all of your raw emotions that come up with people who have clinical or pastoral training in aiding grieving people. My Grief Share group has been absolutely amazing! I have gone through the program three times and am hoping to become a group leader next year. There are days that I have surprised myself in giving advice and counsel to another grieving person and other times when I sit in the room silently for the entire session because I am so enveloped in a grief wave. Either way, having a specific day, time, and group to discuss my emotions related to grief have truly been a lifesaver. Having a good therapist is something I recommend for all faculty moms in general but for young widows especially; self-care (filling your cup) is the only way for you to then have room to assist others (e.g., your children, your students, coworkers, and staff).

Read books; listen to podcasts; join social media groups related to grief, grieving, and being a young widow. These resources will provide you tools, joy, and comic relief, and they will help you to understand that you are not alone, will answer tough questions, etc. They can truly be a godsend. During the first couple months, I read from *Widows Wear Stilettos* or *A Widow's Guide to Healing* every night.[11] These and other resources literally provided me lists that I could simply follow to walk me through the most seemingly simple tasks (for example, which governmental agencies to provide a death notification to—I never would have thought about informing the three major credit bureaus!).

Another good idea is to try to write down lists of things that you need. I find that with my added responsibilities, working through my own grief, navigating my children through their grief, and being a solo parent, I forget things often. I keep a running list of things that I need help with so that when a person offers to help me, I can provide them a concrete thing that I need help with in the moment. I have found this helpful especially when

---

[10]Grief Share is a ministry of Church Initiative. See www.griefshare.org. Grief Share is a Christian-based grief support program designed for those who have lost a spouse, child, family member, or friend.

[11]Carol Brody Fleet, *Widows Wear Stilettos* (Far Hills, NJ: New Horizon Press, 2009); Kristin Meekhof and James Windell, *A Widow's Guide to Healing* (Naperville, IL: Source Books, 2015).

I am feeling overwhelmed. Last, take moments often to recognize how amazing you are, noting that God actually *has* equipped *you* to live through even *this*! One of the intrusive thoughts I often have is that I cannot get through this task, event, or issue on my own.[12] I have learned to trust my subconscious and inner voice because that woman is fierce and she knows what she's doing! I have also learned to acknowledge that while I am doubting myself and my abilities, I am actually accomplishing the task. I have learned that I really can do *all things* through Christ who strengthens me (see Philippians 4:13). Most importantly, take moments to stand in awe and gratitude of God's ultimate provision for you and your children's lives. The thought that will lead me to tears every day is to look back over these last awful months and see how God has continuously provided every single little thing that I've needed time and time again. God knew that it was my husband's time to return home; there was nothing that could be done about that. But God has shown me so much loving kindness as I walk through what had been my greatest fear. From differing groups of friends showing up at my home and packing, to those bringing food for my family to eat, to those texting and emailing me encouraging words or to check in, to those who have committed to meeting me for "fun lunch" dates to help ease my return to work, to those who pray for me without me even knowing, I am firmly rooted in the understanding that I serve a God who cares for this little Black girl who grieves.

---

[12]In these moments, I also practice deep breathing, mindfulness, and thought deconstruction as instructed by my therapist.

NAVIGATING
MARRIAGE AS
THE BREADWINNER

JOY E. A. QUALLS, PhD

SEVERAL YEARS AGO, while lecturing in a class, I asked my students several questions about gender roles: What is great about being a woman/man? What is hard about being a man/woman? One brave young man in the back raised his hand. His name was Billy. He proudly proclaimed, "It is great to be a man because we get to lead women." You could hear the air go out of the room and all eyes were suddenly on me. I team taught this interdisciplinary class with a male colleague who gave me a knowing glance as if to say, "This one is all yours." Ours was a deeply conservative evangelical Christian university, and while I knew that I had a reputation around the university as an advocate for women's leadership and even proudly wore the title of resident feminist, my perspective was not always supported by the majority of our community. As such, I also knew that the room was filled with both young men and young women who expected that I would destroy poor Billy with my response. I did not intend to shame Billy, nor any who viewed the world like he did, but I also felt the weight of responsibility in my answer. So I walked to the front of the large lecture hall and laid my arms on the front tables. I looked up at the room full of intense stares and I said this: "Do you know how my husband leads our family? My husband walked away from years of education and work experience to become a full-time stay-at-home parent to our two little ones. He cooks, he cleans, and he takes care of our children and he does it with a glad and grateful heart. He leads our family because he gave up himself, he died to all of his own ambition so that I could be in front of all of you today. He took on roles that other men (and some women too) mock, and he endures scorn from those who think he is diminished as a man because he stays home and I work for an income." I proceeded through tears to tell that room full of students that I believe my husband is one of the greatest leaders I have ever known because his leadership is the most Christlike I have ever known. My husband gave up everything and daily has to die to self and expectation to love and serve our family. That is leadership.

There were no standing ovations or cheers, just quiet murmurs as students left class that day, but in the years since, I have received notes, phone calls, and private Facebook messages from students in the room that day and colleagues who heard about it from others, both male and female, who have said they had never heard anything like that before, but that they were proud of my husband—and of me too. I, too, am proud of him, and I do believe he is a leader. While my work and my role are very public, the choices that he has made in the way he serves our family are as godly an example of leadership as I have ever known. We navigate a unique dynamic together and as a result, I believe we are stronger and know the faithfulness of God better than we may have in any other circumstances. I am proud of us as a family, too. I know that the God who calls is the One who leads our family so that together we more fully reflect his nature and being.

HOW WE BEGAN

We did not set out in our life and marriage to challenge the status quo or to be some sort of pioneer couple in reversing traditional roles. We did, however, take stock of where we were in our lives, education, and careers. The year we married, I was nearly done with my coursework for a PhD in communication studies and had spent several years working in government and higher education. I came to our marriage with a salary, health-care benefits, and a meager retirement account. Kevin, my husband, had a BA in psychology and philosophy and had spent several years working in social services, where he was overworked and underpaid. We knew that he would need additional education and licensure to grow in his own career, and shortly after our marriage, we would move across the country to continue his education while I wrote my dissertation.

Throughout the years leading up to our marriage, we had several discussions about what it would mean if I made more money, had a title, or progressed in my career in a way that outpaced his. As evangelical Christians, we had both been raised in cultures that spoke openly of the husband as provider and the one responsible for the financial health of the family. Kevin was raised in a more traditional household that met this cultural expectation. His father, a pastor, and mother, a homemaker who did not finish her own education until after her children were in school, were a lot like the families we may have seen in mid-twentieth-century television programming. I was the child of divorce and spent my teen years in a single parent household that included time on government assistance and little in the way of child support. While our family was not unusual—according to the United States Census Bureau, during the period from 1960–2016, the percentage of children living with only their mother nearly tripled from 8 to 23 percent—we were still the minority as 69 percent (47.7 million children) were raised by two married parents living in the same household.[1] While our expectations for our family structure might be different from one another, we knew our lives and family would be our own.

If there were assumptions about our family and our roles, they were that both of us would work and that our long-term plans included careers in the academy for each of us. Yet, like many couples in the twenty-first-century

---

[1] U.S. Census Bureau, "The Majority of Children Live with Two Parents, Census Bureau Reports." April 10, 2018, www.census.gov/newsroom/press-releases/2016/cb16-192.html.

recession, student loan debt and challenging wage stagnation forced us to rethink the ways in which we approached work and family. In addition to economic uncertainty, we became the parents of two beautiful children within thirteen months of each other and in the midst of my defending my dissertation. After four years of adjunct work and time spent as a director of enrollment, I was offered a full-time teaching contract while still in the hospital shortly after having given birth to our second child, a son. While it appeared as if our dreams were becoming a reality, our true reality was one where we were struggling to pay our bills while trying to work and raise a family.

FACING FAMILY REALITIES

After having both finished a graduate degree and achieved licensure in professional counseling, my husband made the decision to join two million other American men and walk away from full-time work and assume the role of primary caregiver for our two children. We made the decision together after considering the culture of the organization he worked for, the out-of-pocket costs for travel and other work expenses that we paid then waited for reimbursement, and the time spent away from our family. Yet the weight of the change was on his shoulders. Our babies were three and two; childcare and household help were stretching us to the limit; and, combined with a challenging work environment, the opportunity for a break was welcome for both of us. Even still, we believed this change was temporary. Kevin quickly secured adjunct teaching assignments that allowed him to be home during the day and still pursue his own career development. Two years later, when the opportunity came for me to accept a role as department chair and be placed on the tenure track, we thought a lot about how a cross-country move and a promotion would once again upend the dynamic of our family. On the face value, a better salary and growth opportunities made the change appealing, but the significant increase in cost of living, lengthy commutes, and differences between state licensure requirements for Kevin would create additional pressures and challenges. The move we would make to California seemed to be one of new opportunities for us both, but once again, we would navigate uncertainty and discover that our lives were never going to fit into some prescribed ideal for life, career, and family.

While we may not have set out to live a life that is "nontraditional" or "upside down," it is the life that we lead, and we have trusted the Lord to guide us in our family choices. Ephesians 5 is often cited as a reference for how husbands and wives are supposed to relate to one another and to their families. In Ephesians 5:21, Paul writes that we are to submit ourselves one to another as unto the Lord. In this mutuality, Paul continues, wives are to submit to their husbands as the church submits to Christ and husbands are to love their wives as Christ loved the church and gave himself up for it. This has been our primary aim as a couple and for our family: that we would live in mutuality toward one another and choose to defer to the other regardless of cultural, societal, or even religious expectation. We believe this honors the Lord and he has blessed us as a result.

THRIVING AS A SINGLE-INCOME FAMILY

Nearly five years into our "new" life in California, we remain a single-income household in one of the most expensive states in the country, and my husband remains the primary member of our family responsible for childrearing and household duties. In many ways this life is challenging, but it is also a life where we have found rhythm and are thriving. We have two healthy and wickedly smart children, we live in a beautiful neighborhood, and we are, for all intents and purposes, a middle-class family. The difference is that I, as the mother who works outside our home, am the only income earner, and my husband is the stay-at-home parent who spends his days meal planning and volunteering at our children's school. While we still dream of lives where both of us are growing in our careers and sharing the responsibilities of home, we accept that this is the life that God has given us, and we are learning to navigate it to his glory, one day at a time.

So what have we learned on this journey together? What does it mean to be a family that is both evangelical and one where the woman is the sole provider and outward leader while the husband tends to the home and family? What have we learned about our relationship to one another, our children, and to the God who called us to these spaces and seasons? Our journey has not been an easy one. But what I can declare is this: the God who calls is faithful. He is faithful to me as a wife, a mom, a scholar, and a departmental leader, but he is equally as faithful to my husband as he leads through care and dedication to our children, our home, and to his own journey of trust that this, too, is just a season.

First, the dynamic of our family would not work if we were not both on the same page and in agreement about the roles we do play. This was not always easy. In the early days after my husband left full-time work, I would often come home to a house that was in chaos and children who had clearly had a day of fun and play. One of the first questions I would be asked when I walked in the door was, "What do you think we should do for dinner?" I fought a lot of resentment and anger as I would go to the kitchen to begin what has become known for many working women as the second shift. We ate poorly thought-out or flavorless slow-cooked meals. We were ships passing in the night who barely had a conversation. I would often cry alone because I was never the one who got to play and have fun. We recognized this quickly and had a very intentional conversation. To be a stay-at-home parent was work. Hard work. But it also meant that care for the home and things like meal planning had to primarily belong to the one who was working at home. We talked, we cried, we prayed, and we planned. From that moment on, my husband assumed these responsibilities with intensity. He acknowledged that "girl laundry" scared him and many a meal resembled those his mom is famous for. But he stepped up to the plate and gave me back time with our kids and each other that was not filled with resentment or anger.

I also had to accept that who I was as a mom would be different than what I see portrayed in popular media, parenting books, or church discussions on motherhood. When one of our kids is sick or has woken up with a night terror, they call for their daddy and walk all the way across the room past me to get to him first. I wrestle with guilt about how much time and attention I give them because of the demands of my work and travel schedule. I am often out of the loop on what is going on at school or in their clubs and sports programs. As with the division of responsibilities, we had to learn to be intentional as parents to share information about our kids' lives and who they are becoming as people. I had to set boundaries with regard to when I leave work, how often I travel, and putting away my phone so email and texts do not steal my time and attention. I melt when my kids tell me that I am the best mom in the world because I often feel like others may be saying just the opposite about me. But I also see the ways my kids are learning to speak differently about Kevin and me as their parents. I am the best mom because I provide for them and give them the life we talk about having. Kevin is the best dad because he provides for them food, laundry, and help with homework. He volunteers in their school and I take them on work trips to fun, new cities. We both parent them and are raising them, but they speak of who we are in ways that are less gendered and more tied to our giftings and actions.

Second, we had to be intentional about our own rhythms as well as our relationships with the Lord. I once read an interview of former first lady Michelle Obama. She talked about her own journey as a working mother and the resentment she had early on as her husband slept soundly while she fed a baby and felt badly about herself. She determined to wake at 5 a.m. and take time for a workout. When their daughter needed feeding, if she was not there, her husband would do it—and sure enough, he did. The story goes that to this day, she still works out at 5 a.m. and that those killer arms are the result, as is a happier marriage and a deeper love for her children and herself. I took Mrs. Obama's words to heart. I do not have the killer arms, but I do wake up at 5 a.m. I walk the dog and I come home to coffee made before I left. For the next hour, until the children need to get up for school and the house comes alive, I sit in a chair in our living room where the Spirit of the Lord meets me in prayer, Bible study, and journaling. My husband is a night owl and long after the kids and I are asleep, his patterns are similar (minus the coffee) and there in the stillness he meets with God. This intentionality of cultivating our own devotional lives has made a tremendous difference because we are both emotionally and spiritually healthy.

My role as department chair also affords me some privileges in terms of time and presence in the office. I choose to take Fridays as a work-from-home day. As a result, we have chosen to take intentional time on Friday either before the workday or after to take "date" time together where we talk about life, work, and finances—and where we dream. It is also sometimes where we fight and deal with the challenges of our lives. According to the National Marriage Project, a comprehensive quantitative study out of the University of Virginia, the study showed improvements for married couples who go on frequent dates across categories such as happiness, commitment, communication, parenthood stability, and community integration.[2] This study also indicates that there are lower divorce rates and a higher perceived quality of marriage among couples who devote time together at least once a week. The research bears out in our experience as well; this time together has become essential to the rhythm of our lives and while it is not always fun and games, it is a time that serves to enrich who we are as a couple and as a team.

We are active in our church and in our denomination. While we consider ourselves evangelicals, we are intentional about belonging to a church that affirms not only our family dynamic but specifically women as leaders. Both my research agenda and my lived experience as a woman in leadership within a Christian context are the result of the distinct call of God on my life. In 2018, I published my first book, *God Forgive Us for Being Women: Rhetoric, Theology, and the Pentecostal Tradition*.[3] In it, I engage in a rhetorical history of my own faith tradition and the theology of women's leadership in the church. The narratives of women and how they have negotiated and renegotiated their roles in church leadership over the last century inspired and challenged me as I pursue God's best for my own

---

[2]Bradford W. Wilcox and Jeffrey Dew, *The Date Night Opportunity: What Does Couple Time Tell Us About the Potential Value of Date Nights?* (Charlottesville, VA: The National Marriage Project, 2012).

[3]Joy E. A. Qualls, *God Forgive Us for Being Women: Rhetoric, Theology, and the Pentecostal Tradition* (Eugene, OR: Pickwick, 2018).

ministry leadership and for my family. My husband affirms my calling and is one of the first to promote my work to others. We were intentional about finding a faith community that would not only support that but provide space for both of us to serve and lead. This is no small task, but we are grateful for pastors (one of whom is a woman) and church leadership who come alongside us to support our family and to share the areas where we still need work.

Finally, we have learned that our family will not succeed or fail based on prescribed notions of roles. Our family will succeed or fail based on how we relate to one another and how we trust the Lord to lead us in ways we are unable to do on our own. We are constantly negotiating and renegotiating the ways in which we use our time, our money, and our talents to serve our family as well as our callings and the command to make disciples of Jesus. Some days are tremendously hard. We have both struggled with seasons of depression and anxiety. We have wrestled with financial challenges. We have not always treated each other with respect for the various challenges that our current roles demand of us. But that is where God is greater than any circumstances we encounter. When we are intentional about a life connected to the Spirit, we navigate the challenges as well as we navigate the benefits. And there are benefits. Kevin is an amazing father to our children. I often brag he is a much better parent than I will ever be. He is attentive and thoughtful to their unique personalities and strengths. His training in child development and family systems helps him address both their needs and their challenges with grace and thoughtfulness. He is a favorite among the faculty and administration of our children's school because he is a faithful volunteer and active in the Parent Teacher Organization. Our kids are secure in who they are, and they are becoming amazing people. That is primarily because of the influence of their dad. Our kids, too, are thoughtful and articulate about who their mom is, and they often express gratefulness for the work I do that provides for them and allows them opportunity to participate in various activities and organizations. Our daughter expresses a clear call to ministry and speaks openly about the Holy Spirit speaking to her. Our son is deeply passionate and intense. He expresses himself creatively and works harder than any child I know to be the best at all he puts his mind to. Our children love Jesus and talk openly of their love for our church.

We are honest with our kids about the struggles and challenges we face as a family. We live in a rented home and things like vacations and time with extended family are rare. The choices that we have made have consequences, and while not all of those consequences are negative, they do come at a cost. Our kids pray that God would lead us and that eventually their daddy would be able to go back to work too.

I think often about that day in class where Billy bravely stated that the best thing about being a man was that men get to lead women. He, as a young evangelical male, had been brought up to believe that he had a specific place and a specific role as a man regardless of the woman he might marry or the children he might raise. The culture he knew was one where men lead and women follow. That includes very specific leadership including work roles, provision of money, and responsibilities in the home. But it also includes a very specific narrative about arbitrary boundaries that limit the experiences of both men and women in relationship to one another. For men and women whose lived experiences do not fit neatly into that narrative, it can create cognitive dissonance for those in the relationship and those outside watching the family dynamic.

As a wife and mother, I am proud of the life that God has given to me and to my family. We may not have set out to be an example family, but we have embraced the example that we do provide. I am privileged to live the life and do the work that I am called to do because my husband has embraced the life and calling that God has given him to do. We take seriously the command of Ephesians 5 to submit ourselves to one another out of our love for Jesus Christ. We also embrace the commands of love and respect for one another in this complex season of our lives. I know that my husband loves me because he dies to self and cultural expectations daily out of his submission to Christ. I also know that he respects me in my role as a teacher, scholar, and leader. I respect my husband for the leadership he demonstrates in our home and in his care for our children. I submit myself to his leadership of sacrifice and my love for him grows as a result. We are certainly not perfect, but the life that we live is a testament to the faithfulness of a God who calls, and when the day comes that we stand before him, our family will be a testament to his faithfulness not to our roles, but to our obedience.

EMPOWERMENT OF PROFESSOR MOMS THROUGH MENTORSHIP

DORETHA O'QUINN, PʜD

AS AN AFRICAN AMERICAN SENIOR PROFESSOR MOM, I often reflect on my own development from adjunct professor to provost and vice president for academic affairs with no formal mentoring opportunities. I was very isolated in the predominantly White evangelical Christian higher education community. As an African American woman, I had no peers who looked like me nor who understood the dynamics of my life and cultural experience, no one who could journey together with me as a professor mom. I can truly say that the Holy Spirit became my personal mentor and revealed leadership truth through gifts (wisdom, knowledge, faith). Books, conferences, and research also contributed to my development. My experience fans the flame of my passionate desire for investing as a mentor in young professor moms to realize what they possess as multitasking, professionally trained, strategic thinkers and planners, equipped for all good work and empowered by the Holy Spirit to influence the academy.

Over the years, I met several young professor moms who were often convinced that they did not fit in as scholars in higher education. They spoke of being overwhelmed with balancing the world of work, motherhood, church, and so forth. They asked, if they couldn't meet the expectations of others, what value would they add? I confess that—after thirty years with the same responsibilities they faced with minimal to no support or encouragement from anyone—I wanted to cynically scream out, "Give me a break!" But I understood what they were experiencing was real and wanted to validate their reality. I recognized the cultural diversity among the group and myself in race, ethnicity, age, social status or class, values, and beliefs. There were years of marriage; child rearing; professor rank and roles; ministry levels; and more between me and these professor moms. Furthermore, higher education has undergone much organizational culture change since I was at their life stage. I came to see that investing in the development and growth of these professor moms could be an opportunity for me to find ways to navigate the challenges successfully together. As a senior professor mom, it was a delight and honor to take this opportunity to invest in these young professor moms. They would never experience aloneness in the academy if I had my say. In this chapter, I describe the process of mentoring as an effective leadership development tool for professor moms and self-care as an essential tool for sustainability in the academy.

WHAT IS THE ORIGIN OF MENTORING?

Mentoring in early society or civilization was uniquely gender-based. It was tradition and commonplace to partner young men in these times with older, experienced males. Often, the older men were relatives, and it was hoped that they would act like teachers and personal friends, instructing the young men in the ways of the world and guiding them in developing values. Generals of the Roman legion worked alongside mentors who advised them at battle. Medieval guild masters instructing apprentices were responsible for the schooling of their craft and, importantly, for the development of their apprentices' social, spiritual, and personal beliefs and values. During the early years of building the United States, mentors were used to train the apprentices (male children) in the workplace as farmers, silversmiths, scribers, factory workers, etc. Mentoring was the chief learning method in the society of artisans; an apprentice spent years at the side of the craftsman learning not only the mechanics of a function, but the "way of life" which surrounded it.[1] Throughout biblical history, mentoring was a common practice in society for developing leaders. Leaders during biblical history saw the value of women leaders in the military, as educators, national leaders, businesswomen, and more. Women of the Bible such as Ruth (Naomi), Esther (Mordecai), and Priscilla (Paul) were developed as leaders using a process that included instruction in the Hebrew Scriptures. Today, women carry on mentoring in various capacities and venues. In Christian higher education, mentoring continues to be practiced in this traditional manner. Conger and Benjamin define such mentoring as a form of socializing the vision, values, and culture of the time to the younger generation.[2]

WHAT IS THE MEANING OF MENTORING?

According to Clinton and Clinton, mentoring is not a single act but an ongoing process.[3] It is a process in which a person with a serving, giving, and encouraging attitude (the *mentor*) sees leadership potential in a still-to-be developed person (the *mentee, future, protégé*) and is able to promote or otherwise significantly influence the mentee along the realization of potential. In my own career, to make this mentoring process a reality and place the definition into action, I chose to set up formal meetings to ensure the mentoring process became intentional. The professor moms took the initiative to make this happen, not knowing the impact it would have on

---

[1]Conger and Benjamin, *Building Leaders*, 79-101.
[2]Jay Conger and Beth Benjamin, *Building Leaders: How Successful Companies Develop the Next Generation* (New York: Jossey Bass, 1999), 79-101.
[3]J. Robert Clinton and Richard W. Clinton, *The Mentor Handbook* (Altadena, CA: Barnabas Publishers, 1991).

their lives as influencers. Professor moms wrestle with many controversial thoughts about their personal ability to excel in the academy because of the traditional mindsets (usually male dominant) that captivate their thinking. Self-doubt, personal sabotage, guilt, or questioning themselves about being an effective mom or competent professor, lack the knowledge of navigating the bureaucracy, politics, and organizational culture of the academy—all these can daily haunt the professor mom. Equipping professor moms through the mentoring process is nonnegotiable.

Clinton and Clinton describe the formal mentoring process I implemented. It consisted of using ten rules, or "The Ten Commandments of Mentoring."[4] The list includes, in order

1. Relationship: Establish the relationship.

2. Purpose: Jointly agree on the purpose of the relationship.

3. Regularity: Determine the regularity of relationship.

4. Accountability: Determine the type of accountability.

5. Communication: Set up communication mechanisms.

6. Confidentiality: Clarify the level of confidentiality.

7. Life Cycle: Set the life cycle of the relationship.

8. Feedback: Evaluate the relationship from time to time.

9. Revise Expectations: Modify expectations to fit the real-life mentoring situation.

10. Closure: Bring closure to the mentoring relationship.

In addition to the process of building mentoring relationships using these ten commandments, I also identified what I called the "Be-Attitudes of Mentoring." They were essential attitudes for developing a healthy mentoring relationship:

1. Be objective.

2. Be a person of honesty.

---

[4]Clinton and Richard W. Clinton, *The Mentor Handbook*, 141.

3. Be vulnerable.

4. Be a good role model.

5. Be a teacher.

6. Be a learner.

7. Be a good listener.

8. Be open and transparent.

9. Be deeply committed.

10. Be available.

The multiple roles of professor moms are often challenging. These challenges, however, can become opportunities of influence. *Leadership* is defined by many as one who influences others, so I began with leadership development and managing the various components impacting the life responsibilities of a professor mom at a relational level. I also reflected on my own personal process of development in leadership, which I could now name and which empowered me as a leader. This process included individual accountability and modeling of my pastor's wife, my maternal grandmother ("Big Mama"), and my mother. During my early years of schooling in the academy, it also included a couple of male and female professors. My leadership development was an unnamed process that we now call mentoring.[5]

In the early 2000s, I taught several courses in mentoring for developing leaders for the twenty-first century. During this time, reports identified continued marginalization of women faculty, and the culture of academia was described as less than hospitable to women as they attempted to navigate the various aspects of their positions and environments.[6] Rios and Lognion described women's view of themselves as "outsiders" in the

---

[5]Ted W. Engstrom, *The Fine Art of Mentoring, Passing On to Others What God Has Given to You* (Newburgh, IN Trinity Press, 1989).

[6]J. Glazer-Raymo, *Shattering the Myths: Women in Academe* (Baltimore, MD: Johns Hopkins University Press, 1999); F. A. Hamrick, "'I Have Work to Do': Affirmation and Marginalization of Women Full Professors." Paper presented at the Annual Meeting of the American Educational Research Association, San Diego, CA, April 1998; N. Hopkins, "MIT and Gender Bias: Following Up on Victory," *Chronicle of Higher Education*, June 11, 1999.

academy.[7] In addition, no assistance was available in gaining access to information networks and organizational systems in the academy that supported women in achieving success. Gibson identified in her phenomenological study the role of organizational politics and culture in the mentoring of women faculty.[8] She found that a mentoring culture for women in the academy (or lack thereof) can promote (or impede) success for professor moms. Gibson's case studies identified characteristics of organizational politics that promoted success, and these included the academy providing a formal mentoring process led by senior faculty; a mentoring committee involved in the interview process; supportive department members dedicated to assisting mothers and their work-life balance needs; and special rewarding of mentors. All these factors supported the development of women faculty and those who are professor moms so they could experience success in the academy.[9]

MENTORING IN PRACTICE

I had the perfect opportunity to apply research and theory into practice when I became intentional about my influence in the lives of the professor moms at my institution. I made myself available to begin the process of developing a professor-mommy affinity group. We set up meeting times for the group and identified a regular location. During the meetings, we addressed a range of topics: insecurities of husbands; carpool clashes; managing meals; back to school nights that conflicted with teaching schedules; housekeeping; wifely duties; personal eating and care habits; childcare challenges; teaching responsibilities; and balancing scholarship for advancing in the academy through writing, conference attendance, etc. The research of Wanberg, Welsh, and Hezlett provided a helpful description and definition of the type of relationships we were developing in the academy. Clearly, they were mentoring relationships embedded in a larger

---

[7]A. Rios and J. Longnion, *Agenda for the 21st Century: Executive Summary*, National Initiative for Women in Higher Education, Minneapolis: University of Minnesota, 2000.
[8]S. Gibson, "Mentoring of Women Faculty: The Role of Organizational Politics and Culture," *Innovative Higher Education* 31, no. 2 (2006): 69-71.
[9]Gibson, "Mentoring of Women Faculty."

organizational context, reflecting the values and attitudes held by organizational members and the organizational culture as a whole.[10] Gibson further posits the need for a variety of human resource (HR) and organizational development (OD) initiatives to address institutional climate issues in support of women's career advancement—in particular young women with families and other life-work balance needs.[11]

During our personal meetings at this Christian university, we discussed church responsibilities because of the requirement in a Christian university to be active in the local church. These requirements consist of, but are not limited to, attending Sunday mornings and midweek worship services and other forms of church ministry leadership. Active involvement was required as a part of the annual contractual agreement as well as promotion in faculty rank. This requirement was often challenging for professor moms, especially those with young children. Additional time away from home, additional childcare, support with homework, work responsibilities, etc., made it difficult to maintain a healthy home and work expectations. There were other topics as well, each of which I related to personally and could present ways in which the mentoring process could address what was unique to each participant.

Each professor mom had individual challenges that allowed me to meet separately in a mentoring relationship. In the area of church responsibilities, I had the opportunity to share ways to manage time and decide which service to attend that would accommodate the family and would not interfere with current schedules. There were issues with husbands who were intimidated by the accomplishment of the professor mom. I had the opportunity to share my husband's story of affirming my identity and how his support for me was support for the family. He recognized we were in this work together, and that gave him such satisfaction knowing I was doing what I was created to do. Each topic discussed involved looking strategically at ways to address their issues with their personal and family

[10]C. R. Wanberg, E. T. Welsh, and S. Hezlett, "Mentoring Research: A Review and Dynamic Process Model," in G.R. Ferris (Ed.), *Research in Personnel and Human Resource Management*, vol. 22 (Oxford: Elsevier, 2003), 39-124.
[11]Gibson, "Mentoring of Women Faculty."

life experience. The time together with the professor moms were so rewarding, but not without lots of prayer, tears, laughter, and definite times of praise for God's revelation of his plan.

Mentoring is a process I take seriously. First, ground rules of trust were established: confidentiality, time commitment, and willingness to be vulnerable. Time and vulnerability were my greatest investment to these moms. I wanted them to take the investment in their lives seriously as an act of reciprocity and respect. The knowledge I was gaining about contemporary motherhood from the professor moms was the act of reciprocity as I invested my knowledge and experience in them. Over the years while investing in mentoring relationships and experiences, there were many stories. I want to share a collective set of experiences in a few combined examples. The stories are not of one individual person but a collective, and "Cassie" is a pseudonym. The first story represents, first, the willingness to be vulnerable at the start of a mentorship relationship.

Cassie came to the meeting very frustrated. She sat down and was out of breath when she said, "That's it. I quit. I can't please anyone. My husband's mad at me. I was just too tired last night. I forgot it was my time to carpool after school today, until the kids reminded me on the way to work and I had to cut my class short. How could I be so stupid? And get this, a student had the nerve to complain to the chair about my class and he took the student's side on the issue. So what do you have to say, Dr. D.? I bet nothing like this ever happened to you!"

In order to use the mentoring process to assist Cassie, it was important that she knew she was not alone nor was she the first professor mom to have this experience. Cassie and I had a personal relationship and based on the intensity of what she was experiencing, she needed validation. I was able to defuse her anxiety by sharing my personal outcome and my plan to journey with her through this mentoring relationship. I used this mentoring relationship as a time to provide personal professional development. We discussed the importance of having systems: living by a calendar (there weren't any cell phones in my professor-mom days); sitting down with the spouse at the beginning of the school year to share schedules; matching teaching days with the other parents to make sure from the beginning of the year systems are in place.

I informed her of a positive development I'd previously made by placing concerns on the faculty meeting agenda that influenced the way my chair addressed student concerns, which resulted in our department developing student policies for filing complaints. I believe in the Matthew 18:15-17 principle, which involves going directly to the person offended or who created the offence for reconciliation. If there's not reconciliation, you bring a third party to hear both sides. If that does not work, it's very probable there will be no resolution and both parties should end the relationship. This principle became our guiding principle.

Calendars, planning strategically, communicating, valuing your voice at the table as you invite others to engage for your personal success, and caring well for yourself—all are characteristics leaders develop. The goal of mentoring is empowerment. Cassie took notes on our discussion and set to work addressing the things she could implement and facilitating department discussions around conflict resolution, both skills she and I have since also shared with other colleagues. When I left that university, several professor moms were well on their way to success and now serve in leadership positions in the academy. Their diverse cases allow me to reflect on my opportunities and my commitment to mentoring professor moms.

Peddy sums up the mentoring process in eight words "lead, follow, and get out of the way."[12] Leading is described as showing the way by role modeling, experience, or example; following, as advising and counseling (when asked); and getting out of the way as the art of withdrawing from a supportive relationship, while leaving the door open for a more collegial one. Peddy's discussion leads to what I consider the outcome of reaching the goal of the mentoring process, which is *empowerment*. James Belasco references empowerment as the key goal for releasing leaders in his book *Teaching the Elephant to Dance*. Empowerment is

---

[12]Shirley Peddy, *The Art of Mentoring, Lead, Follow, and Get out of the Way* (Houston: Bullion Books, 1998).

the igniting of a fire within the mentee that unleashes the latent talent, ingenuity, and creativity to do whatever is necessary and consistent with the principles of an agreed-upon mentoring plan to accomplish the goal.[13]

DEVELOPING A MENTORING PROGRAM

How does one begin a mentoring program for professor moms at the academy? One of the most important contributions to the effectiveness of mentoring in the academy is the support and advocacy of university leadership. The mentoring program's design, in the academies I've worked with, began with the support of the university president. This support contributes to the sustainability, community affirmation, and resources for the program. The positive and supportive relationship I had with each president greatly influenced beginning the mentoring process at each academic institution. I was able to share the need for mentoring of professor moms in my role as a senior female leader. Each were affirming and offered support as well as openness to learn. In one case, I prepared a formal proposal and partnered with human resources to ensure funding for support and sustainability. The desired hope and outcome were to institutionalize the process as life-giving to professor moms and women on campus.

Mentoring groups in the academy can be managed by committee, human resources, academic departments, and other supplemental committees in the institution. Any form of collaboration or working interdepartmentally strengthens the opportunity for institutionalizing the process and ensuring success for professor moms. Each university has its own organizational structure and institutional processes for strategic initiatives. A mentoring program to develop emerging female leaders could be a strategic initiative funded by the institution, which would make the program sustainable. To begin the process, one should know the guidelines for the unique institution.

---

[13]James A. Belasco, *Teaching the Elephant to Dance, The Manager's Guide to Empowering Change* (New York: Penguin Books, 1991), 17-30.

The role of mother involves many qualities of leadership. Professor moms are often not aware of skills in motherhood that translate into skills of leadership. The work of managing schedules, carpools, dinner, and basic household responsibilities are qualities of strategic planning; managing finances at home are skills of budget management; discipline of children is part of the vision planning process; other external responsibilities are skills of multitasking. Many other transferable leaderships skills are discussed in the book *Mothers are Leaders*.[14] Often the assumption is that people are born leaders. But rather, empowerment advances ability, as does discovering the hidden or latent talent that has never been resourced. This is my goal as a mentor of young professor moms. Everything that seems to challenge success in the academy requires an internal look at the professor mom herself and what she brings to all the tables where she sits (dinner, living room, conference room, church table, soccer or cheer, etc.). The target of the mentoring process is empowerment. Many professor mothers know they have talent, gifts, training, preparation, and leadership ability but require a fan for that flame, so they can understand the process of turning skills into action.

THE ROLE OF SELF-CARE IN THE LIFE OF PROFESSOR MOMS

Professor moms will make it by *caring for themselves* while leading others. As a professor mom, the discovery that contributed most to my successful work experience was learning to care well for myself. I often found my focus was meeting the expectations of others and making sure others were satisfied or felt complete in their work, at my personal expense. Areas of personal impact to my self-care included sleep deprivation, guilt, fear of failure, lack of exercise, low personal time with friends and family (especially my husband), lack of consistency in my spiritual disciplines, and no quiet time for myself. I needed self-care. My husband, a pastoral friend, and several written resources I reference later challenged me to consider my personal well-being.

---

[14]Kimberly Walters-Denu and Janet Walters, *Mothers are Leaders* (Abilene, TX: Abilene Christian University Press, 2016).

My journey of self-care began as I had to realize my personal need to forgive myself for not taking care of me. My own self-care had a gradual beginning and continues to be a daily, ongoing process that requires personal commitment. I began with restoration of my spiritual disciplines of worship, prayer, Scripture reading, and church involvement. The internal strength I gained from building spiritual disciplines began my focus on continual external needs. I addressed my physical care by joining a fitness center and changing my eating habits. I also protected personal time for nails, hair, and personal body care. I recognized the need to own my time and placed boundaries on work and home responsibilities. I refused to allow overlapping of work responsibilities and home of any kind. We developed Sunday dinners for adult children and their families, an intentional time to be together as a family. My husband and I developed a commitment to spend a weekend a month to get away and have Saturday standard date nights. I implemented personal retreats, sabbath and solitude for my quiet time at home, hotel, or timeshare. My social and emotional care involved monthly scheduled meals, movies, and other activities with friends and mentors. I made a commitment to have fun! I became involved with several civic community organizations that had nothing to do with work. Learning to care well for myself continues to revolutionize my life. I am intentional about sustaining the changes in my life and guard them as nonnegotiable for my success. Now that I am a grandmother, I often get reality checks from my grandchildren on their observation and their perspective of my work and life balance.

What does it mean to care well for yourself? What is wellness? Barnes and Vanderpool define wellness as the integration of many different components (spiritual, mental/emotional, social, intellectual, physical) that expand one's potential to live (quality of life) and work effectively to make a significant contribution to society.[15] Wellness reflects how one feels about life as well as one's ability to function effectively. Here's how professor moms will make it. The statement below is so important for wellness of

---

[15]Darvin E. Barnes and Kenneth G. Vanderpool, *Fitness and Wellness Strategies* (New York: WCB/McGraw-Hill, 1997).

professor moms as stated earlier and bears repeating: kids, husbands, members of the family, the administration, colleagues, and students are not in control of your success as a professor mom; *you are.*

Caring for yourself is what Rima explains as "God placing more value on the life of the leader than on the practice of the leader." This is a process of self-leadership and grows the ability to lead from the inside-out.[16] Rima speaks of the importance of the leader recognizing two important factors about leading and caring well for yourself.

1. Articulate and embrace your life's values. What are the non-negotiables in your life?

Anything that is nonnegotiable in one's life is considered a value. This is the first stage of self-care. Professor moms must prioritize what values are critical for success as a person, wife, mother, and other roles and responsibilities. They articulate and embrace them. Empowerment occurs when professor moms own their values and identify their goals in each of their roles, which is critical for self-care. Moms' roles will have numerous transitions, but clear values will contribute to sustainability of non-negotiables. Professor roles will also undergo transition or even change, but values can and will often resurface at a different level with diverse responsibilities over time.

2. Connect with your life's calling. How do you acknowledge all the roles that you are tasked with? Do you really understand calling, especially as it relates to a task or assignment from God?

I believe strongly that professor moms must wrestle to answer these questions to resolve how they will own their life's journey. Christian professor moms must recognize they have God leading ambitions. If he is central to their desired outcomes, it won't be hard to ask the serious question, "What would you call me to do?" and listen for God's response. Two other books were influential in my development of strong self-care practices, *Sacred Rhythms* and *Strengthening the Soul of Your Leadership*, both by Ruth Haley Barton.[17]

---

[16]Samuel Rima, *Leading from the Inside Out* (Grands Rapids, MI: Baker, 2000), 47-53
[17]Ruth Barton, Ruth, *Sacred Rhythms* (Downers Grove, IL: InterVarsity Press, 2006); *Strengthening the Soul of Your Leadership* (Downers Grove, IL: InterVarsity Press, 2008).

Barton discusses in *Strengthening the Soul of Your Leadership* the symptoms that manifest when professor moms don't take care of themselves. Forging and maintaining a life-giving connection with God is the best choice you can make for yourself and those you lead. Professor moms must recognize there is a need to make changes when poor self-care behaviors occur. A lack of wellness will impact your life, and those you influence will suffer. The mentoring process in the academy will contribute to the development of healthy leaders who will advance women in leadership in Christian higher education.

CONCLUSION

Over the course of my career, I have mentored and guided many women in the process of becoming successful professor moms. Their unique stories, situations, fields, and family dynamics have sharpened me and helped me see more clearly the common challenges that lie under individual experiences. These challenges can become opportunities for influence.

Two essential skills I consider guiding principles in all mentoring to professor moms are leadership development and practices of self-care. Professor moms are positioned strategically to be able to influence organizational change and uniquely equipped for this task if they draw on the skills mothering builds in them. To have such influence, professor moms must lead in all areas of their lives from a place of wellness—spiritually, physically, emotionally, and in personal care. When professor moms articulate and embrace their life values and connect with their life's calling, they become healthy professor moms. Then they can, in turn, influence and partner with institutional leaders, particularly the university president, to implement mentoring processes that bring mutual benefit and success to the academy and to professor moms.

EPILOGUE

PARTING ADVICE

No, no, my good knight, do not fear for me. The fire is mine.
I am Daenerys Stormborn, daughter of dragons, bride of
dragons, mother of dragons, don't you see? Don't you see?

GEORGE R. R. MARTIN, *A GAME OF THRONES*

WATCHING *Game of Thrones*, I (Nancy) found the character of Daenerys Stormborn, a queen and "mother of dragons," a perfect metaphor for Christian professor mothers. There are days when we soar on wings. We play with our young children, prep a new lecture, cook a meal for the family, and call up a friend to pray for her sick parent—all in the span of a single afternoon. Then there are days when our own fire engulfs us. We are weeks behind in grading, we scream at our kids, we fight with our spouses, and we neglect to even wash our own hair.

There is no magic formula for what we do. We try to rely on God's supernatural love to sustain us when we reach our limits. We love even when it is hard to love because God first loved us (1 John 4:19). We also turn to others who have tread before us and with us. Within this book is a community of professor mothers who want to assure you that you are not alone. We want to leave you with knowledge we wish we had at the beginning of our journeys.[1] Be strong in the Lord. Do not fear, for we too are mothers of dragons.

Being a mother and a professor is like running a marathon, not a sprint (Jenny H. Pak). Like most women, I initially thought I just needed to survive the first few years—until the baby was out of diapers and breastfeeding stopped—and things would get easier. A wise friend warned me motherhood required at least eighteen years of commitment, and she was right. It was for the long haul. Similarly, when I first began teaching, I thought it would get easier after the first few years when all the courses were prepped. My experience was that nothing was static; courses constantly needed to be revised or restructured with curricular and departmental changes, new courses had to be developed, and administrative and committee responsibilities continuously grew alongside research and advisees.

So my advice to women at the beginning of their adventures is that both being a mother and a professor is like running a marathon, not a sprint. It requires planning, training, and pacing through different seasons of life. Just as athletes work with a seasoned coach who can encourage and guide them through the process, mothers in academia not only need emotional support, but more importantly, mentoring from senior-level female academics in leadership positions. Not only do we need more women at the top, but we also need minority mothers in administrative positions, diverse groups of women we can identify as role models. We need not just female academics who joined "the boys club" in positions of power, but women who can conscientiously and compassionately serve as true advocates for mothers in academia, fighting for equity and meaningful structural change.

Do what you need to do to be well (Jean Neely). I plunged into a rather severe postpartum depression the day after our baby was born. I was on a very mild dose of a nursing-friendly antidepressant at the time, but I clearly

---

[1]All of the passages come from contributors in this book. Some have given their names while others want to remain unnamed.

needed something more. Even though my family, my doctor, and friends all urged me to go back on full dosages of medication that I usually took for depression, I resisted. Having heard of how wonderful a mom's breast milk was for babies, I had planned to breastfeed for the first year. I didn't want to fail my child in something so important so early on. I held out for about a month when my condition became critical. I finally gave in, stopped nursing, and went on all the medication that I needed, but for months I felt enormous guilt and regret over this failure to provide something only I could provide for our baby.

Looking back, I'm thankful for everyone around me who pushed me to do what I needed in order to be healthy and present for our family. Even our child's pediatrician at the time, who happened to be a woman and a mom, reassured me that I had made the best decision. I still feel frequent mom-guilt, but more and more, I am learning to accept that it's okay for me to have limitations and needs of my own. My whole family is better for it when I stay true to who I am and embrace the mom I can be, and not the one I can't.

Coping with miscarriage. I started working as an assistant professor and we began trying to have a child since I was already thirty-two. I got pregnant during my first month at my new job (which was sooner than expected). I went in for my first ultrasound at around nine weeks into the pregnancy. They discovered that there was no heartbeat. The doctor called and confirmed that the pregnancy was not viable. The weeks during and after were emotionally difficult, and yet I kept teaching through it. I decided to let the miscarriage happen naturally, so probably the worst part was not knowing when and how it was going to happen. The doctor did not prepare me for the intense physical pain of miscarriage, which basically felt like labor. I debated whether or not to tell my students what had happened. I ended up telling them and will never forget this student who had difficulties with understanding social norms ask me during class, "So, when you miscarried, did you have an abortion? Is that like an abortion?" The whole class looked horrified, and I somehow had to deal sensitively with this student's question while still reeling from the pain of loss. At the same time, I received some handwritten notes from students with prayers and Bible verses that I cherished. I wrote at the time in my journal, "I just go back and forth between sadness and numbness, dwelling on what has happened and trying to move forward, wanting to remember and yet wanting to forget, feeling attached and unattached." Sadly, pregnancy loss is a very common part of the motherhood experience, and there are no instructions for how to deal with it. Once I started opening up to people about the miscarriage, I realized that so many women experience it. As many as one in four pregnancies end this way. I found a lot of comfort in sharing my grief with these women. There were two verses that got me through these times:

> When you go through deep waters, I will be with you. When you go through rivers of difficulty, you will not drown. When you walk through the fire of oppression, you will not be burned up; the flames will not consume you. For I am the LORD, your God, the Holy One of Israel, your Savior. (Isaiah 42:2-3a NLT)

> We can rejoice, too, when we run into problems and trials, for we know that they help us develop endurance. And endurance develops strength of character, and character strengthens our confident hope of salvation. And this hope will not lead to disappointment. For we know how dearly God loves us, because he has given us the Holy Spirit to fill our hearts with his love. (Romans 5:3-5 NLT)

Struggling with infertility. I planned my life well, or at least I thought I had. I completed graduate school, landed a tenure track job, and was working on publications, presentations, and university service by the time I decided it would be great to have children. My husband and I did away with all methods of birth control because surely going off birth control pills would result in a speedy pregnancy. After two years off the pill, ovulation monitoring, timed intercourse, and taking herbal supplements meant to aid in aligning a woman's cycle, there were no pregnancies in sight. As an overachiever, the fact that childbirth was not something I was able to achieve on my own took a huge emotional toll. Being over the age of thirty-five, I ultimately visited a fertility specialist.

Due to my religious beliefs and university affiliation, I had extreme concern about doing this. After all, I wasn't quite sure what God's Word had to say about in vitro fertilization (IVF). What if I had twenty fertilized embryos? I did *not* want twenty children. I was also not sure that I wanted to donate my embryos, which meant sharing my husband's and my DNA with other couples but not having any contact with potential future children. Would I be able to make the choice to destroy the embryos? Would that be considered murder in God's eyes? Does this (IVF) fly in the face of everything I believe? I prayed constantly and consulted with several spiritual advisors. Pondering whether God's plan would include me getting pregnant after all of the exams, medications, etc., took a huge toll on me spiritually, emotionally, and physically. I spent time thinking through why God gave me the particular desire in my heart to have children, juxtaposed to the idea that only God could create a medical procedure like IVF. On the recommendation of my reproductive endocrinologist (R/E), I decided to move forward with the IVF procedure. This decision was huge and the stress, anxiety, mood swings, and cost were even more grandiose than I could have ever imagined. All the while, I hid the fact that I was undergoing IVF from my work colleagues and Christian friends since I wasn't sure how they might respond to my deciding to move forward with this procedure.

Two weeks later, I found out that there was no pregnancy. I plummeted. Depression kicked in so severely that my R/E recommended that I check in with a therapist. When I finally did, I wished I had gone much sooner than this point. My feelings of failure were multilayered. I had failed to accomplish something that I worked hard to achieve for the first time. I had also failed to do the one thing that, according to my belief system at the time, a woman was supposed to do in marriage (be fruitful and multiply). I was overwhelmed, fearing that my husband would leave me for someone who could give him a child. I had damaging questions of whether God loved me, whether I was being punished for something I had done earlier in life, or whether God thought I wasn't mom material. Looking back, this was one of the hardest and lowest points of my life. I cringed, sank lower, and would later cry every time someone asked me when I planned to have children.

Looking back, I now realize that God is the creator of all things, especially science and the advancement of technology. The fact that my IVF procedure failed to result in a pregnancy helped me to understand that no matter what we do in a lab, God is the one who creates life and that life is on God's divine timeline (whether it is for one day, one hour, one moment, or one hundred years). I also learned to extend more grace and not to police women's bodies or their reproductive rights because only God knows the internal struggles they have experienced in life. I now have a more complex faith understanding and belief system that provides room for the hard realities of life. This has made me a better faculty member as I am able to walk alongside and provide encouragement to students experiencing great tragedies. Last, it helped me to love God more as I clung to Job, Jeremiah, Ruth, and Esther during these times.

Ultimately God blessed my family with a beautiful child. The process to get there took a major toll due to my unfamiliarity with infertility. Today, I hope that sharing my story provides you a bit of insight, minimizes for you a bit of the stigma associated with being Christian and going through IVF, and encourages you to seek out experts if you are experiencing infertility.

Don't compare yourself to others. Comparison can rob you of joy in an instant. Rather, what has helped me all these years is this reminder: be faithful to what God has called you to in whatever season of life you are in. Keeping your eyes fixed on God, remember that God is the One who gives true satisfaction. Our measure of success is not in the papers we publish, how famous we become, whether or not our students love us, etc. Our measure of success is faithfulness to God who has called us into this profession. Trust God will use you and be Spirit-dependent every day.

An article from the Huffington Post entitled "My Advice to New Moms" was probably the most freeing and refreshing thing that I read throughout my pregnancy. Here was one of the gems: "All the seemingly divisive decisions—pain meds in labor/newborn sleep arrangements/feeding—are often phrased as moral imperatives from both sides. Screw that. Take care of your kid. Do what works."[2]

Try not to offer unsolicited advice to other mothers. If they are asking for it, that's a different story. But most unsolicited advice feels like judgment and condemnation.

Be in community. Join or create a small group with other families. One of the things that has helped me the most is being part of a small group at my church for families with young children. Many of us had stopped meeting regularly with other Christians because it seemed too impossible with nap times, bedtimes, feeding, and tantrums, but we all craved spiritual fellowship. So we created a system whereby the dads would meet one week while the moms would watch the kids and the moms would meet the next week while the dads would watch the kids and so on. We all still met at the same home and ate dinner together before splitting up. Each week one family would bring dinner for everyone (usually takeout because we rarely have time to cook), and everyone would chip in money. This meant that on most Fridays, you didn't have to worry about dinner. The great thing about it was that the expectations were so low. We all felt so accomplished by just making it there. It was okay if the kids spilled their juice or cried inconsolably or barged into the room during prayer. We all just "got" that this was part of our small group and were thankful that no one judged because the next week, that could be their kid. Small group got easier because the kids became friends and started needing the parents less. This meant that even when we were watching the kids, we were able to catch up on what was happening in each other's lives. Our kids also felt more comfortable with Sunday School because they saw their small group friends there. We went through Paul Tripp's *Parenting* book this past year, and it's cool because we are all kind of on the same page now and can encourage one another in ways that are gospel-centered. There were just a lot of good things that came out of this family small group.

---

[2] JJ Keith, "My Advice to New Moms," The Blog, *Huffington Post*, March 30, 2015, www.huffpost.com/entry/new-moms_b_1850227/.

For everything there is a season. Life has seasons. You will go through a new season in which your spiritual life, prayer life, ministry life, professional life, personal life, and social life looks different than it did pre-kid, and that is okay.

In those early career years, I felt so much pressure to keep the same pace and academic productivity as those around me; but many of the people I was comparing myself with were not professor mothers in a similar season of life (very young children). It encouraged me so much to hear that one professor was 75-percent time for ten years prior to moving into a 100-percent time position (due to the season of life that her kids/family were in). This helped to really take some of that pressure off and find a balance that worked for me in this season of my life.

You may only get eighteen years with these children under your roof. That means when they are six, one-third of that time will be over. When they are nine, one-half. It's true that the days are long (very long sometimes), but the years are short. "To everything there is a season, a time for every purpose under heaven" (Ecclesiastes 3:1 NKJV).

We are power women (the editors). As academic mothers of faith, we are powerful. We are some of the most highly educated women in the world. We are gifted in teaching, writing, mentorship, and mothering. We face a myriad of challenges: societal and institutional obstacles, bigotry, imposter syndrome, imperfect families, limited time, finite energies, heartache, illness, and trauma. We respond with courage, brilliance, innovation, intuition, endurance, wisdom, laughter, vulnerability, growth, grace, hope, love, faith, prayer, community, and God. Always God.

Within these pages are a virtual community of professor mothers of faith who have walked the road less taken. Professor mothers who have struggled, stumbled, overcome, and succeeded. Those who have deconstructed what it means to be a mother, scholar, teacher, mentor, pastor, breadwinner, wife, and child of God. Women who tenaciously research every aspect of motherhood from childbearing to childrearing. Scholars who strive for perfection but live with humility. Teachers who love and mentor students sometimes at the costs of their own families, other times in synergy with being a mother. Ministers who honor God at the pulpit, on the page, at the university, and in the home.

We hope that you find resonance, receive encouragement, and glean tips for your own journey. May we all be clothed with strength and dignity, laugh at the days to come, speak with wisdom, teach with faithfulness, and have our families call us blessed.[3]

---

[3]Paraphrased from Proverbs 31:25-28.

APPENDIX A

INSTITUTIONAL SUPPORT
FOR ACADEMIC MOTHERS

ADMINISTRATORS READING THIS VOLUME are in a unique position to aid in positive outcomes for professor moms on their campuses. While we have come a long way with the addition of FMLA policies, we are far from leveling the playing field and creating true family-friendly cultures and environments for women faculty who have children or are planning a family. Here are a few needs at many institutions:

Parental leave policies. At this point, most universities have parental leave policies that are in practice for both men and women. If your university does not, this is absolutely where you should start. Parental leave should be available for both men and women and should extend to different family circumstances (e.g., childbirth, adoption, etc.). If your institution has parental leave policies, ensure that your campus has a culture of faculty using this leave, (or culture of use[1]). This will communicate to professor moms that their career will not take a social or political hit for using the policy that is designed to aid them.

---

[1] Scott Jaschik, "'Academic Motherhood': Authors Discuss New Book on Academic Motherhood," *Inside Higher Ed*, October 9, 2012, www.insidehighered.com/news/2012/10/09/authors-discuss-new-book-academic-motherhood.

Lactation policies. Similarly, universities should have lactation policies that include facilities (designated rooms and refrigeration) and time (course and meeting schedules that accommodate lactating moms).

Clear requirements for tenure and promotion. Provide resources to aid faculty moms in obtaining tenure and promotion at all career stages. Recognize that the promotion from associate to full professor can be just as daunting for faculty moms as the promotion from assistant to associate professor (e.g. tenure clock promotion).

Childcare. While it is not feasible for all universities to host a childcare facility on their campus, creating a partnership with local daycares, schools, and childcare facilities in which employees can enjoy a discount would aid professor moms greatly.

Financial resources for academic mother support groups centered on professional development. When I (Nancy) facilitated our "professor mommy" group, I was able to obtain funds to purchase lunches delivered to our meeting rooms by our university catering team. This provided a break from having to pack or buy our own lunches. Because professor mothers are especially strapped for time, the lunch meetings did not burden our busy schedules. If possible, provide additional funding for special speakers and professional development workshops. Some topics can include time management, how to get tenure, and work-life balance.

Family-friendly accommodations. Kelly Ward and Lisa Wolf-Wendel provide a list of things to consider which may also be helpful for administrators.[2] Among them are knowing that tenure and biological clocks click simultaneously, instituting more comprehensive family-friendly policies, ensuring policies are equitable and available to all faculty, understanding that one size may not fit all, engaging in conversations proactively, and regularly reviewing policies and practices. Professor mothers of faith bring unique strengths, skills, and experiences to academic institutions and the academic enterprise. These suggestions for institutional support will not only benefit faculty and the academy but also the church and society as a whole.

---

[2]Jaschik, "'Academic Motherhood.'"

APPENDIX B

FURTHER DISCUSSION ABOUT
BEING "GOOD MOTHERS"

IT IS VALUABLE TO EXPLORE our beliefs about what it means to be a "good mother" and a "good worker" in the Christian academy. I have especially enjoyed those moments when I get glimpses into the motherhood ideology of my professor-mother peers. The similarities in beliefs and experience can be incredibly validating. The differences in beliefs and experience can be incredibly illuminating, challenging, and perspective-broadening.

If you are reading this book in a group of fellow colleagues, here are some reflection questions and scenarios that may spark interesting discussion. It is likely that your group will come up with even more questions and scenarios as you discuss.

The following scenarios are presented with intentional vagueness so that different readers may imagine different things based upon their own experiences and backgrounds. Dr. Christina Lee Kim (author of chapter five, "The 'Good' Mother") presents these scenarios as opportunities for further exploration of you and your colleagues' beliefs about motherhood and the role of professor mothers. The intention is not to debate a right or wrong point of view. She encourages readers to discuss with the goal of deepened understanding and perspective-broadening in mind.

Also, Dr. Kim encourages you, the reader, to keep in mind that everyone is not like you. While we might often assume similar beliefs among colleagues, especially if we share background disciplines, similar family life stages, religious views, political beliefs, etc., we actually do not know all of the things that have shaped our colleagues' beliefs about motherhood and the balancing of work and family. Be mindful; assume that the opposite of your beliefs may be present in the room. Speak to share, but also stop and be willing to listen and consider another's perspective. Pay attention to the feelings inside of you as you hear a different opinion. What buttons are being pushed? What are your immediate reactions? Commit to suspending judgment in those moments in order to give space for exploration and attempts to understand. Most importantly, be prayerful and ask God for humility, for greater understanding, and for love.

As you consider each scenario, ponder the following questions:

- What immediate thoughts and feelings arise? Where are these coming from?

- What questions do you have?

- What are the different perspectives that people might hold in this situation?

- What are advantages and disadvantages that you notice about other mothers? About yourself?

- What are you learning about yourself or about others as you discuss these scenarios?

Scenarios

1. A female colleague enters a meeting or classroom with a child.

2. A female colleague is never available after 3 p.m. because she leaves campus to pick up her children. She is also unavailable to serve on committees or participate in events that happen after that time.

3. A female colleague is very productive in her work. She often serves on multiple committees and attends multiple extracurricular and evening events. She is busy flying around the country attending conferences and other professional activities. You are impressed by her productivity, and yet you also happen to know that she has young children in the home.

4. You happen to know that a female colleague has an extensive network of familial support. In particular, you know that her mother often gladly watches her children for her and cooks meals for her so that she can work without worrying about childcare or feeding the kids.

5. Explore thoughts and feelings around housekeeping and chores: for example, feelings around personally cleaning your home versus hiring someone to clean your home, the level of tidiness or clutter in your home, etc.

6. Explore thoughts and feelings around food and home-cooked meals versus store-bought, takeout, or meal-service meals for your family.

7. Explore thoughts and feelings around "playing" or spending time with your children.

8. Explore thoughts and feelings around volunteering at schools, participating in PTAs, etc.

9. Can you think of any other scenarios?

REFLECTION
AND DISCUSSION
QUESTIONS

1 DIVVYING UP LOVE: SCHOLARLY AMBITION
AND MOTHERHOOD AS SPIRITUAL FORMATION

1. Evaluate the season of your life right now: Are you pre-tenure? Do you need to put more time and effort investing in and establishing groundwork for your teaching so that it will yield more dividends of time later? Do you need to sow into your research—even a little bit—in order to reap the benefits in the future?

2. What does your soul care currently look like? Are you prioritizing soul care as much as physical and emotional self-care? Which practices, relationships, or activities are you choosing to invest in that will deepen your trust in Jesus?

3. Is your life characterized by hurriedness? Think about how you can cultivate less hurry in your life.

4. What are the narratives and beliefs you have received about your role as a mother and working woman that you need to lay before the Lord and ask for his light? What assumptions or limits have you placed on yourself that need more processing with the Lord?

2 THE SYNERGY OF LULLABY AND SYLLABI

1. Go through the questions on work-life conflict and work-life enrichment in this chapter. Which do you experience more of? Is this consistent with how you tend to think about your life? Why might there be a mismatch?

2. Work enhancing family: The author shares that the main ways in which academic life enriches her family life is through added skills and perspectives, psychological resources, and flexibility. Do you relate to these in your own life or are there different resources you experience?

3. Family enhancing work: The author shares that the main ways in which family life enriches her work life is through added skills and perspectives and psychological resources. Do you relate to these in your own life or are there different resources you experience?

4. Do you see your Christian faith as creating additional demands or providing additional resources when it comes to work-life balance?

5. Why do you think studies found that women of faith experience less work-life conflict than other women? Do you agree with the explanations given by the author?

6. The author argues that in addition to re-framing our experiences, we need to advocate for policies that provide the institutional support for work-life enrichment. What institutional practices or policies would make work-life enrichment more possible for you and others?

7. How can academic women support one another so that all can experience work-life enrichment?

3 (MIS)PERCEPTIONS OF MATERNITY LEAVE IN THE ACADEMY

1. Why do some faculty have a perception that parental leaves are unfair and what can be done to challenge those perceptions?

2. What can your university or department do to better support faculty who are eligible for parental leave?

3. What advice would you give to a faculty member who is preparing for parental leave?

4 A PRINCIPLED DISCUSSION FOR ADJUNCT PROFESSOR MOTHERS

1. Leaning on one's faith as an adjunct mother professor is critical. How does faith benefit students of adjunct mother professors?

2. Adjunct mother professors with full-time jobs must balance teaching, full-time employment, and family demands. What enables one to remain poised with the excessive demands?

3. Should colleges and universities provide parental leave policies for contingent faculty members?

4. How can college/university administrators support adjunct mother professors in the academy?

5 THE "GOOD" MOTHER

1. Consider the messages about what it means to be a mother that you received from your family of origin, from your church, from formal schooling, from media and the culture at large, from your workplace (feel free to add others). Do any of these messages contradict one another? How have these messages shaped your motherhood ideology?

2. Which of these messages have you adopted? Which have you resisted or rejected? Why? What has been the process for making those decisions? How? What has that looked like in your life at home and in the workplace?

3. How do you manage experiences of internal conflict/tension related to your identity as a professor mother? Do you tackle it head on? Do you avoid it? Do you compartmentalize? Rationalize? What strategies do you use when those tensions arise?

4. Are you aware of times in your career where you have worried about how others view you as a "mother"? Have you felt it from your male colleagues? Female colleagues? Other professor mothers? What did you do with those feelings?

5. At what times have you felt most supported *by* your professor-mother colleagues? At what times have you felt most guarded with your professor-mother colleagues?

6. At what times have you felt most supportive *of* your professor-mother colleagues? At what times have you felt most judgmental, envious, or competitive with your professor-mother colleagues?

7. Where is God when it comes to your "motherhood ideology"?

8. What is your experience when it comes to the continuum of self-sufficiency versus Spirit-dependence? What would Spirit-dependence look like in your daily professor-mommy life?

9. For whom do you work so hard? Who, or what, is at the center of your striving? What does it look like to love God with all your heart, soul, mind, and strength as you live out your identity both as a professor and as a mother?

10. What comes to mind as you consider the invitation to take Jesus' yoke upon you? As you consider his invitation to come to him and his subsequent promise of rest?

6 RECATEGORIZATION: A GRACE FOR WORKING MOMS

1. Have you ever had a time when you judged yourself or other mothers badly? Would you have had the same reaction if the parent in that situation was a father?

2. What is an area of your life where you don't feel the grace of God very much? Is there a "discipline of grace" that you can turn to in those moments?

3. What is the worst failure you have had as a working mother? How does God see that failure?

7 IMPOSTER BLUES AND FINDING REST IN GOD

1. How would you characterize your dominant inner voices? What are the stories you tend to tell yourself about your worth and who you are?

2. Can you think of a time when God encouraged you in an unexpected way, as when the mother in the garden spoke just the words that Jean needed from God when she prayed? Do you find yourself open to hearing from God in these unexpected ways or do you tend to second-guess those affirmations?

3. In this chapter, the author recognizes that God's purpose for her may be different from that of her peers. Do you find that you look more often to God or to those around you as you seek to discover your purpose and measure your success? What challenges does this present?

4. How do you usually imagine that God sees you? Who are the people in your life who have incarnated God's love for you and help you to rest in God?

5. How does the idea of God as Mother differ from what you have learned about God? How might it change your understanding and experience of God's love?

8 JUGGLING MULTIPLE ROLES: NARRATIVE OF A KOREAN PASTOR'S WIFE, A MOTHER, AND A PSYCHOLOGY PROFESSOR

1. Does your calling change when you become a wife and mother? Why or why not?

2. In what ways do you think bicultural identity is common to all human struggles?

3. How is professional psychotherapy similar and different from pastoral care?

4. How is maturity and psychological growth related to the sanctification process in your life journey with Christ?

9 ANSWERING A THREEFOLD CALLING: MOTHERHOOD, THE ACADEMY, AND THE PASTORATE

1. Reflect on your current support system. What arrangements are helping you to flourish right now, and what is keeping you from flourishing? How could better time management potentially create new spaces for you to thrive?

2. What is the underlying motivation that inspires and encourages you in your work as an academic mother?

3. How does your commitment to the life of the church fit into your vocational calling?

10 BALANCING UNIVERSITY TEACHING AND HOMESCHOOLING

If you are considering homeschooling but are not sure where to start, or if you wonder if it is possible given your current work status, I encourage you to make a plan. The first thing to remember is that homeschooling "does not represent a single educational concept beyond its definition as an educational process in which children do not attend conventional schools."[1] There is such a wide variety of methods, curriculum, programs and practical ways of approaching homeschooling. The following are questions and factors to consider that can help you develop a plan:

1. First and foremost, understand why it is that you are choosing to homeschool.

2. Consider your schedule for both work and homeschooling.

3. Will your significant other and/or other family members be involved in homeschooling?

4. What method of homeschooling best fits your vision of how you want to homeschool your children?

---

[1]O. Guterman and A. Neuman, "Personality, Socioeconomic Status, and Education: Factors that Contribute to the Degree of Structure in Homeschooling," *Social Psychology of Education: An International Journal* 21, no. 1 (2018): 76.

5. Will you provide all of the homeschooling yourself or join other families in structured classes and programs to help you homeschool?

6. How can your profession or specific discipline assist you in homeschooling your children? (There are so many academic disciplines that would be an asset to a homeschooling mom.)

11 IT TAKES A VILLAGE: RAISING CHILDREN WITH SUPPORT

1. What does your village look like?

2. Who can you invite into your village for greater support? Or how can you join with others to form a village?

3. What are the ways that God has provided you with support that you might not notice? What are some areas that you feel you need God's help in? Take a moment to release this list to God, then wait and watch to see how God provides these things, perhaps not in the way you were expecting. Journal about how God showed up and what you can learn from living in the fact that God is concerned about your every need.

4. What is your self-care plan? (How do you take a moment to get back in touch with yourself, your calling, and your love for all that you do?)

12 NAVIGATING MARRIAGE AS THE BREADWINNER

1. In what ways can family life be enhanced by focusing on the strengths of each partner rather than stereotypical gender roles?

2. How has God challenged you and your spouse to rethink how you lead together in your family?

3. How does having two incomes help address the challenges of gender roles in marriage? How does it add additional challenges?

13 EMPOWERMENT OF PROFESSOR MOMS THROUGH MENTORSHIP

The Holy Spirit has been an essential resource for me, leading me often from the Scriptures through the uncertainty of decision making, fears, aloneness, and my own personal insecurities. Even though being a professor mom can be very lonely and overwhelming, we are never alone; the Holy Spirit comes to help:

> The Helper will come—the Spirit, who reveals the truth about God and who comes from the Father. I will send him to you from the Father, and he will speak about me. And you, too, will speak about me, because you have been with me from the very beginning. (John 15:26-27 GNT)

1. How have you turned to the Holy Spirit for help in your life? How can you draw from the model of the Holy Spirit as a helper to mentor others?

Motherhood can often become a heavy burden because of all the responsibilities, pressures, and expectations. The Scripture below describes the Holy Spirit's provision for professor moms with promises of comfort through prayer.

> For the Spirit that God has given you does not make you slaves and cause you to be afraid; instead, the Spirit makes you God's children, and by the Spirit's power we cry out to God, "Father! my Father!" (Romans 8:15 GNT)

2. What are you afraid of? By the power of the Holy Spirit, cry your fears out to the Lord.

Professor moms have worked hard for all they've accomplished and are equipped with gifts and abilities to help and complement one another. This Scripture clearly reminds professor moms that the Spirit of God has equipped them with gifts to share:

> But it is one and the same Spirit who does all this; as he wishes, he gives a different gift to each person. (1 Corinthians 12:11 GNT)

3. What are your unique gifts? How can you unlock and honor the unique gifts of others through mentorship?

LIST OF
CONTRIBUTORS

Stephanie Chan, PhD, is an associate professor of sociology at Biola University and the mother of two awesome kids, ages five and eight.

Teri Clemons, MS, SLPD, is a speech-language pathologist and associate professor in the Department of Communication Sciences and Disorders at Biola University. She enjoys sharing life with her husband and two daughters.

Deshonna Collier-Goubil, PhD, is an associate professor and the founding chair of the Department of Criminal Justice at Azusa Pacific University. She solo parents beautiful, vivacious, energetic four-year-old twins.

Christina Lee Kim, PhD, is an associate professor of psychology at Biola University and a licensed clinical psychologist. She is mommy to three daughters.

Jennifer Powell McNutt, PhD, FRHistS, is associate professor and holds the Franklin S. Dyrness Chair of Biblical and Theological Studies at Wheaton College where she teaches the history of Christianity with specialization in the Reformation. The Rev. Dr. McNutt is also an ordained minister in the Presbyterian Church (USA) and parish associate at First Presbyterian Church of Glen Ellyn along with her husband, and they have three marvelous children.

Jean Neely, PhD, teaches in the writing program at Azusa Pacific University. She and her family love hanging out at their friendly neighborhood coffeehouse to read, write, and wonder.

Doretha O'Quinn is the CEO and president of BridgeBuilder Consulting Group providing curriculum design, leadership development and diversity, equity and inclusion strategies, and is the former provost and vice president for academic affairs for Vanguard University. She is the wife of Rev. Michael O'Quinn for forty-seven years, mother of four adult children and grandmother of nine.

Jenny H. Pak, PhD, is an associate professor at Fuller Graduate School of Psychology. She serves with her husband, David, who has been pastoring over thirty years in Southern California, and has two daughters, twenty-five and twenty-one years old.

Joy Qualls is an associate professor of communication studies and associate dean of the Division of Communication at Biola University. Joy is married to Kevin, a licensed professional counselor; they are parents to Blakeley and Soren as well as a fur baby, Madeleine. Joy is the author of *God Forgive Us for Being Women: Rhetoric, Theology and the Pentecostal Tradition* (Eugene, OR: Wipf and Stock, 2018).

Ji Y. Son, PhD, is a professor of psychology and director of the learning lab at California State University, Los Angeles. She can be found doodling on the back of manuscripts with her husband and two lovable boys in the Boyle Heights neighborhood around her campus.

Yiesha L. Thompson, PhD, resides in the District of Columbia where she works full time in education policy, adjuncts at a neighboring university, and spends quality time with her family. In her spare time, she enjoys reading, traveling, and swimming.

Yvana Uranga-Hernandez, PhD, is an associate professor in the Communications Sciences and Disorders Department at Biola University. She has been married for twenty-one years and homeschools four children with ages ranging from eight to sixteen years old.

Maria Su Wang, PhD, is associate professor of English at Biola University, where she researches and teaches first-year writing, world literature, nineteenth-century British literature, and the history and theory of the British novel. She is the mother of two kids (a seventh grader and a third grader), loves to run and walk outside, and is an avid fan of Asian entertainment in all forms.

Nancy Wang Yuen, PhD, is an associate professor of sociology at Biola University and author of *Reel Inequality: Hollywood Actors and Racism* (New Brunswick, NJ: Rutgers University Press, 2016). She is raising a family that makes Good Trouble.